Explosion aboard the *Iowa*

Explosion aboard the *Iowa*

Richard L. Schwoebel

Naval Institute Press
Annapolis, Maryland

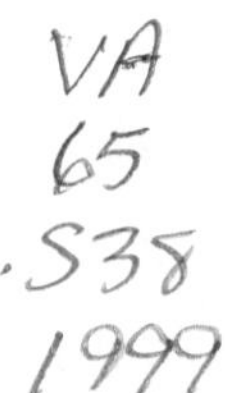

Library of Congress Cataloging-in-Publication Data
Schwoebel, Richard L.
Explosion aboard the Iowa / Richard L. Schwoebel.
p. cm.
Includes index.
ISBN 1-55750-810-0
1. Iowa (Ship) 2. United States. Navy. 3. Marine accidents—Investigation—United States. I. Title.
VA65.S38 1999 98-53484
363.12′365′0973—dc21

Printed in the United States of America on acid-free paper ∞
06 05 04 03 02 01 00 99 9 8 7 6 5 4 3 2
First printing

Title-page illustration: Iowa fires a broadside during gunnery exercises, 15 August 1984.

To the memory of the men
who died in the tragic explosion
aboard the USS *Iowa*,
19 April 1989, to their survivors,
and to the heroic crew
who saved the ship

Contents

Illustrations

Foreword

THIS BOOK is a scientific detective story about the cause of a gun turret explosion that occurred on board the battleship USS *Iowa* during a training exercise on 19 April 1989. The explosion of a 16-inch turret gun was deemed a low-probability event, but when the unlikely happened the consequences were severe: forty-seven seamen died and a stand-down of all the 16-inch guns on board the four battleships then on active duty in the U.S. Navy was threatened.

Was the cause of the explosion an accident? Or was it an intentional act of suicide by a member of the crew? The Navy's own investigation found no direct physical evidence of an accidental cause of detonation, and from this it jumped to the conclusion that the explosion was a deliberate act of suicide by a distraught sailor who, it posited, was motivated by a terminated homosexual relationship.

This conclusion was clearly in the Navy's self-interest, exonerating them of any responsibility for the tragedy due to faulty equipment, procedures, or training. It provided the Navy with a clean bill of health on operational safety, permitting the retention of the four World War II–vintage dreadnoughts in active service. The Navy's investigation and conclusions proved unpersuasive, however, when they were presented in public hearings to the Senate and House Armed Services Committees. Both committees found that the Navy study lacked the rigor and thoroughness necessary to rule out an accidental cause for the explosion. Committee members were also troubled by the Navy's apparent rush to judgment against a dead seaman whose alleged sexual preference provided a convenient scapegoat.

Congress requested an independent inquiry into the incident and its cause. Not surprisingly, this request landed on the doorstep of the Sandia National Laboratories in Albuquerque, New Mexico. Sandia is one of the Department of Energy laboratories in the U.S. nuclear complex that has responsibility for the safety, as well as for the performance and reliability, of our nuclear weapons. The accidental or unintended detonation of a nuclear weapon would be terrifyingly destructive—indeed, of very high consequence. It is therefore essential that U.S. nuclear weapons be designed, built, and maintained to meet exceedingly high safety criteria. The fact that there have been accidents (and even some close calls) but never an accidental nuclear detonation is testimony of the success of the U.S. nuclear establishment in meeting these rigorous goals.

The Sandia National Laboratories' focus is primarily on the many nonnuclear components of modern thermonuclear weapons, in particular their arming, fusing, and firing devices. More broadly, Sandia explores a wide variety of possible accidents and rare scenarios that could lead to an inadvertent nuclear detonation—a process that has led to major safety improvements over the years. It was natural, then, to turn to Sandia for an in-depth, independent probe into possible causes of the *Iowa* tragedy, given its reputation as a scientific and engineering institution with extensive experience and a superb record in the world of low-probability events.

It proved to be fortuitous that physicist Dr. Richard Schwoebel, the author of this book, was chosen to lead the Sandia team in this inquiry. Dr. Schwoebel brought strong and valuable credentials to the task: a long and distinguished career of scientific achievements and technical expertise in studies of surface physics, material properties, and safety issues. His respect for facts and evidence, for objectivity and fairness, both as a scientist and as a technical manager, have earned him the high esteem of many colleagues. This book is his revealing and spellbinding account of an extraordinary scientific investigation by him and his team of expert and devoted scientists. Dr. Schwoebel and his colleagues painstakingly, carefully, and with the highest scientific standards ferreted out crucial clues and bits of data. Just as with the continuing development of nuclear weapon safety, the Sandia team not only examined the expected accident scenarios but also continuously searched for unexpected ones that were not considered by the Navy. Their forensic analyses revealed that there was supporting evidence for a scenario in which the explosion was an accident. The threads of their findings—from physical evidence to lack of adequate crew training and the use of aged high explosives dating to the 1940s and not maintained under properly controlled conditions—together tell a gripping story of how the tragedy aboard the USS *Iowa* could very well have been triggered by accident rather than by deliberate act.

It is important to the nation to get this story right. The Navy left a bad taste in the public consciousness with its rush to both clear itself and put the onus on a ready and defenseless scapegoat. We will never know for certain what actually happened in Turret II on the USS *Iowa*, but we do know that the U.S. government made the best possible effort to find out, and in doing so exposed the Navy's verdict as flawed.

In the long run the Navy, as well as the nation, is fortunate that justice has been served in this case. Otherwise a parallel could be drawn with the notorious Dreyfus Affair in France at the end of the last century. In that case, the French Army accused one of its officers, Captain Dreyfus, of treason. Given the prejudices of the time, Dreyfus, a Jew, provided a convenient scapegoat. It took nearly a decade of dedicated protest, helped in great measure by "J'accuse," Émile Zola's influential letter to the French press, for justice to be done. Fortunately, the work done by Dr. Schwoebel and his team helped save the United States from committing an injustice in this case. We also have Richard Schwoebel to thank for writing the fascinating scientific detective story telling how he and his team did it.

PROFESSOR SIDNEY DRELL
Deputy Director Emeritus,
Stanford Linear Accelerator Center

Acknowledgments

THIS BOOK is the product of the excellent Sandia National Laboratories team that worked so effectively and with such diligence in our investigation of the explosion aboard the USS *Iowa*. These dedicated people gave of themselves many times over in their various activities and brought the highest level of objectivity and integrity to the work and the way in which it was presented. In spite of our widely different conclusions, the Navy team also made significant contributions, and the Sandia investigation would have been far less had it not been for the many forthcoming conversations with and insights and understanding of the Navy's technical team.

Several people directly associated with the incident were most helpful in the preparation of the manuscript: Lt. Daniel Meyer and GMG Steve Brooks aboard the USS *Iowa*; GMG1 Dale Mortensen; FN Brian Scanio, the former commander of the *Iowa*; Captain (ret.) Larry Seaquist; and Nancy Lewis, the mother of Richard Lewis, who was killed in the explosion.

The manuscript was substantially improved by the numerous comments and suggestions of the editors and reviewers at the Naval Institute Press, and I am particularly grateful for their perceptive remarks. Professor Mary Swander provided several valuable insights in development of the manuscript. I also want to acknowledge detailed and insightful reviews of the manuscript by Paul Cooper and Jim Borders, colleagues in the investigation, and Jerry Gorman for preparation of several of the line drawings.

I want thank my wife, Jennie, for her encouragement and patience during the years of writing this manuscript, my sons Eric and Paul for their discerning comments and suggestions, and M. G. Mortenson, with whom I discussed many issues during the investigation.

I was particularly encouraged in this work by my friends Jim Mitchell, Glen Otey, and Tom Green.

Lastly, I want to thank Professor Sidney Drell, deputy director emeritus of the Stanford Linear Accelerator Center, for his perspective and suggestion that a book dealing with this investigation was an important undertaking.

Prologue

AN EXPLOSION occurred aboard the battleship USS *Iowa* during a training exercise on 19 April 1989, a tragic incident that killed all forty-seven crewmen in Turret II. It was one of the most disastrous incidents ever experienced by our peacetime armed forces.

The U.S. Navy conducted an extensive investigation costing approximately $25 million and involving several naval facilities, the U.S. Army Ballistics Laboratory at Aberdeen, Maryland, and the Federal Bureau of Investigation. The Navy concluded that the explosion could not have been an accident but was the result of a deliberate act by a member of the crew. Moreover, they concluded that this deliberate act was "most probably" committed by Gunner's Mate Guns 2d Class (GMG2) Clayton M. Hartwig, gun captain of the center gun of Turret II.

These and other conclusions of the Navy's investigation stimulated significant inquiries into the incident by the Senate Armed Services Committee and the House Committee on Armed Services. These committees generally concluded that the Navy had rushed to judgments that were both speculative and insufficiently supported by specific facts. The House published a report entitled "USS *Iowa* Tragedy: An Investigative Failure."

The Senate committee asked the Government Accounting Office (GAO) to review various aspects of the Navy's utilization of battleships and to seek a laboratory to conduct an independent assessment of the Navy's findings and associated conclusions. The GAO's investigation of the utilization of the *Iowa* and the three other battleships concentrated on issues such as manning and training of personnel. Several deficiencies were noted in these and other areas, and the GAO ultimately recommended that the battleships be decommissioned.

The GAO also sought the services of an independent laboratory to assess the Navy's conclusions related to the cause of this tragic explosion. This independent technical investigation was conducted by Sandia National Laboratories and began in December 1989, about eight months after the disaster and three months after the Navy issued its report on the incident. The Sandia investigation was more circumscribed than the Navy's and probed specific technical questions related to both recognized and altogether unsuspected causes of the explosion.

Sandia found that there was no explicit physical evidence that Hartwig or any other crewman was responsible for initiating an intentional explosion in Turret II using an ignition device. Ordinary sources were identified for all of the "foreign materials" identified by the Navy and claimed by them to be the signature of such a device.

The Sandia investigation also revealed an unrecognized problem with propellant bags that may have been central to the cause of the explosion. The clear implication of this finding was that the explosion could have been an accident resulting from an overram of the propellant into the gun. The overram may, in turn, have been the result of inadvertent actions of poorly trained crewmen or an equipment malfunction.

Although the Navy's interpretations and conclusions from their findings were flawed, the contributions of both the Navy and Sandia National Laboratories technical personnel were remarkable in penetrating the fragmentary evidence that remained following the powerful explosion in the center gun room of Turret II. Although evidence was literally thrown overboard in the cleanup process, misplaced, and at times improperly interpreted, an important safety inadequacy emerged. Important contributions came from both technical teams. Working-level Navy personnel made special contributions to this inquiry and were cooperative and helpful throughout the course of the Sandia investigation.

I have included limited portions of the testimony by crew members about the events immediately following the explosion, but a complete record of such testimony is beyond the scope of this book. Individual recollections surrounding the events on 19 April 1989 are an absorbing record that one is compelled to read and reread. In the case of the enlisted personnel it is a record of courage and perceptive understanding of these huge 16-inch gun systems.

The crew of the *Iowa* deserves substantially more recognition than they have been given up to this point. There were several petty officers and crewmen who exhibited expert knowledge, intelligence, and heroic action following the explosion. Their actions went beyond the instructions and commands of their officers and may have saved the ship and many of their shipmates from further devastation following the initial blast that killed the men in Turret II.

Top echelons of the U.S. Navy could have held up the actions of these men with considerable pride and concluded that the cause of the explosion might never be determined with absolute certainty. Instead, some of them chose, in a series of remarkable judgments, to defend any implication that there had been any fault in either the gun system or the Navy's process for assuring safety. The officers leading and overseeing the Navy's investigation identified a crewman as having committed murder and suicide on evidence that was at best fragmentary and ambiguous and at worst nonexistent. The Navy investigating team's hypothesis of the cause of the explosion became a certainty in some minds, not to be altered by later evidence.

Although some in the Navy found serious fault with a particular individual in causing the explosion aboard the *Iowa*, they were less forthcoming in acknowledging the faults and serious deficiencies in their own processes. The existing management, manning, and training processes did not assure that the battleships were properly manned, that there were responsible judgments by those in control of powerful weapon systems, and that all crewmen were prepared for the stations to which they were assigned. High-level officers of the Navy failed to sufficiently review and control questionable experiments with 16-inch guns, exposing men to possible risks that could have been minimized by using facilities designed for such experiments. They steadfastly maintained that these experiments, poor training, inadequate adherence to safety procedures, and uninformed decision making had no relation to the incident—while the Navy's own report of the incident stated that these issues could "serve as a foundation for disaster."

The Navy failed at the very top to assemble a credible investigative process and appeared to rush to a judgment that sought to exonerate the system at the expense of a deceased crewman. The arrogance and subjectivity of a relatively few in the Navy command was mitigated somewhat in the last judgment of the chief of Naval Operations. In a press conference in the fall of 1991, Adm. Frank B. Kelso II stated that there was no clear and convincing evidence that the explosion had resulted from a wrongful intentional act, withdrew the accusation against Clayton Hartwig, and apologized to his family. There is little doubt that he took this position against the advice of some senior officers,

officers who had been exposed to many of the technical details of the various investigations but insisted on interpreting results of technical studies in terms of an unshaken and subjective belief in their murder-suicide hypothesis.

The Uniform Code of Military Justice, as it was exercised by the U.S. Navy judge advocate general (JAG) in the *Iowa* investigation, deserves review and possible modification. Allegations were made public with, at best, tenuous evidence. The press was used, perhaps all too willingly, by unidentified Navy sources to promulgate defaming rumors that set a public stage for the subsequent U.S. Navy Technical Report. These abuses went unchecked and uninvestigated, either by the Navy or by the JAG process.

The Uniform Code of Military Justice apparently has no provision for appointing an advocate for a deceased service person accused of a serious crime, no option for cross-examination of those who make allegations, no requirement for the substantiation of such allegations, and no opportunity for an advocate to present a defense of the accused or to offer a semblance of due process for those who are convenient and silent targets.

There are several points to be taken from the tragic loss of these men and the subsequent events related to the organization of such investigations. They center on assuring that objective investigative processes are used and that powerful organizations are not investigating themselves, that the media is not used to promulgate innuendo and establishes and adheres to standards for the publication of information from unidentified sources, that basic elements of common law are implemented in military justice in the treatment of service people accused of crimes—particularly those who are deceased—and that the clamor of accusation does not diminish the recognition of the crewmen who deserve great credit for their heroic actions in this incident.

Serving as a counterpoise to these disturbing observations were the insights of an important core of people in the Senate and House of Representatives who clearly wanted to understand what had happened, who wanted to assure that crewmen were now being properly trained for hazardous assignments, and who sought a measure of justice for a deceased crewman accused on fragmentary grounds. There were several who saw injustice and unfairness in a military process in which the momentum of assertion somehow took precedence over meaningful and objective inquiry.

This book is a personal memoir of this investigation based on work performed by the team at Sandia National Laboratories, a view of events and interactions in which several of us were deeply involved. My primary sources of information were the only two official statements made by the Sandia team—the testimony presented before the Senate Armed Services Committee on 25 May 1990 and the House Banking Committee on 8 November 1990. An interim report on our work was presented to the Senate Armed Services Committee as part of our testimony on 25 May, and a final report, "USS *Iowa* Explosion," submitted in August 1991 and published as a report of the U.S. General Accounting Office. The Navy's report, "Investigation into the 19 April 1989 Explosion in Turret II USS *Iowa* (BB-61)," and testimony by members of the crew are also referred to extensively in this book. Other sources include notes, letters, memos, and personal recollections of the meetings and conversations that took place during the approximately eighteen months of this investigation. The testimony, technical reports, and other documents have been used to put these recollections into context and bring authenticity to the narrative.

I have frequently characterized and paraphrased the views, perceptions, and comments of others as I recall meetings and conversations, an imperfect and somewhat subjective process. These meetings include those with Capt. Joseph D. Miceli, director of the NAVSEA Technical Review Team, with whom I worked for about eighteen months, and whom I respect in spite of fundamental differences in our approach to the investigation and our divergent conclusions. Captain Miceli took a major role in formulating and espousing the Navy's scenario for the incident, including the interpretation of the evidence that supported the Navy's position. His scenario was broadly supported by several higher level naval officers directly involved in and responsible for the Navy's investigation.

My objectives in writing this book were to highlight important systemic deficiencies that characterized the investigation conducted by the Navy, to preserve a personal record of our independent investigation, and to acknowledge the heroism of the crew of the USS *Iowa* following the explosion.

Explosion aboard the *Iowa*

Frontispiece

The USS *Iowa* was the first of the *Iowa*-class battleships, a class which also includes the USS *Missouri*, *New Jersey*, and *Wisconsin*. The keel for the *Iowa* was laid on 27 June 1940 in the New York Navy Yard, Brooklyn, New York, and the ship was commissioned on 22 February 1943 with Capt. J. L. McCrea as commander. The other *Iowa*-class battleships were launched in 1943 (*New Jersey*) and 1944 (*Missouri* and *Wisconsin*). Two additional *Iowa*-class ships were authorized (*Illinois* and *Kentucky*), but construction on them was halted in 1945 and 1947, respectively.

These vessels are 887 feet long and nominally displace 57,450 tons. They can cruise at speeds of up to 33 knots and have a 15,000-mile unrefueled range, capabilities surpassed only by nuclear-powered vessels. It is generally agreed that *Iowa*-class battleships were among the fastest ships in the world at the time of their construction and exemplify the pinnacle of dreadnought development.

Iowa-class battleships are immense weapon platforms clad in massive armor and capable of withstanding extraordinary levels of military insult. The turret armor is 17.5 inches thick, and the deck is nearly 5 inches of steel. The "belt," the hull on the sides, is 12.5 inches thick. The hull above the water line and the deck were designed to withstand an onslaught equivalent to that produced by these ships' own 16-inch guns. The hull was fabricated using unique methods, and some claim that the battleships are invulnerable to Exocet-class antiship missiles.

In addition to the 16-inch guns, these ships carry several 5-inch guns, and 40- and 60-millimeter guns for protection against aircraft, one of the ships' most effective adversaries. The modernized battleships carry Tomahawk missiles, which can employ either conventional or nuclear warheads and have a range of over 1,500 miles. Harpoon antiship missiles are also included in the suite of weaponry.

The history of the USS *Iowa* includes many proud moments. The ship served in the Pacific during World War II, participating in key naval battles and entering Tokyo Harbor on the day the war ended. The *Iowa* was decommissioned in 1949 and mothballed in San Francisco, but was commissioned for the second time on 1 April 1951 as hostilities intensified in North Korea. Following service in that part of the world, she was decommissioned for a second time on 24 February 1958 and mothballed in Philadelphia. The *Iowa* was commissioned a third time on 28 April 1984, her massive 16-inch guns once again required by the U.S. Navy to support amphibious assaults and as a powerful show of force in trouble spots around the globe.

All of the *Iowa*-class battleships are now decommissioned.

Photo from Robert F. Sumrall's book, Iowa *Class Battleships: Their Design, Weapons, & Equipment* (Annapolis, Md.: Naval Institute Press, 1988).

1 Incident

19 April 1989

THE RAGGED outline of a huge battleship looms out of the mist-filled dawn, the powerful screws slowly churning the cold waters below. The newly risen sun brightly illuminates the port side of the vessel in a reddish light, casting a dark shadow of the great ship to the western horizon. The dampened Stars and Stripes high above the other standards wave slowly as if in a sad farewell. The bow displays the designator "61," the USS *Iowa.* The ship turns to a true heading of 179 degrees and increases speed to 25 knots as the crew prepares for the day's schedule.

It is not an ordinary day in the life of the USS *Iowa.* It is a day the crew of nearly fifteen hundred will never forget, never fully understand, never recall without pain. The USS *Iowa*, one of four active battleships in the U.S. Navy, is cruising in light seas 330 nautical miles northeast of Puerto Rico early on the morning of 19 April 1989. The true wind is 13 knots from 130 degrees, and the waves are 2 to 4 feet high. The ship is part of FLEETEX 3-89, a training exercise for the U.S. Second Fleet and ships from Brazil and Venezuela. The *Iowa* will conduct "Open Ocean Naval Gunfire Support[,] training her Marine detachment in calling missions and spotting rounds, training gunnery personnel in delivering fire against a point target, and verifying operability of the Main Gun Battery."[1] Vice Adm. Jerome L. Johnson, commander of the Second Fleet, is aboard to observe the gunnery exercise, the firing of the huge 16-inch guns that dominate the silhouette of the *Iowa.*

The exercise will begin about 1000 local time, the ship firing twenty-two rounds from Turrets I and II. The sequence will include single gun salvos from both turrets. The weapons officer may also fire from Turret III if the firing window is still open.

The gun crews for Turret II are called together at morning quarters, but many do not attend, even though the guns have not been fired for over a month and many of the crew are new. The turret officer and turret captain tell those in attendance that Turret II will be firing 2,700-pound projectiles with five bags of D846 propellant. Since that combination—the heaviest projectile and a faster-burning propellant—is specifically disallowed, this information must have surprised some of the crew.

There are several last-minute reassignments of the crew in Turret II, including the substitution of GMG2 Clayton Hartwig for GMG3 Richard Lawrence as gun captain for the center gun. Hartwig, an experienced 16-inch gun captain who normally served in this position, had earlier been replaced by Lawrence for the day. Lawrence had been slated to qualify as a gun captain, but some members of the center gun crew had missed the ship's departure and this argued for a crew more like the original.

BM2 Gary J. Fisk is assigned as the powder hoist operator for the center gun in Turret II. Fisk is relatively new to the ship and has never operated the powder hoist. He was "walked through" the operation by some of the chiefs a few days earlier, but actual use of the powder hoist controls will be a totally new experience for him. Other members of the center gun crew of Turret II are GMG3 Robert W. Backherms as the rammerman, his first assignment in this post for an active firing exercise; GMG2 Richard E. Lawrence as cradle operator; and SR Reginald L. Johnson Jr., also relatively new to the ship, as primerman.[2]

All gun stations are manned by 0830. Turret I is ordered to load its 16-inch guns at 0933. The guns are quickly loaded with 1,900-pound blind-loaded and plugged projectiles, which do not carry an explosive charge. After a projectile is rammed into the breech of each of the three guns, reduced charges of D845 propellant, smaller in diameter than normal charges, are positioned behind the projectiles and the massive breech blocks are closed.

At 0938, a command to fire is transmitted to Turret I. The left gun is triggered, but there is no explosion. A misfire. This is not uncommon with reduced charges because the primer flash in the center of the breech may fail to ignite the black powder patch in the center of the smaller diameter bag.

The crew in Turret I begins the misfire procedure, a part of which is to patiently wait for up to an hour to see if a spark from the primer may eventually ignite the black powder pad at the aft end of the bag. If the breech is opened too soon after a misfire, the exposure of a lingering spark or ember to a sudden draft of air could lead to ignition of the bags and an open breech explosion in the gun room. The left gun is reprimed.

A command is issued to fire the center and right guns of Turret I in sequence, and the two huge guns fire without fail. Concussion from the blasts would be dangerous to anyone standing on a forward deck of the battleship and watchers assure that the decks are clear. The guns are reloaded and, once again, there is an order to fire the three guns of Turret I in sequence. The left gun again fails to fire, but the center and right guns fire normally. A third primer is placed in the breech of the left gun and the barrel is raised to the highest elevation to bring the powder bags back into contact with the breech and very close to the primer. The barrel is then returned to the correct target elevation. The left gun misfires for the third time.

The propellant lots aboard the USS *Iowa* and other battleships were manufactured near the end of World War II. While some of the propellant was stored under acceptable conditions when the *Iowa* was undergoing renovations, other lots were stored aboard barges at the Naval Weapons Station at Yorktown, Virginia, from April to August 1988, subjected to the high temperatures of the summer months. Some experts thought that exposure to high temperatures would reduce the level of stabilizer in the propellant grains, a material that keeps the propellant from becoming autocatalytic and spontaneously igniting at elevated temperatures. Such considerations would later be examined in detail.

The course of action is to continue to try firing the left gun of Turret I. If this fails, the crew will wait an hour until there is only a remote possibility of a lingering spark in the primer area, then open the breech and either replace the aft propellant bag or unload the reduced charge.

Capt. Fred P. Moosally, the commanding officer of the *Iowa*, is on the bridge with Admiral Johnson, observing the firing from that vantage point. Only moments before the firing began Captain Moosally had learned from the weapons officer that Turret II would be using "reduced charges," but he was not told that this would be a combination of a heavy projectile and five bags of an unauthorized propellant. Technically it is a "reduced charge" in the sense that five rather than six bags are used, but it is not a reduced charge in the normal sense of the expression, that is, charges of smaller diameter. In any case, Captain Moosally is misinformed about the nature of the firing that will occur from Turret II.

Captain Moosally is anxious to further demonstrate the firings of these guns. It might be some time before the misfire is cleared up in Turret I, so the order is given to load the guns of Turret II. This order immediately concerns GMG1 Dale E. Mortensen, who is serving as turret officer of Turret I. Normally an officer is assigned to this position, but Ens. Effren S. Garrett IV has only been on board for sixteen days and is observing operations in Turret I. Mortensen doesn't want any of the gun crews or officers to forget that there still is a misfire in the left gun of Turret I. In other circumstances, this would have been resolved before going on to firing in other turrets.

The plan for Turret II is that ten rounds are to be fired, two from the left gun and four from both the center and right guns. All the rounds will be the combination of the 2,700-pound projectile with five bags of D846 propellant.

The D846 propellant cans in the magazine for Turret II are clearly marked: "WARNING DO NOT USE WITH 2700 LB (AP, BL&P) PROJECTILE."[3] Placards posted in the turret carry the same message. The firing plan is clearly in conflict with this warning, which is based on characteristics of the D846 propellant. Once ignited, it burns at a higher rate than the proper propellant for the heaviest projectile. The higher burning rate of a normal load of six bags of D846 will result in an overpressured gun with the slowly accelerating 2,700-pound projectile. To compensate for this overpressure, Navy gun experts had calculated that the use of five instead of six bags of propellant would keep the barrel pressure within acceptable levels.

Certainly this subtlety is not broadly understood by the crew. Only about half of them attended the prebrief, and it was not clear that these deviations from normal firings were ever discussed. This unapproved combination of the heaviest projectile and the faster burning D846 propellant undoubtedly raises questions in the minds of knowledgeable crewmen like Mortensen, Hartwig, and others.

There are forty-seven men in Turret II and eleven in the powder magazines surrounding the turret at the lowest level. The men in the magazines are separated from the powder-handling flat by the annular space—part of an isolation concept developed decades ago. Below decks, a 2,700-pound blind-loaded and plugged dummy projectile is hoisted to each of the three gun rooms in Turret II. When the heavy projectiles arrive in the gun rooms, they are tilted to the horizontal position in the hydraulically operated cradle and positioned to move over the spanning tray extending from the cradle into the yawning breech of the gun.

In the center gun room of Turret II, the gun captain, using a hand signal, orders the rammerman to slowly bring the rammer head up to the projectile. When the rammer head contacts the heavy projectile, the gun captain then gives another hand signal that directs the rammerman to accelerate the rammer to full speed, about thirteen or fourteen feet per second, so that the projectile will be forced to engage the rifling in the huge barrel. (Hand signals are important because the noise level can be deafening during combat.) This same process is duplicated in the left and right gun rooms of Turret II.

Rammer operation is controlled in the center gun room by Robert Backherms using a lever at the left of his seat. Extraction of the rammer from the breech is also hand-signaled to the rammerman by the gun captain, but an experienced rammerman knows exactly what to do and has an unimpeded view of the entire loading process. However, Backherms is operating the rammer for the first time in a live firing and probably watches the gun captain, Clayton Hartwig, carefully for his signals. At each step of the operation, the powerful hydraulic system whines in response to Backherms's movement of the lever.

The upper powder hoist operator for the center gun, Gary Fisk, is operating the controls to bring the five bags of propellant from the powder-handling flat to the gun room. The heavy hoist passes close to his cramped position and he probably attempts to draw back, not expecting this in his first operation of the massive mechanism. In addition, positioning the powder car at the correct of two possible locations is usually a problem for new operators. Fisk likely is given advice by the chiefs standing in the booth behind him, since it is improbable he is able to carry out this task without their help.

Hartwig then signals Backherms to open the powder door, which is located to the left and above the spanning tray in the center gun room. Backherms operates a lever on the bulkhead to his left and above the rammer lever. As the powder door opens, three bags of D846 propellant, each weighing about one hundred pounds, are carefully rolled out and eased onto the spanning tray by the gun captain and the cradle operator.

Hartwig manually slides the most forward bag to his right and very near the breech opening, then pushes the second bag up to the first while placing a silk pouch containing lead foils between the two bags. (Lead foils reduce fouling in the barrel during firings.) Lawrence, standing to the left of Hartwig, simultaneously moves the third bag to his left on the powder tray so the next load of bags from the powder hoist will roll onto the spanning tray between the first three bags. The powder door is closed, and the two-tiered powder car is repositioned for the next (in this case) two bags. Fisk observes the hand signal of the gun captain through a glass pane in the bulkhead and attempts to reposition the hoist for the second load of powder bags. The hoist may have first been misaligned but then went right with the coaching of the chiefs. Backherms may also have had difficulty in opening the powder doors since the operating handle functions in a counterintuitive manner, but he finally manages to get the handle in the right position. The powder doors open and the two bags are eased into position between the three already on the spanning tray. Tens of seconds could easily have been lost in the loading process because the crew has not had the proper training and experience.

This process went smoothly in the left and right gun rooms. In those two gun rooms, the rammer had already been slowly brought up to the sequence of five bags and the five-bag propellant train slowly pushed into the breech at about two feet per second. The cradle operators in the left and right gun rooms then retracted the spanning trays and the huge breech blocks were swung into position and locked.

An aide to Admiral Johnson is standing on the bridge with a video camera pointing forward, recording the scene from that ideal vantage point. The camera records that the guns of Turret II are pointing to starboard. When the order to "load" went to Turret II, the three gun barrels were lowered in elevation. This raised the breech of each gun so that it was in line with the spanning tray and the subsequent movement of projectile and the bags of propellant.

The left gun completed the loading process, as is evident in the videotape by the barrel being elevated. About seventeen seconds later the camera records the elevation of the right gun, but the center gun remained depressed. Two of the three guns are ready to be fired, but the center gun is not yet ready. The videotape captures information that will be reviewed many times in the next several months.

It is not possible for anyone outside the turret to know precisely what is happening in the center gun room of Turret II. While it was later determined that loading of the projectile was normal, something occurred in the loading of the powder bags that caused a delay. Perhaps the inexperienced upper powder hoist operator mislocated the powder car and a readjustment was required. Perhaps the new rammerman was confused by the counterintuitive nature of the powder door handle and this slowed the loading process. Perhaps there was discussion about the use of improper propellant with the 2,700-pound projectile. Perhaps, as the Navy came to believe, the gun captain inserted an ignition device instead of the lead foils into the propellant train and directed an overram to initiate an explosion.

The cradle operator, Gunner's Mate Lawrence, reports over the sound-powered phone, "I have a problem here. I'm not ready yet." His words are overheard by Gunner's Mate Mullahy listening on the sound-powered phones in the magazine several decks below and others on the phone circuit.

Chief Reginald Ziegler in the turret officer's booth is heard to say over the phones, "Left gun is loaded. Good job! Center gun is having a little trouble. We'll straighten that out." Chief Ziegler is widely recognized and highly respected as an expert on 16-inch gun operations and a stickler for safe operations.

The cradle operator of center gun, Gunner's Mate Lawrence, again excitedly reports, "I'm not ready yet! I'm not ready yet!" At very nearly the same time, Captain Moosally and Admiral Johnson stand talking on the bridge. The captain says to Admiral Johnson, "Turret II is my best crew and—"

At that moment, 0955 local time, a powerful explosion rips through Turret II. Nearly five hundred pounds of propellant in the open breech of the center gun has somehow been ignited, spewing deadly fire back into the center gunroom, instantly killing the four crewmen. The hot, high-pressure gases quickly sweep through the aft bulkhead and into the gun house and the left and right gun rooms, taking a sudden and complete toll of the crewmen in those areas. The firestorm flashes into the lower decks of the turret, taking everyone in its path, igniting nearly two thousand pounds of propellant on a lower deck in a second low-order explosion, adding to the intense inferno.

Thick steel bulkheads are twisted and deformed by the immense power of the explosion. Paint blisters and insulation on electrical cables is carbonized in the sudden firestorm. The fireball expands at explosive speed and completely fills the interior of the turret. The overpressure inside the turret quickly climbs to more than a thousand pounds per square inch, perhaps much higher. The bucklers of Turret II, heavy rubber fabric materials sealing the openings between the gun barrels and the turret, are blown away, and smoke and fire burst out of the interior of the turret in a way that speaks of the firestorm raging inside.

Captain Moosally and Admiral Johnson are momentarily transfixed by the horror before them, then the captain shouts to others on the bridge to sound general quarters.

The power of the explosion was largely confined within the turret, but many of the crew feel a sickening shiver course through the ship. They pause and look up from their duties, sensing that something unusual has happened, wondering if all is well—not imagining that a terrible explosion has occurred and that many of their shipmates have just died.

Forty-five bags of propellant had been removed from cans in the magazine for use by the guns of Turret II. Four of the bags were still on trays in the magazine, one was in the annular space, and forty had been passed into the powder-handling flat of Turret II. Of those, five were now in the left gun, and five in the right gun. The five bags just placed in the breech of the center gun had somehow been ignited in the open breech of the center gun.

Gunner's Mate Mullahy in the magazine hears the explosion and, in the small part of a second required for his mind to decipher the meaning, the damage is largely complete. He steps out of the magazine and into the annular space. He cautiously opens the hatch into the powder-handling flat. Fire is raging on the powder flat, but he steps inside calling for survivors. The fire and extreme heat keep him from going farther. Hearing no response, he steps back into the annular space, redogs the hatch, and quickly leaves the turret along with others from the magazine and annular space.

GMG3 Kendall L. Truitt, another of the men in the magazine, hears the explosion and "knew that didn't sound right." He "knew that something was drastically wrong" and climbs the ladders to the upper decks with the others. FR Brian Scanio is one level below the main deck and about fifty feet aft of Turret II, speaking with one of the chiefs. A sound like that of thunder rumbles for some seconds. The chief remarks, "That doesn't sound at all normal. Something is wrong." White smoke from the explosion in Turret II is drawn into Turret I by the ventilation system, alarming Mortensen, his first thought being that something went terribly wrong with the misfire in the left gun. It is several moments before he realizes what has happened.

The loss of life is mercifully quick but tragic in magnitude. Forty-seven men, most of them very young, die in the explosion. The Navy report would say that seven died from blast injuries, ten from "blunt force" injuries, and thirty from thermal injuries. Eleven crewmen in the magazines survived the explosion without injury.

Fortunately, the turret designers had planned for such eventualities by separating the magazines from the powder-handling flat with the annular space. If this design feature had not been included, it is conceivable the magazines would have been ignited and the entire ship destroyed. Too many lives had been destroyed as it was, and even more would be irreversibly changed.

General Quarters is sounded and the ship's crew comes into action. The video camera on the bridge records the rapid and effective response of well-trained fire crews. There are heroic acts during this time; a dozen men sustain injuries in their attempts to save whatever lives are left to be saved and to control a serious threat to the entire ship. The fire must not reach the magazines.

Brian Scanio, a nineteen-year-old sailor who has been on the ship about six months, quickly dons a new one-piece Kevlar fire-fighting suit that was brought on board a few weeks ago. He rushes forward to Turret II. As he arrives, a hatch on the aft starboard underside of the turret is being opened by Capt. Jeffery W. Bolander and 1st Sgt. Bruce Richardson of the USMC. A grating just inside the hatch briefly prevents anyone from entering, but the three men finally force it free. A body is just inside.

Scanio, his youth screened by his protective gear, is lifted into the hatch opening by other crewmen about six minutes after the explosion. He is the first crewman to enter the turret after the explosion. Dense smoke precludes any useful vision of the devastated interior. Only orange glows indicate the regions of active fire inside, particularly in the direction of the center and right gun rooms. Scanio is handed lanterns to help light the interior, and secures trunks from blowers on the deck that begin to clear the smoke.

The crew just outside the hatch bring up a 1.5-inch hose and push it toward Scanio. He slowly begins to work his way forward in the turret officer's booth, directing the stream in the direction of those orange glows. Visions of bodies and body parts come into focus and forever etch his young mind.

Scanio suddenly senses a powerful wind flowing into the open hatch, but just as suddenly, the wind reverses with tremendous intensity and forces him back about ten feet against the bulkhead. It is yet another, but much less violent, explosion that courses through the turret about nine minutes after the initial blast. It probably results from the ignition of combustible gases that formed following the initial explosions. The young fireman is not injured and resumes his efforts.

ENFA Robert O. Shepherd, FR Ronald G. Robb, and MR3 Thad W. Harms soon enter the turret to fight the fire. Scanio replenishes his canistered supply of breathing gas and continues his efforts with the other firemen. They make steady progress and are soon joined by GMGC J. C. Miller, GMG1 Verlin W. Allen, and HT1 Thomas J. Smith.

The fires are quenched in about ninety minutes. Totally exhausted, Scanio is helped out of the turret and crewmen strip off the fire-fighting suit. He is drenched in perspiration. The outside air feels freezing cold and he is unable to stand.

The lower regions of the Turret II are now deep with water from the hoses and intentional flooding. Engineering begins the process of pumping the water out of these areas. As the water recedes, two bodies are found in the annular space, and members of the crew who initiated the flooding are sickened to think that their actions may have caused deaths.[4] Body recovery begins as soon as possible and continues during the afternoon. It is a grim process, and no clear records of body location are kept. Several of the crew, including Scanio, tell their stories to the legal officer.

Word of the explosion had been flashed to Vice Adm. J. S. Donnell, commander, Naval Surface Force, U.S. Atlantic Fleet. He names Rear Adm. Richard D. Milligan as the U.S. Navy chief investigating officer. Admiral Milligan is the commander of Cruiser Group 2 and is familiar with battleships, having earlier commanded the USS *New Jersey* during the operation in Lebanon. Directed to conduct a "One Officer" investigation,[5] he makes plans to be aboard the *Iowa* the next day and will be assisted by Capt. Edward F. Messina, Lt. Cdr. Timothy J. Quinn, Lt. Jeffrey W. Styron, Lt. Benjamin F. Roper, Lt. James F. Buckley II, Lt. Patrick M. Brogan, and Lt. (jg) James T. Black. Capt. Joseph D. Miceli of Naval Sea Systems Command will be director of the NAVSEA Technical Review Team responsible for identifying the cause of the explosion.

The *Iowa* is brought to a southwesterly course to rendezvous with the carrier *Coral Sea*, which will take on the injured personnel for transport by air to a shoreside medical center. The ships rendezvous, and the injured are transferred and an explosive ordnance disposal (EOD) team is transferred to the *Iowa*. The battleship then sets a course for Roosevelt Roads, Puerto Rico. The dead crewmen will be put ashore and the *Iowa* will depart for Norfolk.

When the immediate danger of any recurrence of fire is over, an important and dangerous task remains. This is the critical job of unloading the 16-inch guns that still contain over a thousand pounds of propellant. These are the left gun of Turret I, which had misfired, and the left and right guns of Turret II, which had been loaded but had not been fired when the explosion occurred in the center gun.

GMG1 Dale Mortensen has been thinking about the need to unload these three guns since the explosion. He forms a party including two EOD personnel from the *Coral Sea* and proceeds to remove the propellant bags from the left gun in Turret I. This is the more straightforward task because equipment in this turret is still operational. There are no problems. Mortensen then leads his party in unloading the left and right guns of Turret II, a dangerous and potentially disastrous procedure. Since Turret II and the operating equipment are heavily damaged, the two breech blocks have to be manually opened using block and tackle. No officer directs this operation. It is a job requiring the experience and understanding of the chiefs, the men who operate the battleships.

Mortensen carefully thought through the steps that must take place in Turret II and briefs the small party. As the first breech is opened, crewmen direct streams of water on the powder bags—to keep them soaked during that critical time when they are first exposed to air and can be ignited by residual sparks or embers. This operation goes smoothly because of his knowledge and understanding of the guns and emergency procedures. These same steps are then carefully repeated with the second gun.

Informed of the tragic explosion, President Bush sadly notes, "We lost fine young lives. It's a great tragedy and a matter of terrible sadness and [I want to] express my regrets, especially to the families."

Dick Cheney, secretary of defense, promises "a complete and thorough investigation."

The families of those killed have not yet been informed, and many gather at the Norfolk Naval Station to await news they dread to hear.

The cleanup procedures begin in earnest the next morning, 20 April. The grim job of removing bodies from the turret has been completed, but the location of each body was not carefully documented. Only a crude sketch was made of body location, and identification had to be determined later in several cases. The severity of the explosion and fire greatly complicated the process.

The forty-seven crewmen who died in the explosion are soon identified:

Adams, Tung Thanh, 25, fire controlman 3d class, Alexandria, Virginia
Backherms, Robert Wallace, 30, gunner's mate 3d class, Ravenna, Ohio
Battle, Dwayne Collier, 21, electrician's mate, fireman apprentice, Rocky Mount, North Carolina
Blakey, Walter Scot, 20, gunner's mate 3d class, Eaton Rapids, Michigan
Bopp, Pete Edward, 21, gunner's mate 3d class, Levittown, New York
Bradshaw, Ramon Jerel, 19, seaman recruit, Tampa, Florida
Buch, Phillip Edward, 24, lieutenant (jg), Las Cruces, New Mexico
Casey, Eric Ellis, 21, seaman apprentice, Mount Airy, North Carolina
Cramer, John Peter, 28, gunner's mate 2d class, Uniontown, Pennsylvania
Devaul, Milton Francis Jr., 21, gunner's mate 3d class, Solvay, New York
Everhart, Leslie Allen Jr., 31, seaman apprentice, Cary, North Carolina
Fisk, Gary John, 24, boatswain's mate, Oneida, New York
Foley, Tyrone Dwayne, 27, seaman, Bullard, Texas
Gedeon, Robert James, III, 22, seaman apprentice, Lakewood, Ohio
Gendron, Brian Wayne, 20, seaman apprentice, Madera, California
Goins, John Leonard, 20, seaman recruit, Columbus, Ohio
Hanson, David L., 23, electrician's mate 3d class, Bison, South Dakota

Hanyecz, Ernest Edward, 27, gunner's mate 1st class, Bordentown, New Jersey
Hartwig, Clayton Michael, 25, gunner's mate 2d class, Cleveland, Ohio
Helton, Michael William, 31, legalman 1st class, Louisville, Kentucky
Holt, Scott Alan, 20, seaman apprentice, Fort Myers, Florida
Johnson, Reginald Jr., 20, seaman recruit, Warrensville Heights, Ohio
Jones, Brian Robert, 19, seaman, Kennesaw, Georgia
Jones, Nathaniel Clifford Jr., 21, seaman apprentice, Buffalo, New York
Justice, Michael Shannon, 21, seaman, Matewan, West Virginia
Kimble, Edward J., 23, seaman, Fort Stockton, Texas
Lawrence, Richard E., 29, gunner's mate 3d class, Springfield, Ohio
Lewis, Richard John, 23, fire controlman seaman apprentice, Northville, Michigan
Martinez, Jose Luis Jr., 21, seaman apprentice, Hidalgo, Texas
McMullen, Todd Christopher, 20, boatswain's mate 3d class, Manheim, Pennsylvania
Miller, Todd Edward, 25, seaman recruit, Ligonier, Pennsylvania
Morrison, Robert Kenneth, 36, legalman 1st class, Fort Lauderdale, Florida
Moses, Otis Levance, 23, seaman, Bridgeport, Connecticut
Ogden, Darin Andrew, 24, gunner's mate 3d class, Shelbyville, Indiana
Peterson, Ricky Ronald, 22, seaman, Houston, Minnesota
Price, Matthew Ray, 20, gunner's mate 3d class, Burnside, Pennsylvania
Romine, Harold Earle Jr., 19, gunner's mate 3d class, Bradenton, Florida
Schelin, Geoffrey Scott, 20, seaman, Costa Mesa, California
Stillwagon, Heath Eugene, 21, gunner's mate 3d class, Connellsville, Pennsylvania
Tatham, Todd Thomas, 19, seaman recruit, Wolcott, New York
Thompson, Jack Ernest, 22, gunner's mate 3d class, Greeneville, Tennessee
Welden, Stephen J., 24, gunner's mate 2d class, Bethany, Oklahoma
White, James Darrell, 22, gunner's mate 3d class, Norwalk, California
White, Rodney Maurice, 19, seaman recruit, Louisville, Kentucky
Williams, Michael Robert, 21, boatswain's mate 2d class, South Shore, Kentucky
Young, John Rodney, 21, gunner's mate, Columbia, South Carolina
Ziegler, Reginald Owen, 39, gunner's mate, Port Gibson, New York

Debris and destroyed equipment from Turret II are brought out on deck. No careful documentation is made and only a few photographs of very limited value are taken before it is cast overboard. Even cursory documentation would have been important to the investigation that is now underway. The drive to clean up preempts the concerns of why and how.

The next morning, several members of the crew, including Brian Scanio, are given important but unpleasant cleanup tasks associated with the carnage in Turret II. Some of the crew note that hardware and various debris are being thrown overboard without documentation, that the damage scene inside the turret is not being documented or preserved. Scanio gets his camera and takes several pictures within the turret.

Admiral Milligan arrives on board and immediately begins interviews that will eventually number more than eighty. As the *Iowa* nears Roosevelt Roads Naval Station at Puerto Rico on the morning of 20 April, the ship slows and stands off several miles. Sea King helicopters fly out to *Iowa* from the air station, and the crew solemnly loads body bags containing the remains of their shipmates for the short flight back. The Sea Kings return to the air station and the body bags are unloaded and moved to a temporary morgue in a hangar. The large Sea Kings rise and return to the *Iowa* for yet another load of fallen crewmen.

Back at the air station, each body is placed in a metal coffin covered with the Stars and Stripes. Navy pallbearers in white uniforms carry the flag draped coffins, one by one, past a silent and unmoving color guard to a C5 Galaxy transport. Base personnel silently watch the process, repeated too many times, and the magnitude of the loss becomes terribly apparent. Many are unable to contain their grief and turn away.

At long last the forty-seventh coffin is put aboard the Galaxy and the cargo doors are closed. The huge plane thunders down the runway at noon, slowly climbs, and turns north. Its destination is Dover Air Force Base in Delaware, where the bodies of the forty-seven men will be taken to a military mortuary. Pathologists will examine each body and then release them to heartbroken families for burial.

Meanwhile, the *Iowa* turns north and heads for the home port of Norfolk, Virginia, where it will arrive on Sunday, 23 April. Norfolk holds a memorial ceremony on Friday, 21 April, and about 750 attend. The city manager, James B. Oliver Jr., and Gerald L. Baliles, governor of Virginia, speak briefly, offering sympathy to the survivors. The mayor of Norfolk, Joe Leafe, says, "Even when the tragedy strikes far away from here, it is felt here. That ship is part of our community."

Several of the fallen crewmen's families are interviewed, one of them that of Clayton M. Hartwig, the gun captain. Hartwig's mother says she does not blame the Navy for her son's death: "It was just an unfortunate accident—he often told us how that powder could go up in nothing flat." Hartwig's sister, Kathy Kubicina, says that her brother's death is difficult to accept. He had survived deployment of the *Iowa* in the Middle East only to come home and be killed in maneuvers.

The USS *Iowa* sails into Norfolk late Sunday afternoon, 23 April, with nearly fifteen hundred sailors in white uniforms standing at attention by the rails. Each wears a black arm band in recognition of the loss of their shipmates and friends. About five thousand are at the pier to welcome them, not with music and cheers, but with a quiet and tearful sadness. Turret II is still skewed to starboard and the darkened deck is mute testimony to the terrible fire. The center gun is still depressed in the loading position. The Navy keeps reporters from talking to survivors on the pier.

As soon as the battleship docks the crowd surges forward, family members eagerly searching out and embracing their loved ones, confirming for themselves that they are alive. A cross of yellow flowers appears on the stricken turret, and the tearful gaze of many is drawn to the now cold steel chamber. The ship is officially greeted by Adm. Powell Carter, commander in chief of the Atlantic Fleet. A memorial service—which President and Mrs. Bush, Secretary of Defense Dick Cheney, and other officials will attend—is planned for the next day.

Monday, 24 April, the memorial service is held in the largest hangar at the Norfolk Naval Station. The forty-seven caskets, draped with the Stars and Stripes, stretch across the floor of a nearby hangar with an interspersed honor guard of sailors. About one thousand of the *Iowa* crew are seated together wearing black arm bands, and two thousand family members and friends fill the hangar.

The commander of the USS *Iowa*, Capt. Fred P. Moosally, addresses the mourners: "I remember their faces as they toiled on their guns, sweating an honest sweat that comes from young men dedicated to a great cause. I remember their strong hands as they wielded their great charges with an energy I always marveled at. . . . I remember Turret II. They were the life, the spirit and the soul of our ship. We came together in times of trouble. . . . We shared the good and the bad, the comedy and now the tragedy. . . . But we must go on, the crew of the *Iowa*."

President Bush also addresses the mourners:

> They came from Hidalgo, Texas, and Cleveland, Ohio, from Tampa, Florida, and Costa Mesa, California. . . . They came to the Navy as strangers, served the Navy as shipmates and friends, and left the Navy as brothers in eternity. . . . In the finest Navy tradition, they publicly served a great battleship—the USS *Iowa*. . . . I promise you today, we will find out why—the circumstances of the tragedy. . . . But in a larger sense, there will never be answers to the questions that haunt us. . . . We will not—we cannot as long as we live—know why God has called them home. . . . You must be heroically strong now. . . . But you will find that love endures. . . . It endures in the lingering memory of time together, in the embrace of a friend, in the bright questioning eyes of a child. . . . And as for the children of the lost, throughout your lives, you must never forget . . . your father was America's pride. . . . Your mothers and grandmothers, aunts and uncles, are entrusted with the memory of this day. . . . In the years to come, they must pass on to you the legacy of the men behind the guns. . . . This dreadnought, built long before these sailors were born, braved the wartime waters of the Atlantic to take President Roosevelt to meet Winston Churchill in Casablanca, and anchored in Tokyo Harbor on the day World War II ended. . . . The *Iowa* earned eleven battle stars in two wars. . . . October of 1944, off the coast of the Philippines, I can still remember. . . . For those of us serving on the carriers in Halsey's Third Fleet, having the *Iowa* nearby really built our confidence. . . . I was proud to recommission the *Iowa* in 1984. . . . Now fate has written a sorrowful chapter in the history of the USS *Iowa*. . . . Let me say to the *Iowa* crew, I understand your great grief. . . . I too have stared at the empty bunks of lost shipmates, and asked, "Why?". . . Your men are under a different command now, one that knows no rank, only love—knows no danger, only peace. . . . May God bless them.

President and Mrs. Bush walk to the survivors and offer words of comfort and embrace family members. Many openly weep.

What could have happened during this routine firing to cause this sudden and terrible tragedy?

2 Press Reports of the Navy's Investigation

May–September 1989

STORIES OF the USS *Iowa* explosion occupied front pages and prime-time network television news slots for weeks. Video that captured the explosion was played repeatedly, and the television show "20/20" ran an hour-long program on the history of the ship and the recent tragedy. Stories dealt with a variety of topics, including the return of the deceased men to the United States, memorial services, possible causes of the explosion, the return of *Iowa* to Norfolk, and interviews with the commander and members of the crew. The *New York Times*, for example, published seven lengthy articles related to the *Iowa* during the first ten days after the explosion and over three dozen significant articles before the end of the year. This high-profile treatment was repeated in several other major newspapers. The initial articles provided important information about the ship and the men who had died, but later articles took on a somewhat different tone.

Aspects of the Navy's investigation began to be released to the media by Navy, Pentagon, and Defense Department officials in May 1989, about one month after the explosion and four months before release of the Navy's investigative report by Admiral Milligan. According to a 25 May 1989 *New York Times* article by Bernard E. Trainor, unidentified Navy investigators stated that they were examining the possibility that foul play may have been involved in the explosion. Since no equipment failures or other accidental causes for the explosion had been found, other causes were being considered:

> Pentagon officials said tonight that Federal investigators were also studying the relationship between two sailors aboard the *Iowa*. One of the sailors who survived the explosion was the beneficiary of a life insurance policy on a sailor who was killed, officials said.

> The policy was to pay $100,000 in case of accidental death, but the family of the dead sailor has been seeking to prevent payment of the insurance benefit to the surviving sailor.
>
> NBC News reported today that Federal investigators were devoting their entire effort to the theory that one of the sailors might have set off the explosion either as murder or suicide. The report said the two men had a "special relationship."
>
> Pentagon officials, asked about the NBC News report, would not speculate about whether such a scenario was more credible than other theories under investigation by the Navy, which is getting forensic assistance from the Federal Bureau of Investigation.
>
> At Norfolk, Va., headquarters of the Second Fleet, to which the *Iowa* is assigned, a senior officer of the fleet said it was unlikely that a sailor had conspired to kill a fellow crew member for insurance, but because no definitive cause for the explosion had yet been found, every possibility was being investigated.
>
> "Foul play is the least of about a half dozen possibilities that are being investigated," he said. "But we may never know what caused it."
>
> Pentagon officials said tonight that there were several pieces of evidence at issue. The sailor who died has in the past written letters that could be interpreted as suicidal. The survivor, who was on the life insurance policy, had access to the turret.

The focus of the Navy investigation apparently was shifting from an accidental cause to a deliberate act by a crew member, and the issue of foul play continued to be mentioned by officials and reported in the media.

The 26 May issue of the *New York Times* included the following article by Andrew Rosenthal, based on information from unidentified officials:

> WASHINGTON, MAY 25—The Defense Department announced today that it was transferring a sailor who is under investigation in connection with the explosion aboard the battleship *Iowa*.
>
> At the same time, Federal agents hunted for evidence to support a theory that the explosion in a forward turret of the ship last month may have been the result of suicide or murder.
>
> The sailor, Petty Officer Kendall L. Truitt, has not been charged with any wrongdoing. Pentagon officials said he was being transferred from duty aboard the *Iowa* as "a prudent measure" after newspaper and television reports linked his name to the explosion, which killed 47 sailors. The Navy said Mr. Truitt was being transferred to the staff of the commander of Destroyer Squad-

ron 8, based in Mayport, Florida, because of "the extensive publicity surrounding the *Iowa* explosion."

The Defense Department would not comment in detail on the complex and controversial investigation, in which Government officials said Federal Agents have come up with tantalizing bits of information, some of which have filtered into newspaper and television news account, but little real evidence.

Seeking to Narrow Cause

Pentagon officials who spoke on the condition they not be identified said Navy investigators, assisted by the Federal Bureau of Investigation, have found no physical evidence that the blast was caused by a mechanical or electrical failure or any other material problem.

Without such plausible explanations, the officials said investigators were searching for a human explanation. The officials said the investigators have been studying what they call the close relationship Mr. Truitt once had with Gunner's Mate 2d Class Clayton M. Hartwig, 24 years old, who was killed in the explosion.

Mr. Truitt, in an interview with the Daily Press of Newport News, Va., published Sunday, denied that he or Mr. Hartwig was in any way responsible for the explosion. "In my opinion, they have no idea what's going on, what caused it," Mr. Truitt was quoted as saying. "I think they're trying to find an easy way out."

Government officials said the Navy's inquiry into the relationship arose from events involving a life insurance policy that Mr. Hartwig had taken out, naming Mr. Truitt as beneficiary. The policy was to pay $100,000 in the event of accidental death.

One official said the possibility that the explosion was a form of suicide was being explored, along with a less likely possibility—murder. But the official said no real evidence backed either theory and different explanations for the blast, like a straying spark, were still being explored.

Pete Williams, the chief Pentagon spokesman, said the Navy had decided "as a preliminary matter" that improper storing in barges of the gunpowder for the *Iowa*'s 16-inch guns was not to blame for the blast in No. 2 turret April 19 off Puerto Rico. The gunpowder was subjected to extreme heat last summer after it was removed from the ship for safety and stored in barges while the *Iowa* was overhauled at Norfolk, Va.

Mr. Williams said the Navy was still testing the powder, which is packed in cylindrical silk bags that are stuffed into the barrel of the gun behind a shell. Overheating probably would reduce the effective life of the gunpowder but would not make it more likely to explode unexpectedly, he said.

Still, he said the Navy would remove all the gunpowder from the *Iowa* and replace it before the ship's next sailing, scheduled for June 6.

While the Pentagon has tried to keep an official seal on the investigation, some of the threads being pursued by the Naval Investigative Service have been slowly unraveling in news accounts.

A Report Discounted

One such report, published today in *Newsday*, said investigators had found a crude detonating device and a book, "How to Get Even Without Going to Jail," in Mr. Hartwig's car, which the newspaper said was found in the parking lot of a McDonald's restaurant near the Norfolk Naval Base Monday. The newspaper article said the book described ways to make booby traps and other deadly devices.

But Government officials said the car was parked on the base, where Mr. Hartwig's relatives had left it after a memorial service last month. They said it did not contain a detonating device or the book described in the *Newsday* account. Mr. Truitt, 21, who lived in Tampa, Fla., was presented as a hero at a Navy news conference soon after the explosion. He went into seclusion after news reports that he was under investigation.

Mr. Hartwig's sister, Kathleen Kubicina of Cleveland, where her brother lived, said in a telephone interview that she had been trying to block payment to Mr. Truitt because the two men had a falling-out about six months ago after Mr. Truitt married. Navy investigators have questioned Mr. Truitt and his relatives, along with Mrs. Kubicina and Mr. Hartwig's parents.

Mrs. Kubicina said they [were] asked repeatedly if Mr. Hartwig had been homosexual. "I myself had no personal knowledge that he was," Mrs. Kubicina said. "I can't say for sure and nobody will ever know."

Government officials said investigators had no evidence indicating Mr. Hartwig was suicidal, but that their investigation "created a picture of a troubled man."

The 3 June issue of the *New York Times* included a report by Richard Hallaran that further suggested the shift of the Navy's investigation toward the consideration of an act of suicide by Clayton M. Hartwig:

Washington, June 2—Government officials said tonight that Navy investigators were focusing on a theory that 47 sailors killed aboard the battleship *Iowa* last month died in an explosion caused by a sailor intent on suicide.

The officials said investigators have collected written materials that indicated Petty Officer 2d Class Clayton M. Hartwig was deeply despondent and excessively dependent on a few people.

But the officials cautioned that the investigators had no hard physical evidence that Mr. Hartwig, who loaded the powder in the gun, had committed suicide and no written evidence that he intended to take his own life or the lives of shipmates.

A $15 Timer

NBC News reported tonight that a shipmate had told investigators that Mr. Hartwig spoke to him about how a $15 timer could be used with a battery to cause an explosion in the breech of a 16-inch gun. CBS News had a similar report about a shipmate who said Mr. Hartwig had shown him a timer he had bought. An Administration official said tonight that there is such a witness and investigators are trying to determine his veracity.

"Everything is still up in the air," the official said of the investigation of the explosion inside a gun turret on April 19.

Other Government officials said the investigators were gathering circumstantial evidence that amounts to a psychological profile of Mr. Hartwig and that evidence raised a clear possibility of his having suicidal tendencies.

The officials cautioned that other theories, including a mistake by an inexperienced, hastily assembled crew or a detonation caused by flawed gunpowder, have not been ruled out.

They said the evidence was so fuzzy that a conclusion may never be reached.

The officials declined to describe precisely what the written materials were but suggested that they included Mr. Hartwig's letters to family and friends and a diary or collection of notes he had written.

Sailors Interviewed

The investigators have interviewed sailors on the *Iowa* who know Mr. Hartwig and have found some statements that supported the suicide theory, the officials said.

But they said no one had heard Mr. Hartwig say he planned to commit suicide.

In several interviews, members of Mr. Hartwig's family have vigorously denied that he intended to commit suicide, citing optimistic letters from him just before his death.

NBC said the bodies of victims were in a crouching position, indicating they realized an explosion was coming. The network also said a timing device could have provided such a warning, by smoke or sound. The Administration official confirmed that sailors in the turret were not in the expected positions and said there was no single explanation of this. The official also said there was no hard evidence that a timer was used to cause the explosion.

NBC also reported that Mr. Hartwig was living in a fantasy world, telling his family and friends that he was being transferred to London when, in fact, the Navy had no such plans. But an official said Mr. Hartwig was being considered for duty in London.

The Pentagon said tonight that "despite continuing speculative media reports concerning reported aspects of the USS *Iowa* accident, the Navy's investigation has not been completed." For that reason the Pentagon said it could not discuss specific aspects of the investigation.

Navy officials said an examination of the turret had been completed and all damaged equipment removed. It was not clear if all questioning of people connected with the explosion had been finished. In addition, officials suggested that writing the final report, a version of which is to be made public, would require care because of the publicity surrounding the accident.

A widely held view among officials here was that the investigation will not come to a definite conclusion about the cause of the explosion because critical witnesses were dead and evidence inside the turret was destroyed.

Meanwhile, the Navy issued a carefully worded statement, suggesting that Petty Officer 3d Class Kendall L. Truitt had been cleared of allegations reported in the press that he had caused the explosion.

The Navy did not mention Mr. Truitt by name in its statement. It emphasized that "no charges have been made" in connection with the explosion in a gun turret in a firing-drill northeast of Puerto Rico. Widespread press reports have said Mr. Truitt was being queried because he was the beneficiary of a $100,000 life insurance policy on Mr. Hartwig.

Meanwhile, Navy officials said the *Iowa* was scheduled to sail from Norfolk for the North Atlantic and the Mediterranean on Wednesday.

The Chief of Naval Operations, Adm. Carlisle A. H. Trost, imposed the moratorium on operations of the navy's four battleships after the explosion. Officials suggested that the ban would not be lifted until the investigation had been completed.

The Navy's scenario—suicide by Clayton Hartwig—continued to be emphasized over the next six weeks. The Navy's case was detailed in David Johnson's *New York Times* article, "Navy's Evidence Suggests Sailor Set off Ship Blast to Kill Himself," published on Wednesday, 19 July 1989, three months after the incident. Sources for the information were not identified:

Washington, July 18—A Navy investigation of the gun turret explosion that killed 47 sailors aboard the battleship *Iowa* in April has found strong circumstantial evidence that a sailor set off the blast to kill himself, Government officials say.

The three-month inquiry found no technical flaws in the mechanical or electrical systems in the ship's gun turret that would suggest any other cause of the explosion, said Pentagon and Congressional officials in recent interviews, who spoke on the condition that their names not be used. Nor has it found instability in gunpowder used to fire the 16-inch guns, they said.

In addition, NBC News, citing Navy personnel it did not identify by name, reported today that investigators had interviewed a sailor who told them he had talked with Petty Officer 2d Class Clayton M. Hartwig, who is now suspected of setting the explosion, on the evening before the blast, discussing explosive devices that could sink the ship. Petty Officer Hartwig was among the sailors killed.

Psychological Profile Cited

The broadcast said that a psychological profile of Mr. Hartwig by the Federal Bureau of Investigation, and hundreds of other exhibits, has led investigators to conclude that Mr. Hartwig was a "troubled" young man whose sexual advances had been rejected by other sailors and who took his own life.

One such exhibit was a three-hour videotaped statement by an *Iowa* sailor, identified as David Smith, whom NBC News quoted as having told investigators that Petty Officer Hartwig discussed with him how he could use a 9-volt battery and small timing device to set off a bomb.[1] It was not explained how these components would have been used to detonate the blast in the gun turret.

The explosion occurred in Turret II of the battleship during a firing drill as the ship steamed about 330 miles northeast of Puerto Rico on 19 April. The crew members in the turret, a self-contained cylinder extending down six levels from the main deck, were killed in the blast and ensuing fire.

The Navy has announced that its report on the accident is complete but it would not disclose the findings pending a review by senior commanders. Tonight, Navy officials refused to comment further on reports that the Navy investigation had found that Mr. Hartwig may have been responsible for the explosion.

Family Dismissed Findings

Other Pentagon officials, however, said the Navy had been reluctant to issue a report because it would be another blow to the already demoralized ship's crew and might generate legal action, adverse publicity and possible charges of incompetence or even cover-up.

Mr. Hartwig's sister, Kathleen Kubicina of Cleveland, who has acted as a spokeswoman for the Hartwig family, dismissed the findings. "We don't believe it," she said in an interview this evening. "There is no way."

She also insisted that her brother was not a homosexual and said that 17 of his letters had been reviewed by a panel of psychiatrists who concluded he was a "normal healthy young man."

Immediately after the explosion, a board of inquiry headed by Rear Admiral Richard D. Milligan was named to establish the facts about the ship's 16-inch guns, the condition of the turret, the ability of the gun crew and where things had gone wrong.

Second Inquiry

A second inquiry by criminal investigators from the Naval Investigative Service and the Federal Bureau of Investigation was started when suspicions of suicide or homicide arose after disclosure that a $100,000 insurance policy had been taken out by Mr. Hartwig. He named a fellow crewman, Petty Officer 3d Class Kendall L. Truitt, as the beneficiary in case of accidental death.

After spending $5 million to $7 million and interviewing 400 to 500 people, the investigators were unable to make a case and began a new round of inquiries. Several investigators sailed aboard the *Iowa* when she left Norfolk for Europe on June 6.

When investigators asked Mr. Smith about his conversations with Mr. Hartwig, according to the NBC broadcast, he replied that they talked about "explosions, that kind of stuff. How to set off the powder. All that kind of stuff."

Reports of Rejection

Mr. Smith said the two men were talking in a passageway aboard the ship when Mr. Hartwig told him that he could use a "9-volt battery" and a small timer to set off a bomb. The broadcast said Mr. Smith told an investigator that such a device could "sink the whole ship."

Mr. Smith said that Mr. Hartwig led him to a locker and showed him a timing device. "It was a dark color," Mr. Smith was quoted as saying. "It had numbers like 1, 2, 3. . . . It had a start and stop and a reset button."

The broadcast said that Mr. Smith told investigators that Mr. Hartwig made sexual advances to him, which he rejected, on the night before the blast. Mr. Smith said he did not report the incident immediately because he feared the others would think incorrectly that he was a homosexual.

> The evidence that Mr. Hartwig may have committed suicide has come from letters to his family and notes written to himself, the officials said. The letters and notes, the officials said, indicated that Mr. Hartwig had become despondent when his friend Mr. Truitt married and thus had less time for him.
>
> But there was no statement saying he planned to take his own life or the lives of shipmates, the officials said. Moreover, they said the investigators had no physical evidence that Mr. Hartwig, who helped to load powder into the gun before the explosion, had committed suicide. Nor did they know exactly how he might have set off the explosion.
>
> Mr. Truitt has vehemently denied having had a sexual relationship with Mr. Hartwig. Tonight Mr. Truitt's lawyer, Ellis S. Rubin, said that if American Express, the insurance company, refused to pay Mr. Truitt benefits under Mr. Hartwig's insurance policy because the death is deemed to be a suicide, he would sue the company and "turn the trial into an investigation of what happened on the *Iowa*."

News reports based on unidentified sources became more sensational as release of the Navy report drew near. Navy investigators were quoted by NBC in July as saying that Kendall Truitt told them that his relationship with Hartwig was like the film *Fatal Attraction* in which a spurned lover attempts to kill the other party and his mate. Truitt's attorney retorted that his client had never made such a statement and it was Navy investigators who espoused that view.

The testimony of David Smith, released earlier by a Navy source, was retracted by Smith in September. Smith, according to ABC Radio News, now said that neither his statement about being shown a timing device nor his allegation that Hartwig made sexual advances toward him was true. Smith said that he gave false testimony to investigators in response to intense interrogation. Smith's denial was reported by the paper in its 5 September issue.

The Navy also began to release information to the effect that physical evidence indicated that an igniting device had been inserted into the gun prior to the blast. A statement by "an administration official," again speaking on condition of anonymity, was reported in a 7 September 1989 article by Andrew Rosenthal of the *New York Times* entitled "Fatal Blast Aboard Battleship *Iowa* Was Probably Intentional, Investigation Finds": "The report's conclusions are more general, that it was probably an intentional act. . . . An Administration official said the primary physical evidence indicating the gun was tampered with consisted of 'minute traces of chemical elements' found under a copper ring that is placed into the barrel of the gun before the projectile is loaded.

. . . 'Those elements do not appear in a normal test firing,' the official said. 'The conclusion that people made from that was that something was placed into the gun that shouldn't be there.'"

Such reports were repeated in many other papers throughout the country and continued up to and beyond the release of Admiral Milligan's report of his investigation on 7 September. Vice Adm. Joseph S. Donnell III, commander, Naval Surface Force, U.S. Atlantic Fleet, stated to the House Committee on Armed Services during a hearing on 13 December that "leaks to the media . . . became more than an annoyance and embarrassment and threatened to undermine the investigative effort."[2]

Some elements of these news releases were, indeed, supported by "opinions" contained in the Navy's report. It appears, but remains unproven, that officials involved in the investigation, speaking on the condition of anonymity, used the press to advance a scenario in which a deliberate intentional act caused the explosion and, further, to suggest that the guilty party had been identified and the Navy was not responsible. It also appears that there was too little in the way of verification and corroboration of such stories before they were published.

3 Indian Head Naval Ordnance Station

7 December 1989

I LIFTED the telephone receiver, touched in the number, and waited for an answer, scanning the few notes I'd prepared for the conversation, nervous about this first contact with the Navy. "Captain Miceli," a voice boomed.

"Captain Miceli, this is Richard Schwoebel at Sandia National Laboratories. I'd like to meet with you as we begin our independent investigation."

"Yes, I've been expecting your call. Can you come to Indian Head sometime during the next two weeks? I'd like you to meet the Navy team."

Sandia National Laboratories was established in 1949 at the request of President Harry Truman. The president had written a letter to Mr. Leroy A. Wilson, president of AT&T, and a similar letter to Oliver E. Buckley, president of Bell Laboratories on 13 May. At that time, Sandia was a part of Los Alamos Scientific Laboratory and was responsible for the development of militarized nuclear weapons using Los Alamos "physics packages." Shortly thereafter, on 4 October, the Atomic Energy Commission executed a contract, and AT&T took over management of Sandia on 1 November 1949. Sandia had 1,742 employees at the time, but with the continued development of a nuclear weapons stockpile, the number grew to over 8,000 by 1989. Sandia's mission was enlarged and it became a "multi-disciplinary laboratory" of the Department of Energy (DOE), involved in defense and nondefense-related activities, its laboratories and field test facilities covering many square miles on the southeastern edge of Albuquerque, and a smaller installation in Livermore, California.

I would meet with the Navy Technical Review Team, directed by Capt. Joseph D. Miceli, at the Indian Head Naval Ordnance Station south of Washington, D.C., on the afternoon of 7 December, nearly eight months after the turret explosion aboard the battleship USS *Iowa*. Somehow nearly five hundred pounds of propellant had been ignited in one of the guns before the breech was closed, killing all the sailors inside the turret. The entire ship might have been destroyed had it not been for the superb response of the crew in fighting the ensuing fire.

There had been extensive media coverage of the tragic incident, scenes of fire fighting aboard the ship after the explosion, the memorial service, pledges by President Bush and others to find the cause. I had watched the explosion of the turret caught by a video camera along with millions of other viewers, never imagining that Sandia and I would become involved in the investigation.

There had also been several press reports based on the comments of unidentified officials suggesting that the explosion had not been an accident, but that a member of the crew had deliberately caused the tragedy, that it was an act of murder and suicide. The unsubstantiated press reports further suggested that the explosion was caused by Clayton Hartwig, a member of the center gun crew, in response to a failed homosexual relationship with another sailor. The story was given extensive coverage and widely repeated in newspapers across the country.

The Navy's technical report was issued at a press conference on 7 September by Rear Adm. Richard D. Milligan, the chief investigating officer. It confirmed the Navy's belief that the explosion could not have been an accident but was caused by an intentional act by a member of the crew, "most probably Clayton Hartwig," gun captain of the center gun crew. The Navy's conclusions, in spite of the earlier press reports, stunned the survivors, the public, and Congress. Committees of both the House and Senate held hearings to review the Navy's conclusions, and the Navy's testimony encountered skepticism and disbelief. More hearings were planned in December, when I would be meeting with Captain Miceli and his team.

The Senate Armed Services Committee (SASC), under Chairman Sam Nunn, responded to the hearings with the Navy in November by calling for an independent review of the Navy's findings. The Senate had asked the General Accounting Office (GAO) to find a laboratory to conduct such an independent review, and Sandia National Laboratories was selected. The selection was based in part on recommendations by the National Academies of Engineering and Science, because of our engineering and scientific expertise and because of our work dealing with the safety of nuclear weapons.

I was asked to organize and lead the independent review, a task that impressed me with its varied problems, significant unknowns, and complexities, a task that kept me awake late into many nights, concerned with not only the technical aspects but also the powerful forces that could influence this investigation. Fortunately, there were not even hints of "suggestions" regarding how I was to proceed from either Sandia or DOE, at the outset or at any time during the investigation. Even more fortunately, I found genuine interest among the employees at Sandia who might contribute the most to this investigation and a team was quickly established. The *Iowa* investigation was a unique project for Sandia, the first independent assessment requested by a committee of Congress.

The committee's call for an independent assessment underscored their skepticism of the Navy's findings and must have had a chilling effect on the Navy investigating team. The meeting with Captain Miceli would be the first step in the Sandia review. I had read and reread the Navy's voluminous technical reports on the tragedy but felt deeply apprehensive about this first meeting, about the unspoken expectations of the committee, and about what we could add to what the Navy had already done.

I anticipated a cool reception, bracing myself for remarks or attitudes reflecting that Sandia knew little about naval gun systems, forensics, or criminal investigations. All this was, of course, only too true. On the other hand, although the Navy's technical report was extensive and covered many topics relevant to the explosion, there were issues relevant to their conclusions that had not been fully addressed.

The two-hour drive from National Airport to Indian Head gave me time to review once again my thoughts for the meeting, time to reevaluate the questions that I wanted to discuss with the Navy, time for the inevitable negative thoughts about the obvious down sides of this investigation. I turned into the parking lot outside the Indian Head security gate and saw Jerry Herley and Tim Stone standing near the gate office. The two GAO representatives were obviously waiting for me. I wanted to initiate the interaction with the Navy on my own before other organizations with their various agendas became involved. I was looking forward to a one-on-one with the Navy, and the presence of the GAO would only elevate the tension of this first meeting.

Conscious that I am rarely successful in concealing my thoughts, I put on a friendly face as I greeted Jerry and Tim. "Tim and I thought we'd join you and the captain for the first meeting," Jerry said. "Hope you don't mind."

I asked how they heard about my meeting with the Navy team. "Captain Miceli called us," Jerry laughed. "He wants witnesses, I guess."

We walked into the guard office, and the duty officer called the captain. Chief James P. Tonahill arrived in a few minutes to drive me to the captain's office. The chief explained that he had been assigned to the *Iowa* investigation soon after the explosion and had been working with the Navy team ever since. His normal billet was with the USS *Wisconsin*, one of the other three *Iowa*-class battleships. He had had many years of hands-on experience with the huge 16-inch guns.

It was a short drive to a structure built during the 1940s, needing yet another coat of gray paint, standing among several denuded oak trees. Fallen leaves covered large areas of the asphalt roof, making the building look unoccupied. We parked in a small lot in front and walked up shallow wooden steps to the door, past signs announcing that this was a NAVSEA facility. The entrance was crowded with pictures of recent commanders, flags and pendants, large projectiles, and numerous items related to naval gunnery. A secretary sat at a desk just inside and to the left of the entrance.

I introduced myself and was told that Captain Miceli was on the phone but would be finished in a few minutes. I turned to study the memorabilia in more detail. The walls were neatly lined with dozens of photographs of ships and crews dating back to before World War II. The dark oak floor creaked loudly as I slowly moved from one display to another. Walking carefully was of little value in reducing the noise in the otherwise quiet office. It reminded me of floors in the old school I attended at my home in North Dakota, smelling as though they had recently been oiled. The sun shining through one of the windows reflected brightly off the floor, lighting up the interior of the room, casting my elongated shadow toward Captain Miceli's office.

I overheard the captain on the phone, the same booming voice I'd heard during our earlier conversation, the same falsetto laugh. In a few moments he was out the door to shake my hand, dapper in his dark blue uniform. He was a little under six feet in height but appeared taller because of his girth. His remaining hair was gray, perhaps having become a shade more gray since this investigation began, I thought. He asserted himself with a large voice and a penetrating look accented by his steel-rimmed GI glasses. "I'm glad you were able to come to Indian Head. The *Iowa* is pulling into Norfolk today to undergo repairs."

We talked about the Sandia team visiting the *Iowa*, reviewing the damage, getting acquainted with turret operations aboard the ship. Captain Miceli said it wouldn't be a problem, that he could arrange it whenever we were ready. He glanced toward Herley and Stone, who had been quietly talking to one another near the entrance. He looked back at me as if to say, the GAO is here, too. I realized that the GAO had found out about this meeting from a source other than the captain. He also must have wanted a one-on-one exchange, free of the oversight groups.

He led me past the secretary's desk and into his office at the front of the building. A handful of team members were seated at the table engrossed in conversation. They greeted me in a perfunctory manner and immediately went back to their discussion. While Chief Tonahill had been deferential in the car, I couldn't get a smile out of him as we shuffled our chairs and took papers from our briefcases. The group would say little during the afternoon, leaving essentially all the conversation to Captain Miceli. I took the chair at the head of the table next to the captain's desk, and he sat to my left facing the windows. I'd wondered earlier if from 1:00 to 4:00 P.M. would be enough time for our first exchange. Now four o'clock seemed a long time away.

Captain Miceli blinked a few times, staring into space beyond the windows that were directly opposite him, the light reflecting from his glasses. "How would you like to proceed?" he asked.

I offered to give a brief overview of Sandia and suggested that we spend the bulk of the afternoon going through the Navy technical report.

"Fine, fine," he replied. His gaze shifted toward me. He wanted to skip the "overview" and get on to discussion of the report, about which he was very comfortable. The ten- or fifteen-minute overview emphasized Sandia's mission as a key part of the nuclear weapons complex and capabilities that were relevant to the *Iowa* investigation. My offhand appraisal was that this brief review couldn't have been of less interest to my small and uniformly indifferent audience, staring at me with expressionless eyes, asking not a single question, seemingly anesthetized.

I briefly stated the three tasks of our independent review. Sandia would, as part of the first task, review the Navy work on foreign materials found on the projectile (fig. 3-1). We would assess the background levels of these materials in the turrets, and relate this to the hypothetical device the Navy said was used to initiate the explosion.

Captain Miceli scowled and looked sharply at me. Use of the adjective "hypothetical" had touched a nerve, questioned the Navy's conclusion, indicated that I didn't accept the Navy's conclusion as a fact. I forged ahead.

"In part two of our work, we will also review and perhaps supplement your black powder and propellant sensitivity work. Lastly, we'll review the general methodology used in your investigation. You'll be kept fully informed of our

A

B

Figure 3-1. The 16-inch projectile is approximately 6 feet long and, as in the case of the projectile in the center gun of Turret II on the morning of the explosion, weighs 2,700 pounds. Note in fig. 3-1B the circumferential copper rotating band that is swaged on to the aft end of the projectile. This band engages the rifling of the barrel and spins the projectile for in-flight stability and accuracy of trajectory. *Left*, Department of Energy; *right*, courtesy FCCM (SW) Stephen Skelley, USNR.

progress. I want you to come to Sandia in January and meet the rest of our team. We'd appreciate it if you would give us a detailed presentation of your work at that time."

Captain Miceli brightened. He said he was anxious to meet the Sandia team and looked forward to that exchange. This appeared to be the first minor point of agreement, the captain nodding and sitting back in his chair, contemplating a meeting in which his team would have an opportunity to present all their findings. The captain and I shared a lukewarm smile, but the other faces remained fixed, seemingly immutable, as if they wore masks.

With that as a modest turning point, Captain Miceli took the initiative and launched into an extended overview of the Navy's investigation and the cause of the explosion from its perspective. He emphasized the key points that led his team to conclude that an improvised chemical ignition device had been placed among the propellant bags by Clayton Hartwig: "The improvised ignition device consisted of a container of swimming pool HTH, a second container of a glycol containing fluid, like brake fluid, surrounded by steel wool."

He graphically illustrated this by placing test tubes of the HTH and brake fluid over a wad of steel wool in his hand. He did this with a certain sense of theater, as though he were aware of the motions that would most impress the observer and make plausible the story he told. "This kind of ignitor was placed between the propellant bags and initiated by fracturing the tubes with pressure applied by the rammer," he went on. By this he meant that the rammer, which pushes the propellant bags into the breech, was overextended and compressed the containers until they fractured, mixing the contents, initiating a chemical reaction that ignited a black powder patch and then the five hundred pounds of propellant.

Captain Miceli continued: "We found residues from the ignitor on the rotating band of the projectile, and this foreign material was crucial to the conclusions of our investigation. In particular, we found these residues in the cannelure of the rotating band, a region that was sealed when the projectile was moved forward in the barrel by the explosion (fig. 3-2). The only person who was in a position to do this was the gun captain. Moreover, an FBI team has determined that Hartwig was suicidal." The captain spoke with complete certainty, as though no other conclusion was possible, indicating that there was no question in his mind that this improvised device had initiated the explosion and that all inadvertent or accidental causes of the explosion had been ruled out. Captain Miceli would repeat and further elaborate on this scenario several times in future months, adding a few more details with each telling.

Facing page

Figure 3-2. The circumferential rotating band at the aft end of the projectile is illustrated here in cross-section. The upper illustration shows the cross-section of the rotating band before ramming of a projectile into the gun barrel. The forward part of the projectile is to the right in these figures. Both the cannelure and the forward slots are open to the environment before ramming. The lower illustration shows the configuration of the cannelure and forward slots after the projectile has been rammed into the rifling of the barrel. As the projectile is forced into the narrowing gun breech, the fin closes the cannelure. In the open-breech explosion aboard the *Iowa*, the projectile was forced forward about 30 inches into the barrel, sealing the cannelure as illustrated here. The Navy found "foreign materials" in the closed cannelure that they attributed to debris from a chemical ignition device placed among propellant bags aft (left) of the projectile. Note that the forward slots are sealed from such debris by the fin engaging the rifling of the barrel.

ROTATING BAND NOMENCLATURE

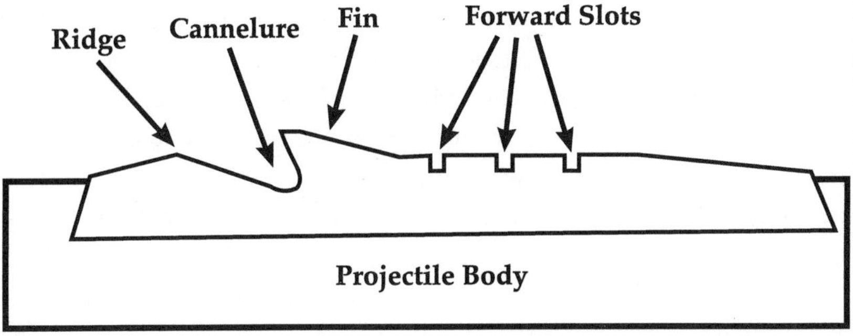

Ridge

Cannelure

Fin

Forward Slots

Projectile Body

Rotating Band Cross Section As Loaded

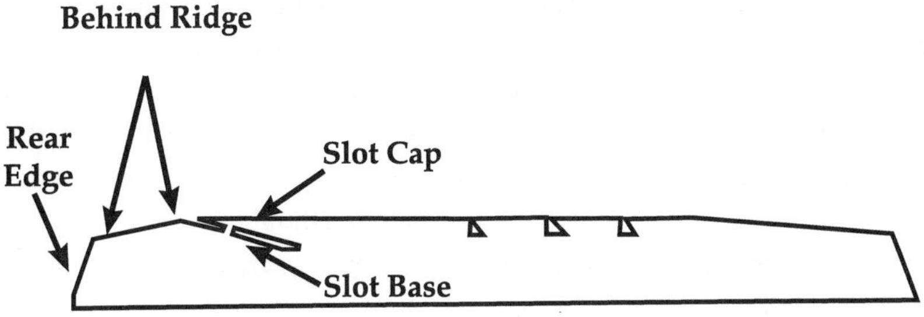

Behind Ridge

Rear Edge

Slot Cap

Slot Base

Rotating Band Cross Section As Recovered

I asked how the gun captain would have learned about such an improvised ignition device.

"This device is common knowledge to anyone who's taken the EOD [Explosive Ordnance Disposal] course, and Hartwig had taken that course. It was also described in *Soldier of Fortune* magazine, copies of which were found in his locker aboard ship. We first found what we believed were residues of an electronic ignitor, but after further investigation, we concluded the residues were consistent with a chemical device. Admiral Milligan's report was not updated before it was released, but it's inconsequential. The important things are that we found no credible accidental causes, the explosion was a deliberate act, and everything points to it having been Hartwig who committed this act."

I pulled out the Navy report. Captain Miceli glanced at it and then piercingly back at me through his steel-rimmed glasses. Not even a hint of a smile, waiting for the first of a series of questions.

"I've read your final report," I said, "and I'd like to ask some questions."

"Fine, fine," he replied, "go right ahead. Anything at all."

I began by citing a section of the report about foreign materials on the projectile. The report stated that "this [foreign] material was only replicated when a chemical device was used to initiate" an explosion. I asked about the uniqueness of this result, the use of the word "only": "Isn't it possible that there are other sources of such foreign materials? How can you be sure that what you call foreign materials were not contamination?"

"What do you mean by other sources of foreign materials?" Captain Miceli replied.

"Well, for example, steel wool cleaning pads might have been used for breech cleaning, and there certainly could be residues of oils in the breech that contain glycol. Also, the projectile had been exposed to the maritime environment ever since it was manufactured—probably many years ago. Chlorine would probably be found on any such surface. Who knows how else the projectile may have been contaminated?"

The captain was emphatic. "Steel wool is not authorized for such cleaning, but has been used by crews for this purpose. [The Navy would later assert that steel wool was never used in cleaning of these guns.] Break-Free [an oil-like material routinely used to clean these guns] is a lubricant that is routinely used in the gun cleaning process. But there is no glycol in Break-Free."

Miceli went on to say that fibers of steel wool will only be coated with a layer containing calcium, chlorine, and oxygen when combustion occurs of the kind produced by such an ignitor. The Navy's view was that these foreign materials could not have come from other sources. It was clear from our discussion, however, that the Navy had not done a thorough study of surface contamination in the turrets, something that had to be done before they could logically put forward the conclusions in their report.

I asked Captain Miceli to describe the overramming of the propellant bags into the gun beyond their normal position: How could this have occurred? "This is also very crucial to our scenario," he said. "Gun captains are instructed to ram the charges to a position such that the last bag of propellant will be just forward of the closed breech." He explained that the rammer had obviously been extended too far into the breech—there had been an overram. The extent of the overram was evident from the fire damage to the rammer mechanism: "The gun captain placed the improvised ignitor between the first and second bags of propellant, and ordered a ram beyond the normal position. This was to rupture the containers and mix the constituents to initiate the explosion."

The captain emphasized that the gun captain had sole authority to order a deliberate overram. The Navy's logic was that since an overram had occurred, the gun captain must have ordered it. The possibility of an inadvertent overram was simply dismissed.

Captain Miceli hypothesized that the gun cradle operator, Richard Lawrence, questioned the obvious overram position and started a discussion in the gun room about the ram position. The captain presented his detailed view of the sequence of events, a view I would hear several times over the next months. At this point, Captain Miceli went on to say that for the first several weeks he and his team had looked for an accidental cause for the explosion. They initially thought friction associated with the overram was the probable cause of ignition.

"Then," Miceli said, "Kathleen Kubicina, the sister of Clayton Hartwig, sent a letter to the Navy about a fifty-thousand-dollar double indemnity insurance policy on her brother. The beneficiary was another crewman aboard *Iowa*. This stimulated Admiral Milligan to call in the Naval Investigative Service, which began an altogether different line of investigation. The Naval Investigative Service raised a question about the possible use of an electronic detonator to initiate the explosion. While we initially found foreign materials that seemed to support the presence of an electronic detonator, further work indicated that there was a much better comparison of the foreign materials with a chemical ignitor."

We talked about the Navy's lab tests and the nature of their conclusions. I noted, for example, that they had conducted ten propellant-bag ramming studies to see if an explosion could be initiated. The Navy's conclusion was that overramming could be "eliminated as a possible cause" for the explosion. I said that I did not understand coming to that conclusion on the basis of only ten tests.

Captain Miceli nodded. "Yes, I understand your point, but none of our studies gave us any indication of another cause of ignition other than the one of a deliberately placed ignitor device. If I used terms like 'probabilities,' that would mean to a senator or a representative that it could happen, and that could easily be translated into it did happen by some low-probability process. I couldn't use words like that with those people. They just wouldn't understand. I was responsible for giving the guns a clean bill of health since all firing of battleship 16-inch guns was prohibited following the explosion. On the basis of our studies, I was able to give that clean bill of health."

In other words, since the captain and his team found no accidental cause for the explosion, they concluded there was no accidental cause. A break in the logic.

Captain Miceli showed a videotape of 16-inch gun loading operation aboard a battleship. He pointed out the key step in the process, where he believed that Clayton Hartwig inserted the improvised device among the propellant bags. He then went on to describe the forensic analysis of the deaths that occurred in the immediate area of the blast: "The crew in the gun room was caught flat footed, there was no warning."

I said that I couldn't imagine forensic analyses of the shattered remains of the center gun crew revealing whether or not the explosion was a surprise. He stood to illustrate the positions of the center gun crew at the time of the explosion as he interpreted the medical examiner's observations, trying to convince me that it was possible to deduce that the crew was not expecting an explosion. I remained unconvinced.

I noted that one of the Navy's laboratory tests had found that shearing of a propellant pellet inside a propellant bag could result in local ignition of the pellet's surface (fig. 3-3). The Navy report stated, however, that the rammer could not deliver sufficient force to shear propellant pellets. Since the two thousand plus pounds of force applied to a small area by the rammer could easily fracture individual propellant pellets, I asked if that couldn't be a possible ignition mechanism.

The Navy people looked at one another and then patiently explained that two thousand pounds of rammer thrust is delivered over the large area of the rammer head, so individual pellet damage can't occur. They nodded at one another, acknowledging what should have been obvious.

I persisted. But how uniform is the loading? The two thousand pounds of force applied by the rammer could deliver extremely high specific loads to small portions of the bag charges if the pellets aren't uniform. Steve Mitchell, an explosives expert, responded. "Yes, I see your point, but even if a pellet fractured and the surface ignited, it isn't at all clear this would propagate into the rest of the propellant. Besides, several overramming tests have been made with no indication of ignition." Within a few months we would revisit this critical point.

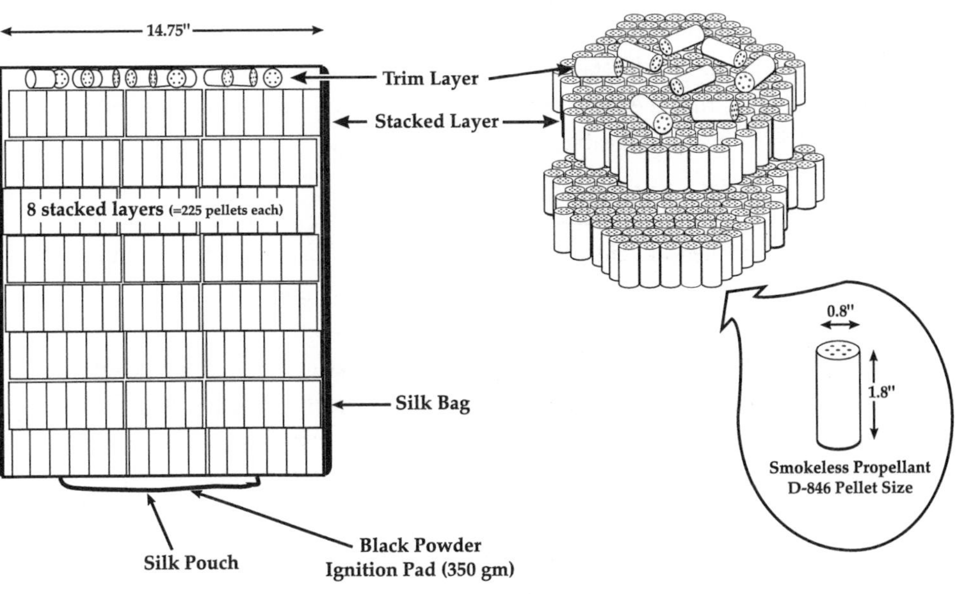

Figure 3-3. A schematic of the cylindrical D846 propellant bag. Eight layers of pellets, each containing approximately 225 pellets, are aligned along the axis of the bag. Each pellet, extruded from a solution of nitrocellulose in ether, is approximately 1.8 inches in length and .8 inches in diameter. The "trim layer" (Sandia terminology) is the single layer of transverse pellets at the forward end of the bag, added to bring it to the correct weight. The bags weigh nearly 94 pounds each and are approximately 14.75 inches wide and 15.5 inches long. The aft end of the bag has an ignition pad of black powder that is ignited by the primer in the breech of the 16-inch gun. The ignition pad in turn ignites the propellant pellets. Normally six of these bags are used to fire the 16-inch gun.

Captain Miceli, in response to my interest in his video on gun loading, said he would provide a copy of the tape. In addition, he offered to send specimens of a rotating band and additional reports that he thought we would find valuable.

I now had little time to make the return flight to Albuquerque. I thanked Captain Miceli and the other team members. It seemed that there had been a modest improvement in the climate of the interchange, a slight increase in the dialogue, a detectable shift of the attitude in a positive direction as the afternoon drew to a close. Captain Miceli and I agreed that we would next meet at the *Iowa* and examine her heavily damaged Turret II, probably before Christmas.

I was impressed with the quantity of work the Navy team had done over the last several months, but there clearly were questions that needed to be further explored, questions that went to the heart of the Navy's conclusions.

I felt more confident about Sandia's involvement, that there was a key contribution to be made at least in the analysis of the foreign materials and turret contamination, that the varied problems, significant unknowns, and complexities were now manageable, not insurmountable.

Captain Miceli's video of turret operations filled my thoughts during the flight to Albuquerque. It formed concrete images of the gun-loading process, reformed and filled in voids of the mental pictures that I had developed in reading the Navy's reports, provided new ideas of things to examine and reconsider, and set me rethinking the incident itself.

I struggled to order and then envision the sequence of events based on this collection of new images, the observations and facts gathered to this point, leading to the explosion and tragic loss of forty-seven crewmen. It was important to reread Admiral Milligan's September report and November testimony before the Senate Armed Services Committee—and to obtain transcripts of the testimony that would be given by the Navy in just a few days to the House Committee on Armed Services.

4 The Navy's Report

7 September 1989

THE U.S. NAVY issued its report, "Investigation into the 19 April 1989 Explosion in Turret II USS *Iowa* (BB-61)," on 7 September 1989. Dated 15 July 1989, it was submitted to the commander, Naval Surface Force, U.S. Atlantic Fleet, by Rear Adm. Richard D. Milligan, U.S. Navy, the chief investigating officer. The Navy's investigation was led by Capt. Joseph D. Miceli, director of the NAVSEA Technical Review Team.

The report was the product of a Judge Advocate General Manual (JAG Manual) investigation and was described by the Navy as an administrative inquiry into the potential causes of the event, a one-officer investigation without a hearing. The report included five main sections: Executive Summary, Preliminary Statement, Findings of Fact (230 in number), Opinions (57), and Recommendations and Endorsements. As will be noted in subsequent chapters, this form of investigation was found inappropriate by committees of both the House and Senate.

Admiral Milligan's report included nearly three hundred enclosures that detailed interviews with the crew, excerpts from operational manuals, and reports relevant to the investigation. Selected portions of the Navy's report are contained in Appendix A, and elements of this appendix will be reproduced and commented on in this chapter.

The Navy's Technical Review Team was assigned three principal tasks: to assess the extensive damage to Turret II, to determine the most probable cause of the incident, and to define requirements to lift the existing restriction on firing 16-inch guns. The Navy team developed a Cause and Effects Analysis to methodically investigate conceivable sources of propellant ignition, conducting extensive tests in each of these areas and concluding that none could have taken a role in the explosion. (These potential ignition sources are listed in Appendix A.)

Below are sections of the Executive Summary, Preliminary Statement, and Opinions that contain the essence of the Navy's conclusions. In addition, a number of recommendations contained in the report are noted.

From the Executive Summary:

> On 19 April 1989 at 0955 local time, as the center gun crew of the USS *Iowa* (BB-61) Turret II loaded five 94-pound bags of smokeless powder . . . into the gun's open breech, the powder exploded. . . . Instantaneously, fire and blast of extreme velocity, pressure and temperature spread throughout Turret II. The blast blew back through the gun house into the Turret Officer's booth, into the left and right gun rooms and down through the powder trunks and vents to the lower levels of the turret. . . .
>
> All forty-seven (47) servicemen in Turret II at the time of the explosion died instantaneously or nearly instantaneously of either blast, blunt force and/or thermal injuries. . . .
>
> Despite written prohibitions and warnings against using NALC D846 with 2700 lb projectiles, Turret II was scheduled to fire ten rounds using five full charge bags of powder from NALC D846 with 2700 lb projectiles. . . .
>
> In preparing for the 19 April 1989 gunnery exercise, *Iowa* held prefire briefs . . . approximately half the people required to be present were absent. The Commanding Officer did not attend either of the prefire briefs. . . .
>
> Of the fifty-five (55) watch stations actually manned in Turret I on 19 April 1989 which required formal PQS qualified watch standers, four (4) personnel were PQS [Personnel Qualifications Standards] qualified.[1] In Turret II, thirteen (13) out of fifty-one (51) personnel were PQS qualified and in Turret III, nine (9) out of sixty-two (62) were PQS qualified. . . .
>
> Neither the Commanding Officer, Executive Officer, Weapons Officer nor the Gunnery Officer knew of the large number of watch stations being manned by personnel not qualified under the PQS program. . . .
>
> In contrast to the poor PQS training program, the damage control efforts of the ship's crew were extraordinary. . . . Although too numerous to list in this summary, in helping to save their ship and attempting to rescue their shipmates, many *Iowa* crewmen distinguished themselves. . . .
>
> Analysis of the reconstructed rammer places the rammer head about 21 inches past its normal point inside the breech at the time of the explosion. At this position the rammer would have pushed the five powder bags up to the base of the projectile while constricting the opening and defining a confined space. . . .

> Despite extensive testing, no anomalies which could have served as an accidental source of ignition have been found in either hardware or ammunition components. There is strong evidence, however, to support an opinion that a wrongful intentional act caused this incident.

Admiral Milligan, the chief investigating officer, then continued his report with the Preliminary Statement, the key element of which was that "on 8 May 1989, after receiving information that suggested motive for a criminal act that could have caused the 19 April 1989 explosion in Turret II, USS *Iowa* (BB-61), I made a formal oral recommendation to the Convening Authority that he immediately initiate a criminal investigation into circumstances surrounding the incident."

The concluding Opinions contained in Admiral Milligan's report were then stated. Again, what follows are key from the perspective of the discussion to follow:

> 7. *Iowa*'s failure to adhere to the formalized PQS qualification process negates structured Navy wide quality control policies designed to ensure uniform and effective training of 16-inch/50 caliber gun battery watch standers. . . .
>
> 13. Ineffective enforcement of safety policy and procedures was the norm within Turret II. . . .
>
> 14. The complexities of turret operations, when coupled with the relative inexperience of main gun battery turret officers, contributed to poor management and administration of maintenance, safety and training programs. . . .
>
> 15. . . . *Iowa* utilized her Main Gun Battery to engage in unauthorized Research and Development. . . .
>
> 26. *Iowa*'s turret crews were not properly prepared for the Main Gun Battery gunshoot on 19 April 1989. . . .
>
> 50. No musters were taken at either the pre-prefire brief or the prefire brief. Firings conducted were inconsistent with the written prefire plan. Accordingly, it cannot be determined that center gun Turret II personnel were adequately briefed and confusion may have resulted from an abnormal configuration of five vice six powder bags. . . .
>
> 52. The investigation into and the analysis of all potential causes of this tragic explosion have been complicated by the issues of improperly loaded munitions in the center gun . . . lack of effective, properly supervised assignment and qualification processes, and poor adherence to explosive safety regulations and ordnance safety. . . . Further, . . . substandard operations and readiness baseline results in systemic deficiencies that can serve as a foundation for disaster. . . .

53. Personnel error could only have caused the rammer to extend about 21 inches past the normal position as the result of an improper signal on the part of the gun captain, miscommunication of signals between the gun captain and rammerman, or improper operation of the rammer by the rammerman. None of these causes are likely in light of the qualifications of the gun captain, the training of the rammerman, and the fact that the rammer was in the proper slow ahead position for a powder ram. The rammer was extended beyond the normal position by the rammerman in response to an overt and intentionally conveyed hand signal on the part of GMG2 Hartwig, Turret II's center gun captain. . . .

54. In the normal course of events, the 19 April 1989 ramming of five powder bags about 21 inches past the standard ram position could not have caused premature ignition. . . .

55. The explosion in center gun, Turret II, USS *Iowa* (BB-61) on 19 April 1989 resulted from a wrongful intentional act. . . .

56. Based on this investigative report and after full review of all Naval Investigative Service's reports to date, the wrongful intentional act that caused this incident was most probably committed by GMG2 Clayton M. Hartwig, USN. . . .

The key Recommendations were:

2. Commanding Officer, USS *Iowa* (BB-61) ensure that no 16-inch/50 caliber firing is conducted using other than authorized and service approved projectiles, propellants and propellant loads without specific prior authorization of Commander, Naval Sea Systems Command, in accordance with paragraph 1266 of OPNAVINST 5100.194. . . .

9. Chief of Naval Personnel take immediate action to fill all Battleship Division Weapons Gunnery billets with second tour Division officers. Such assignments should require all reporting officers to report for assignment as Turret Officers only after successful completion of formal 16-inch/50 caliber training. . . .

11. BB-61 class ships be authorized a Chief Warrant Officer (W-3) ordnance technician to serve as explosive safety officer, special assistant for training, and assistant for technical matters to the Weapons Officer.

12. Implementation of a Navy Wide formal Turret Officer qualification process. Enclosure (279) is provided for review and implementation as appropriate. . . .

21. During the course of this investigation, it became clear that numerous

Iowa service members, in an attempt to save their ship and the lives of their shipmates, distinguished themselves through extraordinary acts of heroism. It is recommended the following officers and crew members of USS *Iowa* (BB-61) be recognized by award of the Navy Marine Corps Medal:

Lt. Timothy P. Blackie, USN

Capt. Jeffrey W. Bolander, USMC

1st. Lt. John A. Brush, USMC

1st. Sgt. Bruce W. Richardson, USMC

GMC J. C. Miller, USN

GMG1 Verlin W. Allen, USN

BM1 Mark A. Tonielli, USN

BM2 Charles P. Smith, USN

BM2 Charles R. Dickinson, USN

HT1 Thomas J. Smith, USN

GMG3 John M. Mullahy, USN

ENFA Robert O. Shepherd, USN

FN Brian R. Scanio, USN

FR Ronald G. Robb

MR3 Thad W. Harms, USN

BM2 Robert M. Burch, USN

This list is not all inclusive. Many other personnel performed heroically on 19 April 1989. Is recommended that Commander, Naval Surface Force, U.S. Atlantic Fleet, in close coordination with Commanding Officer, USS *Iowa* (BB-61), ensure all such personnel be identified and appropriately recognized.

These and several other recommendations will not be discussed, but portions of the Executive Summary, Preliminary Statement, and Opinions merit discussion.

Cause and Effects Analysis

The Cause and Effects Analysis by Navy investigators included a wide variety of recognized or conceivable causes of the explosion, all of which were explored to varying degrees. The Navy discounted some potential sources of ignition after very limited testing and did not develop a continuous and systematic search for new causes of the explosion beyond those contained in the initial Cause and Effects Analysis.

Unauthorized Experiments

A prohibited combination of projectile and propellant was planned for the firings from Turret II to conduct an unauthorized experiment related to firing accuracy. It was understood by experienced gun crews that use of D846 (faster burning) propellant in combination with the 2,700-pound (heaviest) projectile was not allowed because of the danger of overpressuring the 16-inch gun barrel. The USS *Iowa* had not been approved for such experiments, and the commanding officer was unaware of this planned deviation. The weapons officer was, however, aware of the plan and failed to discuss it with Captain Moosally.

Cdr. Eugene J. Kocmich, a former weapons officer aboard the *Iowa*, testified that advocates of these experiments, principally M. Chief Steven P. Skelly, had asked him to approve such firings using *Iowa*'s 16-inch guns on several occasions and that he had refused those requests. Commander Kocmich maintained that these experiments would more appropriately be carried out at the 16-inch gun facilities at Dahlgren, and that *Iowa* had not been approved for studies of this kind. Commander Kocmich stated that while he was on leave in November 1987, and without his knowledge or approval, Skelly conducted experimental firings from 16-inch guns using unauthorized combinations of projectiles and propellants.[2]

The Navy acknowledged the existence of unauthorized research and development activity aboard the *Iowa* on 19 April 1989, but concluded that it had no relation to the explosion. If, as the Navy asserted, the cause of the explosion was the intentional act of a crewman, this conclusion may have been correct. However, if an inadvertent action by the crew led to the incident, the use of prohibited combinations of propellant and projectile may have contributed to the explosion by creating confusion among crew members.

Communications between the Commanding Officer and the Weapons Officer

Communications between the commanding officer and weapons officer aboard the *Iowa* was inadequate and led to the commanding officer not being fully informed of the firing plan for the morning of 19 April 1989 (see Findings of Fact, particularly 27, 30, 31, 33, and 45, appendix A). This included failure of the weapons officer to inform the commanding officer of the abnormal configuration of charges that would be used in Turret II, that these abnormal configurations were unapproved experiments, and that the weapons officer had authorized the movement of charges and firing by Turret III against the specific orders of the commanding officer. Although the weapons officer verbally related some portion of the plan to the commanding officer on the bridge just prior to the beginning of the exercise, this does not alter the fact that command level review and decision making was seriously circumvented with regard to the firing plan for the *Iowa* on 19 April.

Gun Crew Briefings

Briefings on 18 April for the gun crews were poorly attended. Lists of attendees were not maintained, and only GMG2 Richard E. Lawrence of the center gun crew of Turret II is known to have attended. Moreover, the firing plan, which included an unapproved combination of projectile and propellant, was not discussed in the briefing and was first presented to the gun crews just before the firings on the morning of the nineteenth. Because of the nature of the planned firings from Turret II, there is a substantial possibility that the crew was confused as noted in the Executive Summary (see Findings of Fact 21, 41, 44, 50, 175, 179, 193, 201, and 226j, and Opinions 8 and 50 in Appendix A). Moreover, there was a last minute crew change for the center gun of Turret II in which GMG3 Clayton Hartwig was assigned as gun captain in place of GMG2 Richard E. Lawrence.

Crew Training

Training of the gun crews aboard the *Iowa* was deficient, and only a fraction of the men in the three turrets was qualified for the various watch functions. Thirteen of the fifty-one personnel in Turret II were qualified to serve in their positions. Gunnery training was inadequately documented and the commanding officer, executive officer, weapons officer, and gunnery officer were unaware of the large numbers of personnel that lacked basic training in the various assignments within the turret.

Three of the crewmen in the center gun room of Turret II were not PQS qualified for their assignments. BM2 Gary J. Fisk had been aboard *Iowa* only twenty-seven days and had never operated the powder hoist when he manned this position on the morning of 19 April. He may not, in fact, have ever seen the hoist in operation before that morning. According to testimony, Fisk was "walked through his duties as upper powder hoist operator for center gun

Turret II a few days before the accident" (Finding of Fact 201, in Appendix A). Being "walked through" the process would not qualify him to operate the powder hoist, and members of other gun crews reported that improper positioning of the powder hoist at the powder door was a common problem in causing loading delays. This could have contributed to the unknown "problem" that delayed the center gun loading process.

GMG3 Robert W. Backherms, the rammerman for the center gun, was also new to the ship and had been aboard only thirty-three days. The Navy report stated that "although the rammerman in center gun Turret II was not PQS qualified and had never served as rammerman for a live firing, he had observed five live fire exercises (14 rounds) and had practiced operating the rammer prior to filling the position on 19 April 1989" (Finding of Fact 227j). The rammerman has an important sequence of tasks—some of which are not covered in practice operation of the rammer. One of these is to operate the powder door, another potential source of delay in gun-loading operations. It is also important to note that the rammerman can, by his own inadvertent error, overram the powder bags and is not absolutely controlled by the hand signals of the gun captain (as implied in Opinion 53; see Appendix A).

SR Reginald L. Johnson Jr. had been aboard the *Iowa* approximately three months, and while he also was not qualified for the primerman assignment, this task is relatively straightforward and not considered a significant contributor to possible delays in the loading process.

During Commander Kocmich's testimony before Admiral Milligan's team, Captain Messina cited the experience of these three men in the center gun crew. He noted that Fisk had been on board the *Iowa* only twenty-seven days and had no hands-on experience with the upper powder hoist operation. He also noted that Backherms had been on board thirty-three days and Johnson had been on board "roughly ninety days." Before noting these specific lengths of time aboard the *Iowa*, Captain Messina's questions to Commander Kocmich were as follows:

> Q. Would you be surprised that the [center] hoist operator had been on the ship a matter of days? Was brought up to the gunner, up to Turret II a couple of days before the turret walk through, his duties [explained] by Senior Chief Ziegler and GMG1 Hanyecz, sent back to his work station, and died on his station the first time he was ever there? On that job, to do that job?
>
> A. I would be surprised, yes.
>
> Q. Would you be surprised if the rammerman also falls into that category?
>
> A. Yes.

Q. And the primerman?
A. Yes, very much so.

While the Navy acknowledged the poor state of training aboard the *Iowa*, it implied that this was not a factor in the explosion, that the malevolent intent of a lone crewman caused the disaster. Again, if the cause of the explosion was not an intentional act but an inadvertent action, the role of training may be closely linked to the cause. The case for an inadvertent action will be presented in later sections.

Crew Response to the Incident

The crew's response to the explosion and fire was extraordinary, and there were individual acts of heroism. The remarkable response of the crew to this incident, a response carried out at great risk to members of the crew, was not broadly acknowledged by the Navy.

Observation of the Overram

The observation of an overram of the propellant bags in the USS *Iowa* explosion was apparent to Navy investigators in their review of the rammer mechanism. This large mechanism was removed from the turret and set up for examination. The fire associated with the explosion had discolored paint on exposed areas of the rammer in such a way that the apparent position of the rammer head at the time of the explosion could be determined. These observations indicated that the rammer head had pushed the propellant bags approximately 21 inches farther into the breech than is normal. This would have placed the forward bag of propellant near the base of the projectile. The Navy concluded that an overram of the propellant occurred and that the five bags of propellant were pushed approximately 21 inches beyond the normal stopping point. The Navy's report states, "At this position the rammer would have pushed the five powder bags up to the base of the projectile."

In fact, an overram of 21 inches would not have pushed the propellant to the projectile but would have left a gap of about 3 inches between the forward bag of propellant and the projectile. The fact that a gap apparently existed between the propellant and the projectile was inconsistent with the scenario proposed by the Navy in which the hypothetical ignitor would have been activated in the overram. This basic inconsistency between the Navy's observations and their scenario was not brought out in the Navy's report or in their testimony.

Propellant Pellet Fracture

Because of the overram situation, the Navy investigators considered the possible effects of crushing propellant pellets. The exposed fracture surfaces of pellets emit burning particles when the fracture occurs. In spite of this arresting observation, Navy investigators concluded that the strength of the pellets was such that the rammer could not have exerted sufficient force to cause fracture. A significant simplifying assumption was made to arrive at this conclusion—that the rammer force of two thousand pounds would be uniformly applied to all the pellets over the rammer face.

The Navy also concluded that the explosion was probably initiated between the first and second of the propellant bags and produced a high-order explosion with a high-pressure wave.

Propellant Stability

Propellant stability was studied in detail since the material was forty-four years old and a portion of it had been stored on river barges under conditions that resulted in exposure to high temperatures during summer months. Such conditions could lead to loss of a chemical stabilizer, and sufficient loss of stabilizer could result in the propellant spontaneously igniting at elevated temperatures. While the question of propellant stability was frequently raised by active Navy personnel, Navy veterans, and others, the concentration of stabilizers was found to be adequate and stability considerations were assessed to be an unlikely cause of the explosion.

Similarly, studies by Navy investigators of propellant ignition by friction or open flames indicated that these causes also seemed remote. The concern with open flames came about because some of the crewmen killed in the turret were found to have lighters and other smoking items on their remains, items forbidden inside the turret.

Initiation of a Criminal Investigation

The Navy widely explored a number of possible causes for the explosion but found no accidental means by which the explosion could have occurred. They concluded that, since no accidental causes were found, there were no accidental causes. This logic led the Navy to assert that "a wrongful intentional act caused this accident." A portion of the third section of the Preliminary Statement in Admiral Milligan's report, which discusses the Navy's conclusion, is noted here:

> The "information that suggested motive for a criminal act that could have caused the 19 April 1989 explosion in Turret II," was the letter written to the Navy by Kathleen Kubacina, sister of Clayton Hartwig. Ten days after the incident, Ms. Kubicina wrote to the Commander of USS *Iowa*, Captain Fred P. Moosally, stating that the beneficiary of her brother's $100,000 life insurance policy was another sailor on board the USS *Iowa*, GMG3 Kendall Truitt. This letter was an important factor in stimulating a criminal investigation by the Navy Investigative Service on May 8th that pursued the possibility that Hartwig may have been murdered, or that he may have committed suicide and attempted to disguise the suicide as an accident.

The subsequent section of Admiral Milligan's report was labeled Findings of Fact and included 226 statements and concluding Opinions, a selection of which are commented on here.

Opinions 7, 13, 14, 15, 26, and 50 acknowledge the inadequate training, ineffective enforcement of safety policies and procedures, and poor briefings of the gun crews aboard the *Iowa*. This was a serious indictment of the officers, and ultimately of the Navy and its failure to provide adequate numbers of officers and petty officers that could properly train and operate the battleships with a full complement of crewmen. This includes the lack of on-board officers and a higher command structure of sufficient judgment to recognize that an active battleship was not the place to conduct research and development activities when facilities for such studies were available elsewhere. As acknowledged in Opinion 52, the many circumstances surrounding this tragic incident were "systemic deficiencies that can serve as a foundation for disaster."

Opinion 53 concludes that the overram was a result of an intentional hand signal command on the part of the gun captain. This conclusion simply ignores the possibility of unintentional and inadvertent actions on the part of either the rammerman or the gun captain. There is no objective basis for concluding that the hand signal command by the gun captain was or was not intentional, and that the propellant bags may not have been inadvertently overrammed.

Opinion 54 states that an overram "could not have caused premature ignition," a conclusion based on ten tests by the Navy of ignition by overram. This conclusion has no rational statistical basis and was later shown to be incorrect by the Sandia investigation in which overram was demonstrated to be a major safety concern.

Opinion 55 states that the explosion resulted from "a wrongful intentional act." This key opinion derives largely from faulty logic: Since no accidental ignition mechanisms were found, none exist. Therefore the explosion resulted from a deliberate act.

Opinion 56 is the Navy's conclusion following the preceding opinion that Clayton Hartwig deliberately ordered an overram to initiate an improvised device he had placed among the propellant bags. Both Opinion 55 and 56 rest on the Navy team's assumption that foreign materials found on the projectile could only be associated with the hypothetical improvised device, an assumption that the Sandia investigation would demonstrate was baseless.

The following Findings of Fact are worthy of comment. Finding of Fact 229 states that "no accidental cause for premature ignition of powder located in center Gun, Turret II on 19 April 1989 has been identified." As noted earlier, later studies demonstrated that a higher than normal speed overram could cause an explosion and, moreover, an overram at any speed should be avoided.

Finding of Fact 230e states that the "rotating band from the projectile in *Iowa*'s center gun . . . contains traces of Aluminum, Silicon, Calcium, Barium and Iron Wire, all inorganic materials not found in an uncontaminated charge." Finding of Fact 230f states that "spectra show a close comparison between the *Iowa* ring [rotating band] and the ring from a test firing employing a timer controlled explosive device." These findings refer to an earlier Navy hypothesis that a timed ignition device was placed in the powder bags, a hypothesis that was abandoned by the Navy team in favor of yet another hypothesis prior to the time that Admiral Milligan made his report public. The Navy's report, however, was never amended to dismiss the hypothesis of a timed device and to include the hypothesis of a chemical ignition device.

Finding of Fact 230g states that "the equivocal death analysis" was prepared by qualified psychologists from the FBI. The analysis concludes: "Clayton Hartwig died as a result of his own action, staging his death in such a fashion that he hoped it would appear to be an accident." The "equivocal death analysis" performed by the FBI has been unfavorably critiqued by an external panel of mental health experts and will be discussed in a later chapter.

Several of these issues would be reviewed by committees of both the Senate and House of Representatives in a few months when Admiral Milligan and others were called to testify.

5 Admiral Richard D. Milligan Testifies

16 November 1989

STORIES ABOUT the *Iowa* explosion in the media prompted broad concern about a process in which unidentified Navy, Pentagon, and Department of Defense officials had released information in advance of Admiral Milligan's report. These concerns were accentuated by the absence of definitive evidence for the two major assertions that had been made in these releases: that the explosion was the result of an intentional act (Opinion 55), and that GMG2 Clayton Hartwig was responsible for this act (Opinion 56).

These concerns were underscored by open questions regarding the state of training of the gun crews aboard the *Iowa*, several departures from normal safety protocols, experimentation with an unauthorized combination of projectile and propellant, recanting of key testimony by David Smith against Hartwig, questions about the competence of the Naval Investigative Service, and other issues.

Senator Howard M. Metzenbaum of Ohio, the home of Clayton Hartwig, wrote Senators Sam Nunn and John Glenn, urging the Senate Armed Services Committee to hold hearings on the Navy's findings and to explore these and other questions in light of the conclusions put forward in Admiral Milligan's report. The committee agreed to this suggestion and, in addition, agreed to review "the operational planning for utilization of the battleships, manning the battleships and training the crews."

Following are selected portions of the testimony of Admiral Milligan before the Senate Armed Services Committee on 16 November 1989, as contained in the *Congressional Record.* These sections represent key elements of the testimony by Admiral Milligan and the principal concerns of some of the senators.

The Senate Armed Services Committee, chaired by Senator Sam Nunn, met for a "Review of the Department of the Navy's Investigation into the Gun Turret Explosion Aboard the USS *Iowa*," on Thursday, November 16, 1989. The meeting took place in room SH-216 of the Hart Senate Office Building. Committee members present were Senators Nunn, James Exon (Nebraska), Carl Levin (Michigan), Alan J. Dixon (Illinois), John Glenn (Ohio), Richard C. Shelby (Alabama), John W. Warner (Virginia), John McCain (Arizona), Malcolm Wallop (Wyoming), Trent Lott (Mississippi), and Dan Coats (Indiana).

Among those who would testify were Admiral Trost, CNO, and Admiral Milligan, the Investigating Officer. . . .

Chairman Nunn began: The committee will come to order. The committee meets this morning to begin a series of hearings on matters associated with the explosion of April 19, 1989, in the center gun of Turret II of USS *Iowa* which resulted in the death of forty-seven Navy personnel. In addition to the Navy's investigation, the committee will be reviewing the operational planning for utilization of the battleships, for manning the battleships and for training the crews.

Senator Metzenbaum then made an opening statement in which he thanked the committee for calling the hearings and asked Adm. Carlyle Trost, chief of Naval Operations, to discuss the recent series of accidents in the Navy and the forty-eight-hour stand-down to review safety practices.

Admiral Trost discussed the stand-down for all units and activities throughout the Navy. This included an in-depth review of operating procedures, safety procedures, lessons learned from recent incidents, and a review of what he considered to be the excellent safety record in the Navy over a period of several years.

The senators raised several questions: Is the operating tempo unusually high? Is there undue stress being placed on the ships or the men? Are the men getting enough shore time? Is the quality of personnel coming into the Navy adequate for the new assignments? Is there sufficient retention of key personnel? What is the effect of funding constraints on the Navy? Are Navy personnel receiving appropriate training for the jobs they do? Are they PQS (Personnel Qualifications Standards) certified for their watch stations? Do the battleships differ in the extent of PQS certified personnel from the rest of the surface fleet? Is the force structure plan such that the Navy should attempt to better man and train personnel for a smaller number of ships?

Admiral Trost thoughtfully responded to all these queries, but deferred questions related to PQS qualification of battleship personnel to Admiral Milligan, who would be testifying later at this session. This was a key area of concern because initial indications were that many of the personnel in Turret II of the *Iowa* were not properly certified for their stations.

Chairman Nunn: I will be making a brief opening statement and I will open it for other opening statements since people have deferred.

Our witnesses on the *Iowa* oversight hearing will be Rear Adm. Richard D. Milligan, U.S. Navy, the Investigating Officer; Capt. Joseph D. Miceli, U.S. Navy, the Director of the Technical Support Team that was responsible for the various technical testing that sought to identify the cause of the explosion; and Mr. Robert J. Powers, the Director of Criminal Investigations of the Naval Investigative Service, which conducted the criminal investigation into the explosion.

I know the tremendous amount of effort and time Admiral Milligan and his team spent on this investigation, and we appreciate your accommodating our schedule. We express to you our thanks for all of your hard work, you and your entire team.

At the outset on behalf of every member of the committee, I want to express our deepest sympathy to the families and loved ones of the members of the crew of the USS *Iowa* who died in this tragic incident. I also want to express our gratitude to the men and women of the armed services—the Navy and the other services—who perform their everyday duties under dangerous circumstances to preserve the security of our Nation.

The primary purpose of this series of hearings is to determine if the dangers implicit in the operation of this class of warship and others in the fleet have been reduced to the absolute minimum, and to ensure that the Navy had done all that it can do to achieve that result.

The Navy's investigation did disclose a number of discrepancies in the weapons department on board the USS *Iowa*. Those discrepancies include: the use of a prohibited mixture of explosive charge and projectile; the use of an unauthorized round configuration and plans that made the ship essentially a floating research and development platform; improper pre-fire briefs; lack of compliance with personnel qualification standards referred to as PQSs in that in Turret I only four of fifty-five personnel were PQS qualified, in Turret II only thirteen of fifty-one were qualified, and in Turret III only nine of sixty-two were qualified; improper storage of powder in barges; poor adherence to explosive safety regulations and ordnance safety.

Despite these discrepancies, Rear Admiral Milligan opined that they did not contribute to the explosion and that the explosion resulted from a wrongful intentional act and that the wrongful intentional act was most probably caused by GMG2 Clayton Hartwig. This conclusion and others have been challenged, and I know that Admiral Milligan will address those challenges as will the committee during our review.

It is also noteworthy that during the course of the investigation, information was received primarily through the testimony of Captain Moosally, the commanding officer of the USS *Iowa*, and we will be hearing from him sometime in December, which raised questions concerning, number one, the priority of officer and enlisted manning and the quality of personnel on board the USS *Iowa* and her sister battleships; number two, the adequacy of training on the 16-inch guns since there is a lack of hands-on training for personnel prior to reporting to the battleships; number three, the employment plan for battleships and this goes to the overall strategy in the Navy and the Navy deployment; number four, the responsiveness of the Navy to repair requests from the battleship; and number five, the adequacy of various inspections and surveys conducted on board battleships.

Rear Admiral Milligan was not charged to and did not inquire into these matters, as I understand it. I have, therefore, requested the General Accounting Office to look into these matters as well as to review the Navy's investigation as a whole in an attempt to assess its adequacy and to validate its conclusions, particularly those relating to the safety of the ship.

These and other remarks by Senator Nunn were followed by opening remarks by several members of the committee. Portions of these remarks are noted below:

Senator Dixon: . . . Today we are going to hear from Rear Admiral Richard Milligan, who directed the investigation of the tragedy on the battleship *Iowa*. This investigation was designed to tell us what caused the explosion that took forty-seven young lives. Unfortunately, Mr. Chairman, in my view, the report raises more questions than it answers. The report is the culmination of a series of leaks that reflects poorly on the professionalism of the Naval Investigative Services. . . . It is a report that seems based on supposition and guesswork—that is, the naval report—rather than fact and physical evidence. It is, in short, in my view a report that seems to be unraveling. . . . I do not think we can afford to have this investigation stand as the truth of what happened. . . .

Senator Glenn: . . . I do not question the thoroughness of the investigations that were done, but I did question some of the conclusions. I have basically two related concerns. First, given the numerous weapons-related safety and training deficiencies that existed aboard the *Iowa* on the day of the explosion, the Navy's report describes these deficiencies as, and I quote, "a foundation for disaster." Is the Navy correct in concluding then that the explosion was most likely caused by a wrongful, intentional act? Second, given these deficiencies, is Gunnersmate Second Class Clayton Hartwig being unfairly blamed?

These remarks were then followed by the statement of Admiral Milligan, portions of which are noted below:

Admiral Milligan: . . . I arrived on board *Iowa* on the 20th of April off of Puerto Rico. I immediately conducted my initial inspection of Turret II. . . . My immediate investigating team inspected the damage in search of a cause. . . . I must say, Mr. Chairman and members, that I did not go into this investigation considering foul play as a reasonable likelihood. On May 7, three weeks into the investigation[,] . . . I received a copy of a letter from Mrs. Kubicina, the sister of one of the deceased. That letter surfaced an insurance issue. Specifically, an accidental death policy on her brother's life, Petty Officer Hartwig's life, for the value of $100,000. Petty Officer Truitt, a survivor from the magazine in Turret II was the beneficiary of that policy. A few days earlier I had learned of Petty Officer Truitt's involvement in an auto theft back in 1987. I must point out, while Mrs. Kubicina's purpose was to seek help in getting assistance for her parents to become the beneficiaries of that insurance policy, I had to consider, with the information I had, the possibility of a criminal act.

Admiral Milligan then described the gun room and loading operation, emphasizing that the gun captain is in "full control" of the operation. He also stated that although there were significant administrative deficiencies in maintaining the PQS records, the center gun room crew in Turret II was "qualified." This statement was incorrect. As noted before, the rammerman, powder hoist operator, and primerman were not PQS qualified. Only the gun captain, GMG2 Clayton Hartwig, and the spanning tray operator, GMG2 Richard Lawrence, were PQS qualified.

A key finding was, he said, that the rammer was 21 inches too far into the breech at the time of the explosion. A wide variety of tests were conducted and, "after twenty-thousand tests, we found no plausible accidental cause for ignition." He went on to establish Clayton Hartwig's knowledge of explosive devices and the characterization of Hartwig by "hundreds of interviews that were being conducted by the Naval Investigative Service."

Admiral Milligan: . . . It is important to remember at this point that the explosion takes place inside the breech of the center gun. One has to take a look at who has access and who has opportunity to do something, and it is the gun captain who has that access and that opportunity. He is the one who controls the loading of the gun up in the gun room. He controls the ramming of the propellant and the projectile with his hand signals to the rammerman. He is the one who places the lead foils, two of them, in between the first and second bags in the propellant chain.

The logic of Admiral Milligan's presentation was essentially summed up by two statements contained in his written report:

1) " . . . portions of this investigation which I have alluded to clearly demonstrate that an accident did not cause this explosion."

2) " . . . if this tragedy was not an accident, then it must have been the result of an intentional act." (Opinion 55 of the Navy's report)

With the logic thus established, it then simply became a matter for Admiral Milligan and his team to determine who had committed the intentional act. This last step was taken by Milligan's team when they concluded in their report that "the act was most probably committed by Gunner's Mate Guns Second Class Clayton M. Hartwig" (Opinion 56).

When Admiral Milligan finished his statement, he was first questioned by Senator Nunn.

Chairman Nunn: Thank you, Admiral. Do either Captain Miceli or Mr. Powers have anything they would like to say at this point?

Captain Miceli: No, sir.

Mr. Powers: No, sir, Mr. Chairman.

Chairman Nunn: Admiral, you made reference in your statement that your overall code of inquiry basically calls for finding of fact, and you say that they must be specific and as indisputable as possible. Is that right?

Admiral Milligan: Yes, sir.

Chairman Nunn: Then you go on to say that opinions, however, are logical inferences or conclusions which flow from the facts.

Admiral Milligan: Yes, sir. Every finding of fact in my report, by JAGMAN procedures, must be backed up conclusively by an enclosure within that report, and my report now totals something on the order of 298 enclosures that support the findings of fact.

Chairman Nunn: Are you required to come to conclusions, or if the facts were simply too uncertain and not indisputable, would it be within your prerogative simply to say, "I have no opinion"?

Admiral Milligan: Yes, Mr. Chairman, I could say that.

Chairman Nunn: You do not feel pushed to come to what you call a conclusion based upon your opinion, then?

Admiral Milligan: What I felt obligated to do was to develop all of the facts that I could, all of the information, and build the findings of fact and then the opinions in the effort, to the best of our ability, to find the cause of this accident so that we could take whatever corrective action was required to ensure that we never experience it again.

Chairman Nunn: But you are not under the code of what we would use in the courtroom, or what you would use in courts-martial, are you? You are in a different kind of circumstance in your investigation, is that right?

Admiral Milligan: It is an administrative process, Mr. Chairman, with the goal of developing all of the information as far as you can possibly go to come to the opinions that are needed.

Chairman Nunn: You do not use criteria like "clear and convincing evidence," or "preponderance of evidence," or "beyond reasonable doubt"? You are not using either civil or criminal terms for your conclusions?

Admiral Milligan: It is an administrative process, not a criminal process. However, all of the findings of fact must be backed up by very supportive and convincing enclosures, or information in the report itself, and my report does that.

Chairman Nunn: I do not want to belabor this, but when you come to an opinion, are you saying that that opinion is probably what happened, or are you saying that this is possibly what happened?

Admiral Milligan: All opinions, of course, cite in the report the findings of fact which those opinions are based on. Some of my opinions, such as opinion number fifty-six, are "probably" issue-based on all of the information.

Chairman Nunn: Let us take two specific ones. You say the incident was a result of a wrongful intentional act. This is an opinion is that right?

Admiral Milligan: That is correct.

Chairman Nunn: Then you go on to say, "most probably GMG2 Hartwig was the individual who caused it."

Admiral Milligan: That is an opinion also.

Chairman Nunn: But they are based upon the facts?

Admiral Milligan: They are based upon findings of fact which are then supported by all of the enclosures in the investigation. They are based on literally many, many issues.

Chairman Nunn: Are you excluding the possibility that other things could have happened or could have caused this, when you come to those opinions?

Admiral Milligan: The conclusion I come to—

Chairman Nunn: Are you saying this is one possibility that could have happened, or are you saying this is what you believe probably happened?

Admiral Milligan: I think to answer your question, Mr. Chairman, I have to say that we have excluded all other possibilities and have come to this as the only possible conclusion.

Chairman Nunn: So you have excluded other possibilities?

Admiral Milligan: Yes sir. All of the programs on the ship, all of the twenty-thousand tests that we conducted from a technical viewpoint, we found no other cause for this accident.

Several senators questioned Admiral Milligan regarding discrepancies with the FBI's findings on foreign material in the cannelure of the rotating band (this will be discussed later), the psychological profiles that indicated that Clayton Hartwig was suicidal and preoccupied with death, and the certainty with which the Navy had dismissed all possibility of some form of accident.

The senators also inquired about the Navy's first conclusion—that the ignitor was electronic in nature—and the Navy's later shift to the assertion that it was a chemical ignitor. Other questions were raised: Why hadn't the FBI's involvement in foreign materials analyses been continued? Wouldn't it have been useful to have the FBI follow up and corroborate the Navy analyses?

Senator Dixon: . . . And what a remarkable thing, I think, that a young man who, the night before, spent over three-quarters of an hour discussing the good time on his next vacation or leave, or whatever you want to characterize it to be, and who, the next morning, was not listed to be the gun captain in that turret, somehow, through some extraordinary manipulation of events, was able to put into play this terrible tragedy that transpired. I find that difficult, Admiral Milligan, to understand how that could occur.

Admiral Milligan: Mr. Dixon, that is what the facts of this investigation draw you to. . .

Senator Glenn: . . . You see that is where I have always had a problem coming back and reaching the same conclusion, that you reached out of this thing. . . . That requires a leap of faith I have trouble making on that one. . . .

Senator Levin: Thank you, Mr. Chairman. You [to the witness] talked about data points. Is it fair to say that you feel that there is evidence which raises uncertainty as well as evidence, which leads you to your conclusion?

Admiral Milligan: There is findings of fact, and evidence, certainly. There is evidence to support my findings of fact. And there certainly are findings of fact to support my opinions. I left my opinion number fifty-six, which is the issue with regard to Petty Officer Hartwig, as the most probable on the basis that there was—

Senator Levin: Is there also evidence which raises uncertainty? Those other points, data points you made reference to? There is no certainty here. Is there?

Admiral Milligan: The totality—

Senator Levin: Not the totality. Just, is there evidence that raises uncertainties in your mind?

Admiral Milligan: There is no evidence that raises uncertainties with regard to the shipboard program review, with regard to all of the—

Senator Levin: Fifty-five and fifty-six, is there any evidence which raises uncertainty in your mind relative to fifty-five and fifty-six?

Chairman Nunn: Tell us what those are, Senator Levin.

Senator Levin: Fifty-five is that explosion resulted from a wrongful intentional act, and fifty-six is that it was most probably committed by Hartwig.

Admiral Milligan: No, sir. If there was uncertainty I would not have those opinions.

Senator Levin: So, for instance, the material that Senator Glenn went over with you, that we are not ready yet, I have a problem here. That does not raise any uncertainty in your mind at all?

Admiral Milligan: They were facts that are in the report that I considered in my opinions and ultimate conclusion. And they were of importance. And I think they gave me some insight into the fact that there was, in fact, a problem in the gun room. But they do not tell me what the problem was.

Senator Levin: My question is, does it raise any uncertainty in your mind? It is a simple question.

Admiral Milligan: No, sir.

Senator Levin: Thank you. You are certain, also, I think at one point, that the elements found in the timing device and associated batteries were found under the USS *Iowa* rotating band. Have you changed your view on that?

Admiral Milligan: Let me ask Captain Miceli to answer that.

Captain Miceli: Would you repeat your question, sir?

Senator Levin: You changed your view that elements found in the timing device and associated batteries were found under the rotating band?

Captain Miceli: Yes, sir.

Senator Levin: You have changed your view on that?

Captain Miceli: In the process of the analysis with help from the Army and the FBI, we have ruled out that there was an electrical device with batteries.

Senator Levin: That is my whole point. You were certain, back on July 28, that elements found in the timing device and associated batteries were found under the rotating band. And now you are satisfied that that is not so. Is that correct?

Admiral Milligan: Mr. Levin, let me answer that—

Senator Levin: I do not need long answers. I just need short ones. Are you now satisfied that that is not accurate?

Admiral Milligan: We are satisfied that it was not an electronics device. I am satisfied foreign material was in the band. My report is based on foreign materials, sir.

Senator Levin: Yes, but your report of July 28 also said that you were satisfied that the elements found in the timing device and associated batteries were found there, which means you were satisfied that there was foreign material consistent with an electronic device. Is that correct?

Admiral Milligan: If it is read that way, it is not intended that way. My report is based on the fact that there were foreign materials, something foreign to the normal propellant charge in the center gun of Turret II on April 19. That is the issue. . . .

Senator Levin: Admiral Milligan. Let me just ask you about finding fifty-five. You seem to be more certain in finding fifty-five than you are in fifty-six. Is that fair?

Admiral Milligan: I said most probably in fifty-six.

Senator Levin: But not in fifty-five?

Admiral Milligan: That is correct.

Senator Levin: And is it also some probability involved in fifty-five?

Admiral Milligan: No. Fifty-five says it was a deliberate act.

Senator Levin: That is not probability, it is certainty?

Admiral Milligan: That is my opinion, yes, sir. . . .

Chairman Nunn: Admiral, this has been alluded to several times, but let me make sure I understand the sequence here. As I understand it, your technical team initially believed, and maybe this ought to go to the Captain, initially believed that the explosion was caused by friction or compression. And then you later believed it was caused by an electronic device. And you ultimately believe it was caused by a chemical device. Now, were these really conclusions you reached as you came along. Did you change your opinions as you went along?

Admiral Milligan: Mr. Chairman, let me answer that. The effort was an iterative process. We looked at all of the possible ignition sources and, yes, at one point in time we were looking at friction as the most probable cause, but we conducted all those tests, and we frankly ruled out friction. We could not create a friction event. . . .

Senator Levin: What troubles me, I must tell you, is not so much your conclusion. I think people can differ on conclusions, and you had an obligation to reach the best conclusion you could. You do your duty the way you see it, and that is what you have got to do, that is what you take an oath to do, and I think you have done a good job of carrying out your oath. What bothers me is the certainty of your conclusion that you do not acknowledge that there are some factors which raise some doubts. Now, you can resolve those doubts the way you have, and I understand that. Whether I agree with it or not is not the point, but you can in good conscience, I believe, reach the conclusion you have and resolve the doubts in the way you have. But what troubles me is that you do not acknowledge the existence of any doubt. And even in a criminal trial a jury can convict, although there is a doubt, not if there is a reasonable doubt, but a doubt. There are factors pointing in different directions here which trouble me, including the fact that he was not assigned to be there that day. That is a troubling fact for me.

Admiral Milligan: He was there and we have conclusive evidence he was there.

Senator Levin: A premeditated, purposeful act of suicide when you were not supposed to be there is a little difficult for me to accept. It raises a doubt in my mind. That is all I am saying. I might resolve the doubt the same way you resolve the doubt.

Admiral Milligan: I understand.

Senator Levin: But you do not acknowledge any information at all that raises a doubt, even though you have resolved your doubts the way you have. What troubles me about your conclusion is that it is so absolute and unacknowledging of any factual material pointing in a different direction. If you had said, look, I have got 250 facts, 220 of them point this way, and I have got ten of them, or whatever, pointing the other way, I resolved it that way. If you had done that, I would feel a lot more comfortable. But the inability to acknowledge any doubt is what troubles me. Also, I do not know why the question about the inconsistency between your finding and the FBI finding cannot just simply be acknowledged. It is not something which is not explainable in the way you have tried to explain it, but there is an inconsistency. So you went back and looked and sent out this material to a different lab, and they came back with a different conclusion, which still supports your ultimate conclusion. That seems to me to be the way to answer that question. I am just expressing my own feeling. I think you have carried out your duty according to your best conscience, and that is what you are supposed to do. And it is a tough job, and I think all of us ought to, by the way, appreciate that you have got a very difficult job and you do not relish the finding that you have made. It comes through very clearly in your testimony and otherwise. And I think we have to acknowledge you have a very, very difficult job. Those are my difficulties with your conclusion. Thank you. . . .

Senator Dixon: Now, I am advised that the rammer had a considerably bad performance record in the immediate past; that, in fact, it accelerated sometimes and sometimes it stuck, and that there was substantial mechanical difficulty in the past with that rammer. Is that information available to you?

Senator Dixon's question was stimulated by testimony of the crew, which contained indirect references to erratic performance of rammers. However, according to the Navy investigators, none of these references led to specific instances in which this kind of rammer malfunction was documented or corroborated by others.

Admiral Milligan: Our inspection of the turret and all of the maintenance records associated with Turret II show no materiel problems in that turret.

Senator Dixon: But did you have information from other members of that crew who had operated that rammer in the past, that they had difficulty with that rammer?

Admiral Milligan: None that I recall, but I would have to go back and review all of that, it has been a long time.

The hearing ended shortly after this last exchange. These portions of the hearing highlighted the principal aspects of the Navy's position as well as the concerns and reservations of Senate Armed Services Committee.

The obvious concern of the committee with the certainty and inflexibility of the Navy's conclusions was a key factor in the eventual involvement of a third party to conduct an independent assessment of the Navy's investigation.

6 House Committee on Armed Services Hearings

12, 13, and 21 December 1989

JOINT HEARINGS by the House of Representatives were held to review the Navy's investigation of the USS *Iowa* explosion. Chairman of the House Investigations Subcommittee, Representative Nicholas Mavroules (D-Massachusetts), organized the joint hearings before the subcommittee and the Defense Policy Panel of the Committee on Armed Services. Chairman of the Defense Policy Panel was Representative Les Aspin (D-Wisconsin).

The committees heard testimony from Vice Adm. Joseph S. Donnell III, commander, Naval Surface Force, U.S. Atlantic Fleet; Admiral Milligan and Captain Miceli; Kenneth Nimmich, Dr. Richard L. Ault, and Robert R. Hazelwood, all of the FBI; Dr. Richard C. Froede, Armed Forces Institute of Pathology; GMG3 Kendall Truitt and GMG2 John Mullahy, former *Iowa* crew members; and Dr. Bryant L. Welch, executive director for professional practice, American Psychological Association. Portions of the testimony by Admirals Donnell and Milligan and Captain Miceli will be iterated in this chapter, and Appendix C includes portions of testimony given at these hearings by others. A report of the House hearings, "USS *Iowa* Tragedy: An Investigative Failure," is summarized in a later chapter.

The first witnesses were Admiral Milligan and Captain Miceli. Representative Mavroules queried Admiral Milligan about the Navy's allegation that Clayton Hartwig was responsible for the explosion, and the associated evidence for this charge:

Mr. Mavroules: Admiral, let me ask you right up front here, can you, in your best judgment or opinion, with the evidence you have before you—and I am looking for documented evidence—without any doubt in your mind, make the accusation, allegation, charge, that Mr. Hartwig indeed was responsible for this explosion? Can you make that without any doubt whatever?

Admiral Milligan: Sir, my position is, and I stand behind it as written in my report, based on all of the facts that this was an intentional act most probably done by Petty Officer Hartwig.

Mr. Mavroules: Most probably. But you cannot say without any doubt whatsoever that it was Mr. Hartwig?

Admiral Milligan: I believe that is a difficult bridge to make because we have no living witnesses of what exactly took place in center gun Turret II.

Mr. Mavroules: Therefore you cannot make the statement?

Admiral Milligan: That is why I made the statement probably.

Later in the hearing, Representative Joseph E. Brennan (D-Maine) returned to the choice of words used by the Navy in their accusation of Clayton Hartwig.

Mr. Brennan: You concluded your one-officer investigation, and you found that Mr. Hartwig most probably committed an intentional act that caused the explosion?

Admiral Milligan: I found the accident was the result of an intentional act most probably committed by Petty Officer Hartwig.

Mr. Brennan: Those words I am sure were chosen carefully, "most probably committed" and "an intentional act."

Admiral Milligan: Yes, sir, Mr. Brennan. This has been one of the toughest assignments of my thirty plus year career. Those opinions were very difficult to come to. . . .

Mr. Brennan: You understand in the American criminal jurisprudence system that you have to prove your case beyond any reasonable doubt, otherwise you can't convict; isn't that a fair statement?

Admiral Milligan: Yes, sir.

A second point of inquiry by the committees was the form of investigation used by the Navy, a one-officer investigation versus one that would have involved an investigative board, and a related question regarding the absence of involvement of the Naval Investigative Service at the beginning of the investigation.

Representative Mavroules noted that "Navy instruction 5520.3 requires the Naval Investigative Service to investigate unattended deaths, fires, and explosions," and that it appears that the NIS should have been called in at the outset of the investigation, on 20 April instead of 8 May, when the possibility of a criminal act occurred to the Navy. He opined that "significant physical evidence on the ship could have been lost or destroyed [in the cleanup process], and the issue of contamination of evidence will never be resolved." Admiral Milligan noted that the cleanup process was important to "prevent any further disaster . . . and that some evidence may have been lost, but that was a decision I had to make and I did it."

Representative Larry J. Hopkins (R-Kentucky) questioned Admiral Milligan on the selection of JAGMAN procedures:

Mr. Hopkins: Admiral, let me ask you on the selection of JAGMAN procedures, that being the Judge Advocate General, as I understand it, there are really three levels of investigation under the Navy process. I may not be saying this exactly right, and you correct me if I am wrong, one [the first] is the board of investigation which includes hearings.

Admiral Milligan: Yes, sir.

Mr. Hopkins: One [the second] is the board of investigation with no hearings, and then finally we come to [the third] the one-officer JAGMAN investigation. Who selected that [last] process over the other two, which seemed to carry more weight?

Admiral Milligan: The convening authority directed that I conduct that investigation, sir.

Mr. Hopkins: Who is that, please?

Admiral Milligan: The convening authority. That is Vice Admiral Donnell, who you will hear tomorrow, who is the commander of the Naval Surface Force, U.S. Atlantic Fleet. . . .

Mr. Hopkins: Is it not true the [one officer] JAGMAN process did not carry the weight or the authority of the other two? It would seem like you would not be quite as important as the other two, and my question is, what would have to happen of more importance than the death of forty-seven sailors that we might elevate this up to a higher procedure?

Admiral Milligan: I don't believe that it is a matter of importance. We could have, and certainly Admiral Donnell made available to me the opportunity to come to him if I felt that we needed to shift it from the investigation type that was conducted to a formal investigation, which would have then required that anyone who was suspected of any violations have a lawyer present and all of the testimony would have been taken with all those people present. . . . We just made it possible to get into the real facts and get the best information we could from the people who knew whatever they did about this accident, I am sure that is why he elected the type of investigation that he directed.[1]

Another line of questioning centered on the Navy's assertion that the initiating device was a timing device. They later asserted that a chemical initiator was placed in the propellant train. This line of inquiry was carried forward by Representative Mavroules:

Mr. Mavroules: . . . If my colleagues would only bear with me, there is a line of questioning we need clarification on some of your own charts, Admiral. We are going to put a couple charts up there, but let me just give you some background. The two charts were made by the Navy, and to the best of my knowledge they are reproductions. If there are any mistakes on that, please point them out to us. They show significant elements found in the *Iowa* rotating band [of the center gun projectile] compared to elements found on the test bands [from projectiles used in field tests]. The chart labeled chemical and metallurgical analysis of rotating bands which appeared in your August 11 report, showed the greatest similarity in elements found on the *Iowa* band and on the band of a test shot using a Radio Shack timer, with a barium magnet. The Navy described the most significant elements: antimony, barium, calcium and silicon, indicating the likelihood that a timing device caused the ignition. Do you follow me up to this point, Admiral?

Admiral Milligan: Yes, sir, we are following you.

Mr. Mavroules: Let me just continue. The second chart used in a Navy September 7 press conference purports to show similarities between the *Iowa* band and that of a test shot in which ignition of propellant was caused by a chemical detonator of brake fluid, HTH, swimming pool cleaner, and steel wool. The Navy indicates that the most significant similarities is the finding of iron wires, indicated by the asterisks coated with calcium, chlorine, and oxygen. Yet, why was the chlorine not identified on the *Iowa* band in the first chart, but shown in the second chart? Why did the August 11, 1989 Navy technical report show that chlorine had not been found on the *Iowa* rotating band although the chart used in the September 7 Navy press conference presented chlorine as an element that was found?

Mavroules also identified other inconsistencies. The chart used by the Navy in August indicated the presence of iron particles, but not iron wires. The chart in September indicated the presence of fine iron wires, but not iron particles. The presence of antimony and barium were noted on the August chart, but not on the September chart.

Captain Miceli explained that the Navy had listed various constituents based on their understanding of what was important at the time, but his response did not resolve the issue for the committee. The implication of the committee's questions was first, that the Navy put forward selected evidence to support their conclusion, and second, the evidence put forward varied depending on the current conclusion. The open and unresolved question was, Why wasn't all the evidence presented?

Several questions dealt with the particular scenario that the Navy chose to articulate, and the absence of any competing concepts for how the explosion could have occurred:

Mr. Pickett: One final question, Admiral. You indicated that in coming to your conclusion, you sifted through and evaluated all of the data and all of the different possibilities about what could have caused the explosion. I take it that in that process, you had different scenarios of what may have happened, and you had to rank those in some order and decide which of those were best supported by the facts that you had at your disposal. You came to the conclusion that it was an intentional act and one person was most likely to have been responsible. What was the next most likely cause in your mind for this, had you had to rule out the one you selected?

Admiral Milligan: Well, we chased down and investigated every suggestion, every idea that was brought to our attention by the hundreds of people involved in the investigation including the fifty or so ordnance experts that were working for Captain Miceli, incoming mail, whatever. If we had any suggestion whatsoever of what might have caused that explosion, we chased it down and ruled it out in hopes that we would find one we couldn't rule out. The fact of the matter is that we could not find any that could be considered even a possible accidental cause. We ruled them all out. So that is a big part of the whole issue of gathering all the data and looking at the data points of fact that drove me to the conclusion that it was an intentional act. We literally ruled out every other possibility.

Mr. Pickett: So you are saying that there is no number two scenario that you consider?

Admiral Milligan: No, sir. I think we have the evidence and the facts that support the conclusion and opinion that I came to. If I didn't have that, didn't take that position, then I would have to say that I couldn't make that conclusion, but I feel comfortable in doing so.

Mr. Pickett: Thank you.

Mr. Mavroules: Mr. Chairman.

Mr. Aspin: Let me follow up on Owen Pickett's questions, Admiral, because I think there is a jump here that is being done and it is a jump over proving a negative. I don't know that it is, what the conclusion of it is except as you were responding to Congressman Pickett. The position that you have taken is, because we couldn't find a technical explanation, therefore there is no technical explanation.

Admiral Milligan: Well, the position is that we have looked at every possible—

Mr. Aspin: I understand that. But it is a jump. The jump is, because we couldn't find the technical explanation, therefore there is no technical explanation. There is no explanation of an accident because we could not prove any of the theories about how an accident could occur, therefore there is no accident; it was not accidental. That is a jump. . . . But I would just like to say that the really only fair conclusion that you ought to draw is that we found no technical explanation for an accidental cause. You cannot prove a negative. . . . I would just like to point out that the right thing to say is that we could find no evidence of any technical malfunctioning or accidental problem. . . . It is just that a little bit of humility is required here to say that there was no technical explanation found does not mean that no technical explanation exists.

Representative Aspin's logic did not move the Navy.

Admiral Milligan was also questioned about why he signed his report on 15 July, approximately a month before the Navy's technical report was finished and a number of months before other technical work was completed. The thrust of these questions was that, since several changes in the Navy's perspective had occurred after the fifteenth, with the result that certain of its conclusions were now invalid, shouldn't the Navy revise its report? Admiral Milligan stated that, in his view, no revision of the report was necessary.

Also testifying on 12 December was Vice Adm. Joseph S. Donnell III, commander, Naval Surface Force, U.S. Atlantic Fleet. Admiral Donnell noted in his opening statement that he had convened a one-officer investigation without hearings, rather than a formal board of investigation or an investigation with a hearing. When Admiral Milligan gave him the letter written by Petty Officer Hartwig's sister discussing her brother's accidental death policy, Admiral Donnell considered for the first time the possibility that the explosion may have been the result of a "wrongful intentional act." The NIS was asked to open an investigation, and from 9 May onward, both the one-officer JAG Manual investigation and the NIS investigation proceeded. Admiral Donnell stated that "reconstruction of the rammer unequivocally established that the powder had been over-rammed about twenty-one inches beyond its normal breech position at the time of the explosion, and it was established that the rammer mechanism was functioning properly. . . . The facts point to the powder having been over-rammed about twenty-one inches, thereby pressing the powder bags against the base of the projectile, probably to activate the detonator."

What Admiral Donnell and previous testimony by the Navy failed to acknowledge was that a 21-inch overram would not have been sufficient to press the powder train up against the projectile and initiate the hypothetical chemical ignitor, a crucial part of the Navy hypothesis. Measurements clearly indicated that an overram of about 24 inches would have been required to bring the propellant train up to the projectile.

Admiral Donnell went on to say that there was "strong evidence that a detonating device was the source of ignition." He failed to say that the FBI did not agree with that analysis, and did not explain why the FBI was not asked to participate in the analysis in the case of the chemical ignitor scenario. He stated, "The NIS investigation, which you have also heard about in detail, developed considerable background information about Petty Officer Hartwig, the center gun captain, at the time of the explosion. Based upon that information, an FBI Equivocal Death Analysis indicated Petty Officer Hartwig did, in fact, commit suicide." In response to a question about an NIS psychologist's report, which was substantially less certain in its assessment of a suicide by Hartwig, Admiral Donnell said he was unaware that a report by a Navy psychologist had been prepared or why it was not included in the NIS report.

Admiral Donnell also noted in his written statement his "annoyance and embarrassment" with leaks to the media that "threatened to undermine the investigative effort" by the Navy: "The number of people who had access to information about the investigation was limited to a very few on my staff . . . and I do not believe that leaks emanated from my staff. I do not have any idea where the leaks occurred."

Representative Mavroules also probed Admiral Donnell's logic in his endorsement of the report which described the first scenario involving a timing device. Mavroules noted that since later findings led to a second scenario in which the Navy proposed that a chemical ignitor had been used to initiate the explosion, the report should be changed to reflect the new results. Admiral Donnell disagreed, asserting that the kind of device was a detail and had no substantive effect on the report or his endorsement.

Representative Mavroules then returned to the certainty with which the Navy had singled out Clayton Hartwig:

Mr. Mavroules: I am an individual, Admiral, as you are. I have three children. I have grandchildren. I would assume that most of us here are the same. I find it quite irresponsible, frankly, personally, that the Navy would issue a report of a probable cause rather than having documented evidence that they could prove. What I am saying is that [neither] you, [nor] Admiral Milligan, nobody can point the finger and say, "Petty Officer Hartwig, you were the cause of that explosion."

Admiral Donnell: I think my statement says that, doesn't it, sir? It says probably.

Mr. Mavroules: I realize that, but don't you think it is unfair to leave that innuendo hanging out there without documented proof?

Admiral Donnell: I could say the most probable person to do it was the gun captain.

Mr. Mavroules: Is it possible someone else could have done it?

Admiral Donnell: Sir, in this world, anything, I guess, is possible. I can't rule out absolutely that nobody else could have done it.

Mr. Mavroules: I realize that, so when you cannot rule it out absolutely, isn't that pointing the finger toward one individual?

Admiral Donnell: Yes, sir, it certainly is, but we have to take the facts of evidence as they exist and arrive at a conclusion.

Mr. Mavroules: If that were my son, I would be all over you like a hound dog, Admiral. You wouldn't hear the end of it.

Admiral Donnell: I am sure.

Mr. Mavroules: If that were your son, you would be all over me or the Navy.

Admiral Donnell: I would be heartbroken like the family is; yes, sir.

Mr. Mavroules: The point is, you cannot point the finger and say "Clayton Hartwig, you are the guilty one. You committed suicide, and you committed murder."

Admiral Donnell: No, sir. I would not make that kind of statement. I can't. I can say most probably he did.

Admiral Donnell's testimony closed with questions by Representative Brennan and Warren L. Nelson, a member of the professional staff to the joint committee. Brennan questioned Donnell with regard to the qualifications of Admiral Milligan to lead such an investigation. Admiral Donnell defended his choice and said that he was "extremely satisfied; very satisfied" with the quality of the Navy's investigation. Representative Brennan also commented on the certainty of the Navy's position that an accident had been ruled out:

Mr. Brennan: Are you satisfied that the cause of the accident, that it was accidental, is fully ruled out?

Admiral Donnell: Yes. We are going to deal in absolutes here. Fully? We have looked at every known way that we can possibly conceive of that that powder could be detonated. If you could tell us of some, we will be glad to go out and—

Mr. Brennan: I am just looking at your prepared remarks. You said "By mid-July, I knew that Rear Admiral Milligan's inquiry had eliminated virtually all conceivable accidental causes for an explosion."

Admiral Donnell: Absolutely.

Mr. Brennan: You said "virtually all." Were there some you hadn't ruled out?

Admiral Donnell: I just got through saying I hesitate to deal in absolutes. I didn't want to deal in absolutes. You couldn't say I know for a fact, somebody is going to pin me down. They say how do you know for a fact? You weren't there? There is nobody alive who was there. So I guess there is, since all things are possible. I should say, that there is a possibility that we have overlooked something, but I seriously doubt that. I know nothing, and neither does any other expert in DOD that I am aware of, know of any other test we could do.

The last witness on 12 December was Dr. Richard C. Froede, armed forces medical examiner, of the Armed Forces Institute of Pathology. Dr. Froede, as the armed forces medical examiner, was not employed by any of the armed forces or the Department of Defense, but rather was a scientist with the American Registry of Pathology working for the Armed Forces Institute of Pathology. A portion of Dr. Froede's testimony dealt with the identification and position of the various crewmen at the time of the explosion:

Mr. Hopkins: Dr. Froede, a review of the Navy's investigation shows that there was some initial confusion over the identities of several of the crew members' bodies, including that of Mr. Hartwig. I understand that another crew member's body was initially misidentified as that of Mr. Hartwig; is that correct?

Dr. Froede: I believe there was some confusion.

Mr. Hopkins: Could you run through that for me?

Dr. Froede: When these bodies are brought to the Dover Air Force Base, the mortuary there, they have tags with some names on them . . . by the end of forty-eight hours all positive identifications were made either by fingerprints using the FBI fingerprint teams or by dental records or by anthropometric studies. At the end of the forty-eight hour period, all were identified positively. . . .

Mr. Hopkins: . . . several Naval officials have made comments describing Hartwig as having been in an unusual position, for a gun captain, at the time of the explosion. For instance, some accounts have him reaching into the gun barrel for no clear purpose, while others have him standing to the side with his arms extended. Is that correct?

Dr. Froede: . . . we were asked about the second day by Captain Miceli, is it possible, once we have made identification, to position all of these people, whether it is in the gunroom or in the projectile room or other areas. We would then take a look at the pattern of injuries that were present on each of the bodies, the amount of injury and any of the extraneous finding evidence that we might have. We were able in this case to place four people into that gunroom and put them in positions that were consistent with the patterns of injuries.

Mr. Hopkins: I am not doubting what you are saying to me, but I want to explore that further. I have a difficult time trying to imagine an explosion going off in a confined area, creating four thousand pounds per square inch, thus creating temperatures of three thousand degrees, followed by flooding of the area, followed by draining of the area, I have a hard time in my own mind determining how you can say for sure where these people were located.

Dr. Froede: All right, if we take two of the four had powder undeposited, burn powder deposited on their bodies, these two were Hartwig and Johnson. The position of the powder that we found on Hartwig was found on the anterior, anterior right shoulder and right arm . . . then we . . . put them closer to the breech where the alleged explosion took place. . . .

Mr. Hopkins: Back to my original question or one of my questions a little bit earlier. Some accounts have him reaching into the gun barrel. Other accounts have him standing to the side. Where was he? Which one of these do you agree with?

Dr. Froede: I cannot really give you an answer. All I can say is that he was near the breech at the time, closer to the breech than the other two with his hands extended and looking at that breech area. I cannot say whether his hands were inside or whether his head was inside.

Mr. Hopkins: Whose opinion was that?

Dr. Froede: I don't know. It is the first time that I heard it that he was reaching in.

Mr. Hopkins: Does staff know where that came from?

Mr. Mavroules: That was the Navy.

Dr. Froede's testimony was relevant to Sandia Laboratories' questions about the details of Hartwig's position, which Captain Miceli had described to us in January 1990. That is, Froede was only able to ascertain general characteristics of Hartwig's position at the time of the explosion, and these general characteristics were within the realm of what might be expected for the tasks of a gun captain.

7 Visiting the USS Iowa

20–21 December 1989

I WAS anxious to visit the *Iowa*, to see the damaged turret, and to talk with the crew if at all possible. Captain Miceli's graphic description of the incident while I was at Indian Head occupied my thoughts, but I was more impressed with his apparent total commitment to the Navy scenario than the technical rigor with which the Technical Review Team had explored each point. It was clear that we would have to conduct a thorough survey of surface contamination in turrets and relate this to the Navy's foreign materials analysis, which was key to their conclusions.

Initial repairs aboard the *Iowa* had taken place before the ship was deployed to the Mediterranean Sea, and further and more extensive repairs were soon to begin in Turret II. With Captain Miceli's help, I arranged for the first visit to take place 20–21 December. Along with me on this trip would be Mark Davis, Dennis Mitchell, and Paul Cooper. Mark Davis was a member of the materials group, and we had worked together for many years. Mitchell was in an explosive components division of my group, and Cooper was an explosives expert with broad experience relevant to the *Iowa* study. The four of us had examined the Navy's reports in great detail.

We arrived at the hotel in Norfolk late on the nineteenth and briefly met Tim Stone and Jaime Dominguez of the GAO. The GAO people would accompany us aboard the *Iowa* as a continuing part of their coordinating role as requested by the Senate Armed Services Committee.

The lobby was empty early the next morning, the brightness of the day revealing a decor from a much earlier time. Captain Miceli was at a corner table of the coffee shop, and I went in to greet him. Davis, Mitchell, and

Cooper joined us in a few moments, and we arranged to follow the captain's car first to the pass office and then to the ship.

It was 8:30 A.M. when we left the pass office and fell in behind the captain's Cadillac as he led the way to the pier. The day was cold under the gray overcast, and I felt a deep chill as the brisk wind whipped around us while we made our way to and from the pass office. The pier access road, covered with cables and hoses, was the picture of activity, with vehicles, workmen, and naval personnel moving in every direction. An aircraft carrier dominated the view, impressive in size and height above the roadway, and was moored starboard side to the pier. The *Iowa* was across the pier from the carrier, low and squat by comparison. The center gun of Turret II drooped below the left and right guns, a vivid and mournful reminder of the reason for our visit. The appearance of the somber gray battleship seemed to deepen the overcast, the two shades of gray reinforcing one another.

We turned left onto the pier and parked at the base of the gangway. The ice-coated metal steps took us to the main deck and allowed us to visually gauge the massive ship for the first time. We stood under the guns of Turret II as we waited for the group to gather and a few officers and petty officers came on deck to welcome us. The wind raised white caps on the bay, sharply snapping the flag overhead. We hunched our heads into inadequate collars, seeking protection, torn between wanting to see as much as possible and getting off the wind-swept deck.

When the group assembled, we entered a passageway on the starboard side that led to the wardroom. We shared coffee and words with the officers who would be with us the next two days. The overhead was low, and I kept my head tilted to avoid contact, moving from one short conversation to another, reassessing the height of the overhead each time. The vintage of the ship was evident in several ways. One of the things that struck me was the electrical wiring and fixtures that filled the overhead space. Some of it was clearly of another age.

The ship's commander, Capt. Fred P. Moosally Jr., entered the wardroom and greeted the visitors: a few members of Captain Miceli's team; Chief James P. Tonahill; Tom Doran, a civilian employee of the Navy at Dahlgren; and Steve Mitchell from Indian Head. Other *Iowa* personnel on board included Lt. Cdr. Larry Dotson, a gunnery officer, and Lt. (jg) Dan Meyer, who was in Turret I at the time of the explosion in Turret II. Captain Moosally had provided important testimony to the Senate Armed Services Committee just eight days earlier, and it would be some time before we became aware of his remarks (see Appendix D).[1]

Captain Miceli motioned Captain Moosally aside for a private conversation, Miceli gesturing broadly, facing away from the rest of us. (Such public/private conversations by Captain Miceli would be a common occurrence in the weeks ahead.) Cdr. Robert Kissinger, the weapons officer, handed us white coveralls to don before entering Turret II and, after we had struggled into them, led us on a reverse path through the passageway, up a ladder to the turret (fig. 7-1). We entered a large port at the rear of the turret. I noted a smaller hatch on the aft starboard side, the one that Brian Scanio and the other firemen must have entered when they came forward to control the fire. Just inside the turret, a crewman asked us to put our watches, coins, smoking paraphernalia, and any spark-making materials into a red box—the reinstitution of a safety procedure that had not been carefully followed by the crew during operations prior to the explosion.

The gun house, the visible part of the turret that stands above the main deck, was crowded with heavy equipment, leaving limited walking area. The interior was poorly lit, and it was difficult to immediately see obstructions on the floor, cable trays, piping, and other hardware. There were many places to trip, bang your shins, or bump your head.

The smell of lubricating and hydraulic fluids filled the space. We were out of the wind, but the cold steel surfaces radiated another kind of chill. I avoided looking in the direction of the open hatch, and my eyes began to adjust to the low light level. I thought of Scanio trying to move through this area in his protective gear, unable to see in the fire and smoke, and then gradually seeing a veritable hell all around him.

Captain Miceli described operation of the equipment in a louder than normal voice to cover the din of machinery. While restorative work had been done in the form of cleaning and painting, significant damage was evident in the forward part of the gun house, where the three gun rooms were located. Heavy steel bulkheads separating the gun rooms were blown out or severely deformed. The residue of damage offered the imagination a starting point to what must have been the condition of the booth after the explosion.

Following a brief look at the right and left gun rooms, we entered the narrow space of the center gun room, where the explosion had occurred. The center gun, an immense steel weapon, appeared undamaged (fig. 7-2). The equipment aft of the gun had been removed, and the blown-out bulkhead had been replaced with temporary plates. Forward in the gun room a wooden

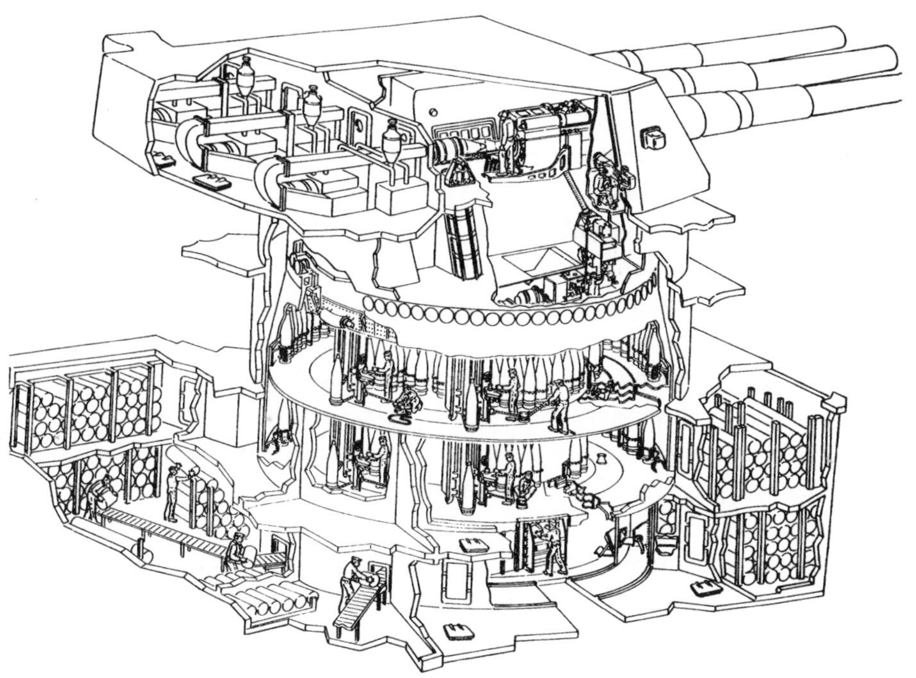

Figure 7-1. Drawing of the turret on *Iowa*-class battleships. The three turrets that give the battleship her characteristic silhouette are actually cylindrical structures that extend from above the main deck to the keel. The weight of each of these turrets is approximately 1,800 tons, nearly equivalent to the weight of an entire destroyer.

The gun house, the portion of each turret above the main deck, contains three gun rooms, the left and right sight-setter stations on each side, and the turret officer's booth aft of the gun rooms. The gun rooms and booth are separated by a bulkhead with flame-tight hatches. In the gun house there are powerful hydraulic rammers, which assist in the loading of projectiles and powder bags into the guns, and a host of other equipment integral to the function of the turret's three guns. Below the gun house is the electrical deck, which contains large motors and gears that drive the rotation of the turret and elevation of the guns.

The massive projectiles are stored on the projectile decks and are moved by crewmen using lines and capstans to slide upright projectiles on an oiled deck. Still lower, just above the keel, is the powder flat. It is here that a crew of about a dozen men load powder bags on hoists that lift the propellant to the gun rooms. Magazines partially surround the powder flat and are isolated from the turret by two heavy concentric bulkheads that form an annular space.

In the gun-loading procedure, projectiles from one of the two projectile decks are raised to the gun rooms. (A portion of the right gun room is shown in this drawing.) Propellant bags from the magazines, at the lowest two levels, are removed from hermetic cans and passed through the annular space into the powder flats at the lowest level. The propellant bags for each gun are placed on a powder hoist and raised to the gun room and moved into the breech behind the projectile. The three rammer mechanisms are partially shown inside the turret booth at the upper left.

scaffolding stretched over the yawning space above the equipment deck, the deck that held the large electric motors that rotated the turret and elevated the gun. There was clear evidence of the explosion, even though the crew had cleaned the carnage with special materials and repainted several sections. An unpleasant odor distinct from that of lubricating and hydraulic fluids filled the room. I could not identify it.

I found myself staring at a particular section of the gun room and then slowly turning to stare at another section, trying to project back to the time of the explosion, listening with half an ear to Captain Miceli's continuing litany. Occasionally my gaze would meet and briefly search the eyes of a companion, and then move on to another section, trying to envision the events, to imagine the unimaginable. The gun room exuded an even deeper and lasting chill. I couldn't suppress an occasional violent shiver that seemed to emanate from deep inside.

Captain Miceli stood at the center of the small room recounting the incident from his perspective point by point. His recollection was detailed as he

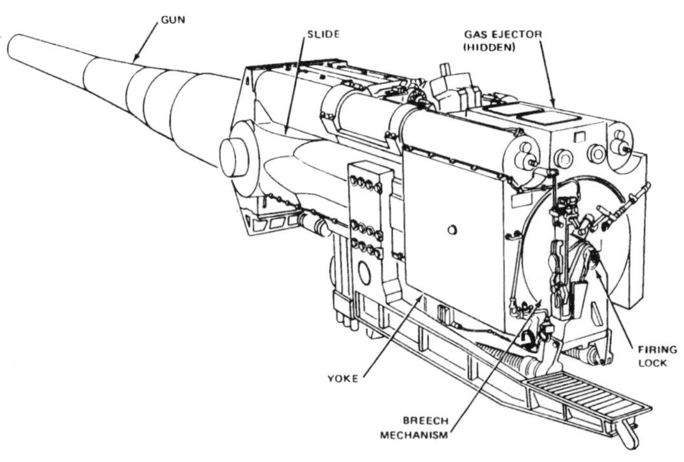

Figure 7-2. A drawing of the 16-inch gun, three of which are mounted side by side in each of the turrets on *Iowa*-class battleships. This gun weighs 120 tons and is capable of shooting 2,700-pound projectiles over 20 miles with remarkable accuracy. The massive projectile leaves the barrel with a speed of approximately 2,500 feet per second and can penetrate 26 inches of armor. Two of these projectiles are equivalent to the total nonnuclear ordnance that can be delivered by a modern combat jet fighter.

cited the forensic findings and demonstrated the positions of the men at the time of the explosion. He abruptly cut off a comment by one of the Navy crewmen and instructed all of them to not make any statements to "our visitors." He clearly intended to control the conversation, to be the sole source of information, to not have the Navy's story modified in anyway by anyone.

Captain Miceli described the insertion of the hypothetical ignitor into the powder train by the gun captain, adding a graphic display of how the gun captain must have hand-signaled the overram and then faced the breech (fig. 7-3), "expecting the blast." He sat in the rammerman's seat and asserted that rammermen watched only hand signals from the gun captain, not the position of the powder train as it was advanced into the breech by the rammer. I thought again of the rammerman sitting in his seat on the morning of 19 April, never having served in this position for a single live firing, totally inexperienced. We listened and asked a few questions but realized that the captain was not clearly stating the actions of an experienced rammerman. An experienced rammerman would use the hand signals as a guide but watch the readily visible rammer (fig. 7-4) to properly position the propellant train in the breech—that is, to position the aft powder bag so that the mushroom of the closed breech would just "kiss" the aft powder bag for trouble-free ignition. Captain Miceli was underscoring a point that was important to the Navy's scenario—that the gun captain had absolute control over the rammerman.

Commander Kissinger led us out of the gun house and through several passageways and ladders, down several decks. We encountered a number of crewmen on this trek. I studied their faces and wondered what they thought about the Navy's investigation, what scuttlebutt had made its way to them about us.

We eventually emerged on the powder flats, the lowest deck of the turret just above the keel. Evidence of the explosion was impressive. Not only were bulkheads warped, but large steel beams supporting the bulkheads had been substantially deformed by the explosion. Effects of the fire on electrical and other equipment were apparent in spite of efforts by the crew over the past several months. I recalled that a number of bags of propellant had been ignited on the powder flat by the flames of the explosion reaching down from the gun room several decks overhead. Several men had died here. We climbed up one deck on a ladder and walked around the projectile deck and projectile elevators. The overhead was low and the light level was dim, perhaps due to damage of the lighting system, adding to a sense of poor footing I felt on the oiled steel deck.

Figure 7-3. The breech of a 16-inch gun in the gun room. The gun spans the width of the gun room and the three gun rooms are separated from one another by heavy bulkheads. The circular breech opens downward during the loading process. In the foreground is a portion of a folded cradle mechanism over which the projectile and propellant bags are slid into the breech by the rammer. The open breech and extended cradle is shown in figure 7-5. Robert F. Sumrall, Iowa *Class Battleships: Their Design, Weapons, & Equipment* (Annapolis, Md: Naval Institute Press, 1988).

The projectiles used in the 16-inch guns are sizable, about 6 feet long and, of course, 16 inches in diameter. They weigh either nineteen hundred or twenty-seven hundred pounds and were stored on the base, secured to the outer bulkhead with chains. They were color coded into several types—blanks, armor penetrating, fragmentation, etc. The process of moving the projectiles on the oiled deck would be demonstrated the next day.

We continued the climb inside the turret and eventually found ourselves on the equipment deck, just below the scaffolding we had seen in the center gun room. I examined a pair of headphones hanging from a selector switch that had been damaged by the fire. The cables were charred and stiff, and I tried to imagine the high-temperature gases from the explosion quickly cascading from one region to another. The massive size of the motors and drives for the turret and guns greatly restricted the space for moving around. It was clearly the province of young, flexible, and agile men.

From this point we looked up to the gun room where the explosion had occurred, to the large steel breech that had been open when ignition took place, looked up much as the primerman must have done, watching the crew load the gun. It was at this position that the primerman inserted the primer, which looks like a 30-caliber shell without the bullet, into the breech block. The primer had been found by the explosive ordnance disposal team after the explosion and thrown overboard. They reported that it had not been fired.

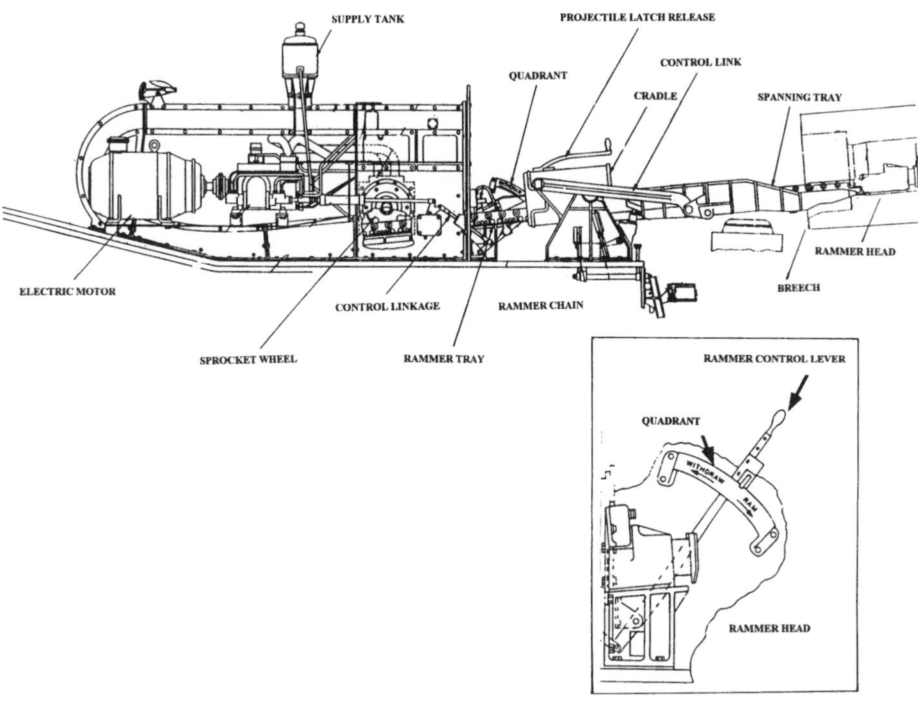

Figure 7-4. The rammer mechanism used to (fast) ram the projectile and (slow) ram the propellant bags into the breech of the 16-inch gun is shown in the upper drawing. The quadrant (barely visible in the upper drawing) and rammer control lever is shown in the inset. This hydraulic mechanism is controlled by the rammerman, who operates the rammer control lever that, in the case of the center gun of Turret II, is to the left of the rammerman. The rammer control lever is connected through control linkage to a stroking control, which delivers hydraulic fluid to rotate a sprocket wheel. The sprocket wheel drives the linked rammer chain. The rammer chain terminates in the rammer head, which contacts the projectile or, alternately, the series of propellant bags. Speed of the rammer is controlled by the rammerman and the position of the hand lever.

The last stop of the day was one of the magazines adjacent to the turret on the lowest deck. The magazine was separated from the turret by an annular space, another of the safety features of the thoughtful designers. The magazine for Turret II would have been crowded under any conditions, but seven of us squeezed into the constricted space. The brass tray on which the bags were moved by the crew divided us into two compressed groups. The contour of the lower hull was evident in this part of the ship, and I could visualize the water line on the other side of the thick hull well over our heads.

Two of the powder tanks, aluminum cylinders each containing three bags of propellant, were opened with a special wrench by one of the crewmen. "GMG Zion" was stenciled on his faded blue dungarees, and his shirt was so thin I felt that he must be terribly cold. He was a pale and lean young man, which seemed strangely appropriate in this deep recess of the ship. He removed the round covers and slid five of the six propellant bags onto the tray, where the second crewman moved them in front of us. Ether had been used as one of the solvents of the nitrocellulose at the time of pellet manufacture, and the fumes were quite strong as the bags lay before us on the tray. He explained how the propellant bags were passed through flame-tight doors into the annular space, and then again into the powder flat area.

I found the magazine an inhospitable space, crowding all my senses. People spoke in lower tones, and I sensed that we all felt discomfort, that the combination of ether vapors, confinement, and chill touched each of us in this forbidding space. We made our way out through the upper part of the turret and the hatch that we had entered earlier that day. We collected our belongings on the way out and headed back to the wardroom. It would take awhile to rid myself of the deep coldness, a coldness that derived not just from the weather but also from the tragedy that had taken place here.

After a short conversation and discussion of tomorrow's activities—a demonstration loading in Turret I—we made our way back to the gangway and down the icy steps to the car. The tempo of activity in the shipyard had picked up even more during the day. Captain Miceli motioned me to ride with him. I mocked a smirk at the others as I closed the door on the Caddie. I thanked the captain for the fine tour, noting that the crew had clearly gone out of their way to be helpful, and that I knew he'd worked hard to help bring us up to speed.

"Good, good," Captain Miceli said, "glad you liked it. This is a fine crew, and Captain Moosally is one of the best. He had been slated for a flag but all that's over with now. The captain takes the responsibility for everything, you know."

We talked about that for a while. I thought a commander who had such an experience could emerge a more effective leader, certainly not one to automatically cast aside if, as the Navy asserted, this was an incident beyond his control.

I asked Captain Miceli what his long-range plans were. "I was planning to retire when this explosion took place aboard the *Iowa*," he replied. "One of the admirals asked me to stay on and do the investigation, which I've done. As soon as this is over, I'll retire. I've thought about starting a company to carry out investigations, just as I've done with the *Iowa*. I think I could get a lot of support for that, based on what I've done in this investigation."

I could easily imagine that in his mind our independent study was of no significance, only a token review to placate skeptical senators. I could see that it was a small step to his perspective that all information of value had already been developed by the Navy team. All that remained was broad recognition of the rightness of the conclusions. The Navy's conclusions.

"You know," he said, "Hartwig and Truitt were real scuzbags. They were actually caught one night wrestling with each other. Can you imagine that? While Hartwig was on watch?" He glanced at me as he laughed. "The NIS [Naval Investigative Service] really tagged them."[2] The captain clearly had a fixed opinion about these two crewmen. I didn't respond. I knew nothing about these men, except that the media, particularly the papers, had said many disparaging things, largely based on unidentified sources.

We arrived at the hotel and I thanked the captain again for the informative day. I was exhausted from the combination of cold, climbing around inside the turret, and the depressing recollection of the incident. We agreed to meet tomorrow at the ship rather than the restaurant.

I took a long shower to shake the chill and called the others to make plans for dinner. We opted on the dining room and welcomed the quiet evening—only two other parties were there. The tension of the day faded as we compared our impressions, impressions that were remarkably similar, and enjoyed the first of many dinners in which we would continue to share our various observations.

I didn't sleep well that night, thinking of things we might do on board ship the next day, weighing them against one another, periodically rising to make notes.

I became even more convinced that it was essential that we take surface samples, swipes, of as many areas as we could in Turret I as soon as possible. One of the significant defects of the Navy study was that the "foreign materials" were not discussed in terms of the background levels of these same materials in the turrets. If the background levels were comparable to levels observed on the projectile, the significance of the "foreign materials" observed by the Navy would be altogether different. It would be necessary to sample Turret I because Turret II has been subjected to extensive cleaning and painting.

I had earlier talked with Mark Davis about the need to do a broad background survey. He had agreed and put together a sampling kit for the trip. Davis was a "generalist" with broad knowledge in many technical subjects. He had an instinctive sense for the unspoken thoughts of others and discerning motives. At breakfast I explained what we should try to accomplish in the sampling process. Davis and I would go to Turret I to swipe as many surfaces as possible. Paul Cooper and Dennis Mitchell would talk with Captain Miceli about other issues. We all needed to be mindful that Captain Miceli would not want us to be moving around the battleship unaccompanied, talking with the crew when he was not present.

We arrived at the ship before Captain Miceli and went directly to the wardroom and donned our overalls. Commander Kissinger was amenable to our taking surface swipes from inside Turret I. "No problem. I'll ask Lieutenant Meyer to take you to all the decks. Would you like to start right now?"

It couldn't have worked out better. We explained our intent, and Lieutenant Meyer took us to the powder flats of Turret I, where we entered the magazine. We took swipes starting with the brass trays that the propellant bags were moved on, next the scuttles into the annular space, and then we reentered the powder flat. We proceeded up through the turret, taking samples from a wide variety of surfaces, including from projectiles on the projectile deck. Our last stop was in the left gun room of Turret I, where we sampled surfaces of the breech, breech block, and a brush that was used to clean the bore. Almost all of the sampling materials had been used.

We passed the center gun room, and GMG Steve Brooks, the gun captain, was there. He was aware of our effort and obviously interested in being helpful. It was a unique opportunity to talk with both a gun captain on the *Iowa* and Lieutenant Meyer in an informal way. I asked Brooks about the full sequence of events in the gun-loading process. "What kinds of situations would cause you to report 'I have a problem'?"

“One of the main things I think of,” Brooks replied, “would be a ram creeping out from the fully retracted position so that it would interfere with refolding of the gun cradle. When that occurs, I make eye contact with the ram operator and ask him to secure the ram. Other things might be delays in correctly positioning the powder hoist so the bags could be rolled out onto the cradle. If the hoist is in the wrong position, you can’t open the powder door. You have to reposition the hoist to unload both levels. It can be tricky, especially for someone who is inexperienced.”

“Was the upper hoist operator in the center gun of Turret II inexperienced?”

“We didn’t know the man—he was new to the ship.”

“According to the testimony, he had never operated the powder hoist before that day and had only been on the ship a short time.”

“That could be a serious problem. It’s not a position that can be filled by an inexperienced operator.”

“Could bags being put on the hoist backwards be a problem?”

Brooks said he had never seen this happen. “We check them very carefully,” he added.

“Would ramming the bags too far into the breech be a reason to say, ‘I have a problem’?” I asked.

“If that were the case, I would have said ‘the charge has been moved in too far,’ not that ‘I have a problem.’”

“Do the various gun crews generally stay together as units?”

“Generally they do, but there is some mixing. I started out on the right gun in Turret I, and I’m now captain of the center gun.”

Lieutenant Meyer added,

> We don’t mix the right and center gun crews with the left gun (it is a mirror image of the other two) because of possible confusion. The center gun crew of Turret II was a very good crew. The rammerman on the center gun had been with the group about two months, so he was relatively new. Rammermen can be heavy-handed. It’s a touchy job and you have to develop a feel for it. I couldn’t do it. I tended to run the rammer too fast, and the deck plate lore is that fast ramming of propellant bags is not good. The crew is very touchy about this, and the lore is that you can initiate bags by fast ramming.

Davis asked about misfires, such as occurred in Turret I the morning of the explosion. Lieutenant Meyer said,

Turret II had a record for the fewest misfires. In fact it was zero, which was phenomenal! I have the record [in Turret I] for the most misfires, and I don't really understand this. But we were doing better and our turret was catching up to Turret II in total shots. We were behind about fifty shots in total and had crept up to about seven shots behind Turret II when the explosion occurred. The only misfire Turret II had was when a visiting secretary of the Navy goofed up in triggering a salvo.

We also position the propellant bags very carefully to get the most consistent IV [initial velocity]. I always ram the bags to a point about two inches beyond the end of the cradle, and then reach in and pull the last bag back just a little so it will just touch the mushroom when the breech is closed. Slight differences in position will give variations in IV.

Consistency in the initial velocity of the projectile (which is measured from the sighting positions) is crucial to shooting accuracy. I asked if it was possible to hear in the center gun room when the other two guns had completed the loading sequence. Were the crews under pressure to load as quickly as possible? "The noise level is pretty high in here," Brooks replied. "You can't tell by sound when the guns on either side of you are ready to go, but the cradle operator hears all the chit chat on the headphones and tells us when the others are ready. At one time we were under time pressure to load as fast as possible, but our current CO told us he wants us to do the job right and not be concerned about time. Captain Moosally doesn't want us to rush this."

I asked if there was a tendency to operate the ram faster if they were trying to catch up. Without hesitation Brooks said, "No. We do it right and we won't be rushed."

"Are we asking the right questions of you?" I said. "Are you aware that there was an overram in the center gun? What are the other important things from your perspective of the explosion and gun operations?"

Lieutenant Meyer answered,

One thing I think may be important are the electrical fittings in the gun room. These fittings are all original stuff, installed in 1943. Once I had a gun captain hit the air switch and it came apart. Before I could stop him he reached in with a screw driver to actuate it and a short blew sparks right across the width of the gun room. Right over the powder tray! It scared the hell out of us. In my opinion, electrical safety is more of a problem than homemade bombs.

My off-the-record view—the deck plate view—is that fast ramming is very risky. When I came on board, the crew was terrified of 16-inch bags and treat-

> ed them with a lot of respect. We know about the studies of fast ramming at Dahlgren, but we don't believe there is just "no problem" with overramming. What I'm telling you is not the party line—and that's all you hear around here—but that's the deck plate view.

We asked Meyer and Brooks to go through the sequence that takes place when they get the command to load.

"We get permission in advance to have a projectile brought up to the gun room," Brooks said. "If you wait until the last minute, you can get one projectile on top of another in the hoist and that is a real problem. When the order comes to load, I open the breech and look up the barrel to see that it is clear. We then extend the cradle and ram the projectile. Bags are on the powder car at the powder flats and ready to go. When the load order is given, the powder car starts up and arrives almost immediately so the propellant bags can be rolled out on the cradle."

The conversation with Meyer and Brooks continued for some time in the gun room, a memorable exchange, clear, direct, forthright. It was now about midmorning, and we felt we had touched on several major questions that had been on our minds. We expressed our thanks to Meyer and Brooks and headed back up to the wardroom. There was a refreshing authenticity to their remarks and observations.

Just after we returned to the wardroom, Captain Miceli said the crew was ready to demonstrate the loading process. I expected some comment about our heading off on our own, but there was none. We reversed our path and headed forward to Turret I again. The demonstration began on the powder flats with simulated propellant bags from the magazine coming into the area via the scuttles through the annular space.

We had asked a number of times if it was possible that a propellant bag could be placed in the gun in the reverse direction, with the black powder pouch forward instead of aft, and each time we had been assured that this was "impossible." We were about to witness how "impossible" can become possible.

The simulated propellant bags used for this demonstration were painted red on the end that simulated the red colored pouch on actual powder bags. The crewmen on the powder flats would place the roughly one-hundred-pound bags on the powder tray with the red end toward the lower end of the inclined tray. A red circle had been painted on that end of the tray as a reminder of the proper orientation.

I was standing next to Captain Miceli when a young crewman walked in front of us and placed the first bag in the tray. The bag was in the reversed position. At first I thought the sailor would pick it up and reverse it. But instead, he walked straight back to a scuttle to get another bag.

I glanced at Miceli with a "did you see that?" look. He had been following my eyes and saw exactly the same thing. His face darkened and he wheeled toward the crewman and said in a loud voice, "Sailor . . . hey, sailor! You just put that bag in backwards!" He also directed his remark to Commander Kissinger, the weapons officer, who was standing nearby. The commander grimaced and went over to correct the crewman.

Captain Miceli marched over to the tray, picked up the bag, reversed it, and replaced it in the correct position. He was flushed and obviously irritated. What he said was impossible happened with the very first bag placed on the tray. The action caught the attention of Davis, who instantly began to enjoy the discomfort of the situation.

I walked over to the powder tray and said to Captain Miceli, "Let's leave this bag in the reversed position on the powder flats and see what happens when it gets to the gun room." I picked up the bag and reversed it again so it was backward on the tray, just as the crewman had placed it. Davis turned away to chortle. Captain Miceli was infuriated and vented his wrath on the hapless crewman, who, it turned out, was new to the ship and on his first assignment. It must have been an unforgettable welcoming party.

We went up to the projectile deck and observed how the large projectiles were moved onto the elevator that would take them to the gun room. Straight manual labor with line and capstan, just the way it had been done during World War II. Crude but effective. The projectiles were unsecured from the bulkhead and a special projectile-handling line was looped around the base of the upright projectile sitting on its base. One of the crew then circled the line around a slowly spinning capstan near the elevator. The crewman used the capstan to slide the 2,700-pound projectile over the oiled deck to the elevator. The elevator was basically a heavy chain inside a metal cage. The chain was fitted with ears that would catch and lift the projectile. We acknowledged the crew's obvious skill with smiles and nodding of heads.

We climbed up to the left gun room. There must have been six or eight additional people in these already crowded quarters, and it took a while for everyone to find a secure place for at least one foot and a good hand hold. When we were ready, the gun crew called for the projectile and we watched as it emerged at the aft end of the gun room on the elevator. Since this was a demonstration of the loading process (fig. 7-5), the projectile was not tipped over into the ramming position on the spanning tray (that would have created extra work for the crew as the projectile was not going to be fired). Nothing was lost in the demonstration by omitting this step.

The powder hoist was actuated and the powder car arrived at the left gun of Turret I. Simulated propellant bags have a loop at the forward end that can be used to pull the bags out of the breech in practice loadings. Because the loop is at the forward end, the crew is supposed to reverse the bags as they came off the powder car onto the powder tray. In the reversed position, a loop on the forward end of the bags could be reached with a hook and the bags withdrawn from the breech after a practice ram.

The powder door opened and the bags rolled out, one already in the reversed position because of the miscue on the powder flats. The gun-room crew started to reverse the bags so the loops would be facing aft. They came to the bag that was already in the wrong orientation. They first reversed it, then turned it again, realizing that the loop was forward. They became completely confused.

"What the f——?" one of them muttered.

A side glance told me that Captain Miceli's blood pressure was clearly on the upswing again. Those of us who were aware of the problem the crew was struggling with let them cope with the ambiguities for a while. Then we told them that one of the bags was reversed on the hoist. In a few seconds they had all the bags oriented as they should be in a practice of this kind. The crew looked up at us, laughing and shaking their heads at their confusion. We laughed with them, all of us except the captain, who was thinking that this never should have happened in the first place.

The gun-room crew then rammed the powder bags at a painfully slow rate, so slow it was clear someone had given them instructions to be extra conservative for the benefit of the visitors. It was hard to suppress a smile. I noticed that Captain Miceli was taking a face vote on whether or not we accepted this as an authentic ram speed. I followed his eyes to the other grinning faces . . . his referendum failed.

The crew then retracted the rammer, folded the spanning tray, and closed the massive breech. They looked at us with a silent "that's it." We all thanked them for their fine demonstration and shook their hands, very fine young men, eager to please and display their skills. We slowly withdrew from the crowded gun room through the narrow hatch. We were almost getting used to the cramped spaces and scraped shins.

A

B

C

Figure 7-5. These three photographs show the full sequence of loading the 16-inch gun. In fig. 7-5A, a projectile is brought up in the hoist to the spanning tray. Note the folding action of the tray to bring the projectile into alignment with the bore. When the tray reaches the fixed loading angle of 5 degrees (fig. 7-5B), the projectile is rammed and seated in the bore. Last (fig. 7-5C), the propellant bags are placed on the tray and rammed into the breech. The bags are constructed of Wearsaver material (polyurethane foam). The quilted ignition pad may be seen at the aft end of the last bag. Courtesy FCCM (SW) Stephen Skelley, USNR.

We went to the wardroom again, always the common rallying point, and visited the nearby head. An officer explained that President Roosevelt had used this head and bathtub during World War II, that it had been installed when the *Iowa* took him to a meeting with Churchill. We silently regarded the white painted tub for a few moments, acknowledging this piece of *Iowa* history, and went back into the wardroom for lunch. We sat in small groups among the crew, who were courteous but essentially uninterested in us. There were many contractors aboard when the ship was in port, and we just blended into the background of civilians on the ship.

Commander Kissinger arranged for a quick tour of the ship after lunch, something we were all looking forward to. He led us to the bridge, engine room, and several other parts of the ship. The ship had been modernized in many areas, something particularly evident in the fire-control center. One of the fire-control computers was an intriguing mechanical device that worked so well it hadn't been replaced with an electronic version. There were small windows here and there to watch the gears and other mechanisms, and we spent some time peering into this remarkable device. One of the crewmen, apparently anticipating some remark about his computer, said, "Hey, don't knock our computer. It works just fine . . . and it's radiation hard!" We enjoyed his good humor and obvious knowledge of Sandia's efforts in making radiation hard electronics.

After we regathered in the wardroom, I thanked the officers and crew for the informative visit and special tours over the past two days. It was impossible to not think about the terrible tragedy that had occurred, and the further tragedy of several of these men's lives being irreversibly changed by forces beyond their control. We left the ship for the last time on this trip, clambering down the gangplank, not quite so icy as before, to the cars. With what was left of the afternoon, we would visit the shipyard civilian personnel who had done an analysis of the overram. Captain Miceli again invited me to ride with him in his Cadillac. I reiterated how much we appreciated the crew's cooperation in acquainting us with the relevant activities on board. The captain expanded on the impact of the explosion on various crew members—the damaged or ended careers—and his thoughts paralleled mine.

The shipyard was an extensive complex of rail spurs, old equipment, parked vehicles, and many vintage brick buildings that were not identified with signs. The captain led the parade of four cars in a series of wrong turns, impromptu U-turns, and minor traffic violations. All this was at a slightly excessive speed, fine for the captain, but too fast for the other cars to really keep up. On one or two of the reversals, we passed the last car heading in the opposite direction, and I could see a puzzled look on the face of the driver.

While Captain Miceli felt free to park his Cadillac wherever he wanted, the other drivers searched for designated spaces. Without waiting to regroup, Captain Miceli and I headed for a totally undistinguished doorway midway along an old brick building. The building looked like a warehouse with a few windows, and I wondered at first if the captain had erred. I fully expected the sole door midway along the building to be locked when he tried it, but it opened and I followed him inside.

I hoped some of the others were watching and knew where we had gone. Just inside we met the people we would be spending the rest of the afternoon with. We talked with them while the other cars parked and the group of ten or twelve found their way to the doorway. Inside we found the building to be just what it looked like, a giant warehouse. It was literally filled with assorted equipment from another age. Our host led us down some long aisles bounded by heavy wire-mesh dividers that extended upward from the floor to at least a two-story height. They took us up to a second-floor conference room. There were introductions, but our attention was taken by a display to our left.

Spread out on a table was the badly distorted rammer head and chain from the center gun of Turret II. The rammer chain was massive and looked like short hinged segments of a narrow-gauge railroad track. The explosion had blown the rammer against the aft bulkhead. The deforming effects of the explosion on these heavy segments were impressive. Also on the table was the spanning tray, which showed several deep gouges from the rammer chain. Those gouges were to take on special significance for Karl Schuler, one of our colleagues, and send us off on an important odyssey. Our hands quickly blackened from the various residues as we picked up and examined the heavy pieces.

We listened to and discussed two or three informal presentations about the various analyses the Navy people had carried out. They were helpful and open in these discussions, clearly trying to make our efforts as effective as possible. My impression was that they told us absolutely everything they knew about the rammer system and related analyses.

Our exhaustion from two full days of activity began to show as we headed to the airport. The exposure to so many details stimulated a lot of ideas, and we shared these with one another continually, even as we boarded the aircraft and went to our separate seats. The discussion continued in the airplane all the way back to Albuquerque. We thought about the miscue with the propellant bag on the powder flats and the subsequent confusion in the gun room. It was a small thing in itself, probably of no major consequence. But it was a reminder that it's difficult to account for human action, or to assert that certain kinds of errors are impossible when humans are involved.

While the Navy had steadfastly maintained that training was not a factor in the explosion, adequate training of the crew would certainly have reduced the probability of misunderstanding and inadvertent error.

8 The Navy and Sandia Technical Teams Meet

16 January 1990

KEY MEMBERS of the Navy Technical Review Team visited Sandia on 16 January 1990, the first of a number of meetings of the two teams over the next eighteen months.[1] Members of the Navy team who did not attend this first meeting included individuals from other Navy facilities, Army personnel at Picatinny and Aberdeen, the FBI forensic lab, and the Armed Forces Institute of Pathology and Forensic Services. We would meet a number of those people over the next year. A sizable group of Sandians was in attendance, including many directly involved in the *Iowa* investigation at Sandia.

Captain Miceli opened the Navy's presentation: "Committees of the House of Representatives have reviewed the findings of the Navy team and were unable to find flaws in the technical investigation. The problem we have with these committees is our assertion that Hartwig committed the crime. If we had said it was sabotage without a specific accusation, our results and conclusions would have been accepted."

I looked up from my note taking. The GAO people had given me their version of the House hearing just a few weeks ago. Captain Miceli's characterization of the House perspective on the Navy's investigation had to be the kindest possible interpretation. We had not yet seen the transcript of the recent hearing. (A summary of the House report, "USS *Iowa* Tragedy: An Investigative Failure," published on 5 March, is reviewed in chapter 10.)

Turning to me, Captain Miceli continued: "I understand that the Senate Armed Services Committee will make their report when you have completed your investigation. I was given authority to determine whether or not the moratorium on 16-inch gun operation should be lifted, and on August 11 the guns were, on my recommendation, recertified for operation." He paused a few moments as if he was giving us time to fully grasp the significance of his responsibility in this matter, slowly scanning the entire group. "The Navy technical team began with about forty personnel and grew to about sixty, the principals of which are here today. In addition, we had a 'cause analysis team' that was completely independent of the technical group."

The captain discussed the chronology of events from the initiation of the investigation up to the issuance of the Navy's final report. It was clear the Navy team had been very busy over the past several months. In fact, the fatigue of the Navy group, which I sensed came from being driven to further buttress their assertions, became evident over the next two days. The Navy had obviously been stung by the Senate and House hearings' probing questions and skepticism.

Captain Miceli described the scene in the center gun room just before the explosion, noting the position of each of the crewmen: "The gun captain was looking into the open breech. That was the key. When I went through the operations with other gun captains, I just couldn't get them to do that." The implication of his remark was that the center gun captain of Turret II knew that an explosion would occur and was expectantly "looking into" the open breech of the gun. Captain Miceli had apparently read more into the pathologist's report than was there. The testimony by the pathologist indicated only that Clayton Hartwig was facing the breech—not an unexpected position during this part of the gun-loading process since the next step was to close the breech.

Captain Miceli discussed use of the lead foil pouches that are inserted between the first and second bags, the purpose of which is to reduce fouling of the barrel by copper residues. The Navy hypothesis was that the gun captain, who normally inserts these pouches, had instead inserted the ignitor that the captain had described during our 7 December meeting.

Captain Miceli continued: "The forensics indicated that all the crewmen in the gun room were standing flat footed, that no one was alarmed. That is, the gun crew were not alerted to any emergency or impending explosion."

I was again skeptical of this improbable conclusion from the pathology examinations. I later learned that the Navy's testimony before the House included no such assertions.

The captain continued, "This was the only incident of this kind in the history of 16-inch gun operations. All others have been different."[2] This statement referred to the fact that although open-breech explosions had occurred before in 16-inch guns, the *Iowa* incident was unique since the gun had not been fired prior to the explosion. The residual burning ember theory (a means of igniting the propellant) was a possible explanation for those earlier incidents.

Captain Miceli continued with his interpretation of the events. "Lawrence [the cradle operator standing to the left of Hartwig] is heard to say over the sound-powered phone system that he's 'having a problem.' Subsequent interviews with those who heard him say this indicated that Lawrence was talking to Hartwig. There was a twenty-second delay. Again, Lawrence reports, 'I'm having a problem.' Almost immediately the explosion occurred. We first focused on a low-probability event, like initiation of a bag by friction. We found no evidence of a malfunction that might have initiated the bags in the breech. We found in our experiments that we could only get initiation by friction using extreme measures, but we could not get ignition by friction in the gun environment. We also considered a flareback. The abnormality we eventually found was that there had been an overram. It took us about a month to determine this through our studies of the rammer."

Captain Miceli briefly described how the explosion and fire-damaged regions of the rammer indicated to them that the rammer had been overextended into the breech, that is, that there had been an overram. He then discussed the chemical ignitor that he had described to me in his office. He said that Hartwig had worked with EOD (explosive ordnance disposal) for three years and was very knowledgeable about such devices. He quoted Hartwig as saying, "I am an expert in making improvised explosive devices," but did not offer a source for this quote.

"Hartwig had books on dirty tricks and how to get even," the captain continued, "and he had lead foils and propellant pellets in his personal effects. The weight of such evidence blows you away in comparison to low-probability events such as initiation by friction. Truitt did not have an EOD background, but he also had lead foils and propellant pellets in his possession."

In fact, the possession of propellant pellets by sailors aboard battleships was not unusual. Pellets could easily be removed from the bags without actually opening the bags, and were souvenirs. A subsequent inspection aboard the *Iowa* revealed that several sailors had propellant pellets in their possession, even after all the turmoil associated with the explosion.

An extended discussion of Captain Miceli's interpretation of the sequence of events followed. I listened to this with interest, realizing that the captain understood from the nature of the questions that many of the attendees had not read the Navy's report, that this left him a certain latitude in the way in which he could answer their queries. In fact, the impression of many Sandians was that the Navy's analysis had been exhaustive and covered a broad variety of accident forms.

After a short break, Captain Miceli continued: "The primer of the center gun had not been fired and was found by the EOD people after the explosion. We considered the possibility that the primer fired in the open breech block might have triggered the bags after they had been rammed. We demonstrated by open field experiments, however, that this could not occur." He showed the video tape of experiments at one of their explosive sites, and that a primer fired in an open breech would not initiate the last bag charge since the primer was pointed in the wrong direction. Moreover, even if the last bag were ignited, a flare would occur, not an explosion. I thought these were valuable experiments and that excellent information had been obtained indicating ignition occurred further forward in the breech. We would return to this subject.

Captain Miceli also noted that there had been rumors of electrical malfunctions in gun rooms. "We have reviewed the logs and found no records of malfunctions," he said. "Furthermore, we have inspected all switches in the gun rooms and found none that suggested some malfunction." Mark Davis and I exchanged a glance, thinking about our conversation with Meyer and Brooks, and of Meyer's personal experience with a faulty switch in a gun room. There was a discrepancy between the logs and what these crewmen had told us.

I asked Captain Miceli about the last words of GMG1 Ernest E. Hanyecz, turret repair, who was reported in testimony by GMG1 Dale E. Mortensen to have called out, "Mort, Mort," just before the explosion. Dale Mortensen was serving as turret officer in Turret I and was wearing sound-powered phones that connected him with Turret II. Captain Miceli said, "We chased that for a long time but couldn't make anything of it. I don't believe that report. I think it was speculation. I think Mortensen thought he heard this." Some months later we would talk directly with Dale Mortensen about this. Known as "Mort" on the ship, Mortensen was convinced that Ernie Hanyecz in Turret II was trying to tell him something over the phone system.

Captain Miceli said that the letter by Kathleen Kubicina, Hartwig's sister, telling about the $100,000 insurance policy with Truitt as the beneficiary, stimulated the criminal investigation by the Naval Investigative Service about three weeks after the explosion. In accord with this new investigative thrust, he and his team began to look for evidence of intentional ignition of the propellant. "We first pursued the possibility of an electronic ignitor," he said, "but we couldn't find the fingerprint of an electronic device [in the analyses of foreign materials on the projectile]. However, Crane [a Navy facility in Indiana) started finding iron fibers and calcium and chlorine and oxygen—that was very strange chemistry. We eventually concluded we were looking at remains of a chemical device and started tests along this line about the twenty-sixth of August. Shot number twenty-five [in which an ignitor of the kind proposed by the Navy was used to initiate an explosion] produced foreign materials that matched those found on the center gun projectile from the USS *Iowa*." By this, the captain meant that a field test with the proposed ignitor produced the same kind of chemical residues on the projectile used in the experiment as were found on the projectile in the center gun.

"How long does it take for the chemical ignitor that you described to actuate?" I asked.

"It might take a minute, but glycerin based hair creams [which also contain glycols] act much faster, maybe twenty seconds."

Dave Anderson, manager of our explosives group, asked, "What was the purpose of the five-bag experiments?"

Captain Miceli spoke briefly of Master Chief Skelly's interest, along with a group at Dahlgren, with shots using D846 propellant. More accuracy from such shots was thought to be possible.

Again, Captain Miceli went through the basic elements of the scenario, and then concluded his remarks. He seemed pleased with the questions and interest in what he had to say.

The next speaker was Bob Sloan from Crane. He reminded us that the D846 powder bags on the USS *Iowa* were normally restricted for use with only the 1,900-pound projectile. However, on the day of the explosion, the guns in Turret II were loaded with the 2,700-pound projectiles, and five, not six, bags of D846 were to be used to fire these heavier projectiles. Authorities on 16-inch guns had determined that five bags of the D846 could be used to accelerate the 2,700-pound projectile without overpressuring the barrel.

Sloan went on to discuss the propellant aboard the *Iowa*: "The powder bag canisters, each containing three bags, had been aboard the USS *Iowa* a little over two years. All the bags were examined after the incident. A 100 percent visual and X-ray inspection was performed for timers and ignitors. Nothing out of the ordinary was noticed. The stabilizer level was also checked throughout the lot of propellant with no deficiencies being found. I thought we might find some deficiencies, but this was not the case." Sloan also said that the storage of propellant bags over the years had been of concern, because some of it had been stored at high temperatures during the summer.

Nevertheless, measurements showed that stabilizer levels in the propellant were adequate and within specification.

Steve Mitchell of Indian Head talked about his ignition studies of black powder and propellant, and his ether level tests: "We examined black powder from the patch or pad on each propellant bag. This included powder from twenty ignitor pads from the USS *Iowa* bags and twelve pads from propellant stored on shore. In our impact initiation studies, there was no reaction in drop tests up to the highest levels on the testing equipment, and this indicated that the material was quite insensitive to impact."

Mitchell noted that the propellant was made in 1944, and although the stabilizer level of the *Iowa* propellant was about half the level of new propellant, it was still within specifications. Their studies indicated that the *Iowa* propellant would be good for at least twelve more years under normal storage conditions. "We found, however, that the propellant could fracture and give off hot fragments in drop tests. The fractured surface often had a burned appearance and smelled like it had burned."

Captain Miceli interjected, "This kind of thing [ignition of propellant surfaces by fracture] can't be duplicated during the actual loading operation. This result is not relevant to the explosion." This was a key point, and we would reexamine it in detail in a few months and find that the explosion could have occurred because of propellant fracture.

Mitchell continued. "We carried out sliding friction tests using a fabric covered wheel sliding against either the pellet or the black powder. Extremely high forces were needed to get ignition. These forces were so high that it was difficult to imagine how friction might have been involved in the explosion. We also carried out other sliding tests with various combinations of materials, various loads, in ether atmospheres, et cetera, and observed no reactions."

Mitchell went on to discuss electrostatic discharge (ESD) tests and the possible effect of ether in the environment. He related detailed information regarding ether levels at various stages of the loading process, and his assessment that ether levels were not a significant concern with respect to the *Iowa* explosion. Sandia researchers eventually came to the same conclusion. The studies he summarized were thorough and well documented.

Tom Doran from Dahlgren then spoke about the testing that had taken place at their facility. He began by noting that the *Iowa* incident was unique in that an explosion had occurred. Previous, related gun-room incidents aboard battleships had produced intense burning of the propellant in the gun room, not explosions. The two incidents aboard the USS *Mississippi*, in 1924 and

1944, were of this nature and may have been initiated by a source of ignition near the open end of the breech.

Doran reported Dahlgren's detailed examination of the gun system, rammer, general turret equipment, and handling of ammunition, all with no particular results relevant to an accidental cause for the explosion. He said the propellant is very insensitive to high levels of radio frequency (RF) radiation, but the primer is susceptible. However, RF levels in the turret are extremely low and the primer was found not to have been fired in the center gun. A member of the EOD team had observed that the primer was unfired, and then the primer along with many pieces of equipment was unfortunately thrown overboard in the cleanup process. Similarly, based on many measurements within the turret, Doran had found little evidence for the influence of electrostatic discharge in initiating the explosion.

Doran also discussed requirements to initiate either the black powder or the propellant in terms of open flames. Such long times were required to bring about ignition in each case that it seemed unlikely that the crew would not have reported such a circumstance. The video tape of their ignition studies were convincing. In addition, frictional heating studies had been conducted in which a cylinder was covered with silk, Wearsaver (a polyurethane cover on the propellant bags), steel, and so on, and then the cylinder was rotated at various surface speeds. The Navy concluded that the conditions to produce ignition were such that friction was an improbable source of ignition. Doran's studies on all of these subjects were thorough and well documented.

Doran also discussed the Navy's studies dealing with overram. They had rammed simulated bags (bags filled with wooden pellets), but with regular black powder pouches against a seated projectile. No reactions were observed. They had even cocked a bag at an odd angle and, again, no reactions were observed. This was the first time we had heard that the overram tests were not performed with all bags containing actual propellant.

The Navy had also performed low- and high-speed rammer tests in which they had stalled the rammer and bags against a projectile one hundred times at low speed. Real pellets had been used in these studies. There was no reaction. This had been repeated at high ram speeds. They found that the bags would begin to break up after a few rams, and that there was "no damage to pellets in the forward bags, but the pellets do break up in the rear bags." This latter observation clearly countered statements at the Indian Head meeting in which it was asserted that the rammer couldn't deliver enough force to fracture propellant pellets.

The Navy team showed us a photograph of these tests that arrested my attention. It was taken after ram number seven of bag number four, and showed a broken pellet protruding through the black powder pouch. I asked Captain Miceli for a copy of the picture. As it turned out, we would show this picture to the Senate Armed Services Committee in May. It was an excellent example of what could have occurred in the USS *Iowa* incident in which an overram might have taken place with a fractured pellet having access to the black powder.

Captain Miceli opened the meeting the following day by showing a C-Span videotape of Ken Nimmich of the FBI Laboratory testifying before the Senate Armed Services Committee. Miceli commented on Nimmich's testimony as it unfolded and did little to conceal his disdain for what the FBI had contributed to the Navy's investigation. Senator Nunn's questions to the FBI were of a searching nature, asking for comparisons of the capabilities of the two laboratories, whether the FBI disagreed with the Navy or not, why the FBI did not continue their work.

Captain Miceli turned off the tape. His arched eyebrows and expression underscored his view that the FBI Laboratory's contribution was of essentially no value. "My intent in getting the FBI involved," he said, "was to get the USN out of the investigation of physical evidence. But after we started to get some of the FBI's results, I decided it was important to continue with studies by Navy experts. Nimmich called me and said the FBI didn't have the resources for this job and they couldn't be of further assistance. I was surprised when he testified that the Navy didn't want to continue FBI involvement in the investigation."

There was an extended discussion on the various specimens of rotating band from the projectile from the *Iowa*, where the "foreign materials" were noted, and the location of each of these specimens. It appeared that Sandia had received a section of the rotating band that had first been examined by the FBI. This section had been cut into several pieces and the cannelure opened on all those pieces. Disturbingly, the Navy could not clearly identify the section we had received, and we would need to contact the FBI directly to try to identify the section.

In these few minutes, it became apparent that there were no untouched portions of the rotating band on which we could perform analyses. This was discouraging since an important premise of our involvement was the existence of some untouched samples of the rotating band from the center gun. The record keeping on the disposition of the rotating band had been inadequate, and it was clear that we would never have a complete description of the specimens of rotating band that we would be dealing with. Moreover, the samples we had received had all been poorly packed in small plastic boxes that had come open in the parcel sent to us. It was clear that critical evidence from this important investigation had been mishandled.

Next we went into a series of questions and answers about the sampling of the rotating band and the observations that had been included in the Navy report. Captain Miceli emphasized that "seeing steel wool by itself was not significant—you must have the association of HTH and glycols from brake fluid or some other glycol containing material." These questions only heightened the interest in what Dave File from Crane would have to say. He was the Navy's expert in the foreign materials work that had been carried out at Crane.

File went through a viewgraph presentation that centered on a number of things we already knew from the Navy reports. The evidence that he felt substantiated the presence of a chemical ignitor was: (1) the existence of steel wool, "with encrusted regions of high calcium content," which he associated with the hypothetical chemical ignitor; (2) the presence of glycols, which he also associated with the chemical ignitor; and (3) a single fragment of plastic film that he associated with a food baggy in which the chemical ignitor might have been contained.

Jim Borders, a supervisor of the materials analysis organization at Sandia, and I had looked through his section of the Navy's report carefully, and File had essentially reiterated the contents of the report. On the face of it, the work seemed competent and thorough. The devil was in the details, and it was clear that the materials experts in the two teams would need to have additional meetings to examine all those details.

File concluded his presentation and the meeting turned to general discussion, which continued for the rest of the afternoon. At the conclusion, I thanked the Navy team and commented on the candor and openness of the conversations.

Captain Miceli said he was anxious to have us visit Crane and Indian Head to review the work there. "The Navy's report was written for a general audience," he noted, "not for experts. I want to stay close to your investigation to help provide the details which may not be there because of the way we wrote it."

With that, the first meeting of the two technical teams concluded.

9 The FBI Laboratory

24 January 1990

AFTER MEETING with the Navy team at Sandia, it was essential to visit the FBI Laboratory in Washington, D.C., to get a firsthand report of its work related to the *Iowa* investigation. There were two aspects of FBI work that were germane to the investigation. The first related to the materials analysis work that Captain Miceli had described. Ken Nimmich's responsibility at the FBI included oversight of this work, and he had been the primary contact for materials analysis requests by the Navy investigators. I found it difficult to accept that the FBI had not been fully supportive in the investigation as Captain Miceli had indicated. The basis for the conflict between the Navy and the FBI was unclear to me. I wanted to understand the FBI's concerns with the Navy's analysis of "foreign materials" found on the projectile, one of the areas of particular responsibility in the Sandia assessment.

The second aspect of the FBI's work on the *Iowa* investigation related to the Equivocal Death Analysis performed by personnel who were not part of the FBI Laboratory. I did not intend to explore this work at the FBI since we had no expertise in this area and it was not a part of independent assessment activity. I was, however, interested in Nimmich's general view of the value of this analysis.

I arrived in Washington late on 23 January. Early the next morning I boarded the Metro for the stop nearest the FBI building, reviewing again my notes on Captain Miceli's comments on the FBI participation in their investigation. I arrived at the huge building shortly after 8:00 A.M. and climbed the broad steps to the main entrance, which I might have guessed was not the right one. I was directed to an underground garage entrance half a block away.

The guard called Ken Nimmich's office, and in a few minutes he came into the badge office and introduced himself. It was apparent from the beginning that he wanted to help in any way he could, as if he had been waiting for the opportunity, extending his welcome in several ways. We had exchanged only a few words when he began telling me of his experience with the Navy. He said that Captain Miceli had played everything so close to the chest that Nimmich and his people at the FBI never really knew what was going on in the Navy's investigation. The captain had insisted on compartmenting the information and, in Nimmich's view, had not made the FBI a partner in the investigation.

The initial request the FBI received from the Navy was to look for residues of an electronic or electrical initiator on an approximately 16-inch section of the rotating band from the projectile in the center gun. The focus of the search was the cannelure of the rotating band, the region that had been sealed by the forward motion of the projectile resulting from the explosion. The search would focus on residues of wires, insulating materials, fiberglass, and other debris that could be associated with an electronic device.

Nimmich recalled, "We received a piece of rotating band from the Navy and sectioned it into several pieces for examination. We opened the cannelure and found it loaded with what we later found to be Break-Free [a liquid used to clean and lubricate 16-inch guns]. The first step was to separate this liquid from other debris in the cannelure."

The FBI was not able to identify anything that they could definitively associate with an electronic initiator. Nimmich said he'd requested samples of "normal" rotating bands that would give the FBI technical people a background reference with which to compare the *Iowa* samples, but these were never provided. Nimmich's request was very reasonable. Many modern analytical techniques can detect extremely low levels of, for example, calcium and chlorine, and the levels of such elements on other projectiles would be germane to establishing their significance in the cannelure of the 16-inch projectile from the center gun.

Nimmich said they were concerned about overinterpretation of results by the Navy without good reference information. I mentioned that we also were concerned about the lack of information on background levels, and that we had begun establishing background data during our first visit to the *Iowa* in December, taking numerous swipe samples throughout the turret.

An obvious irritating factor to Nimmich was that Captain Miceli frequently called Nimmich's two principals, Fred Whitehurst and Bob Halberstam, to query them on the latest results. These phone conversations were of a one-way nature with the captain insisting that they "just answer the questions."

Nimmich was rankled by being bypassed, and said his two investigators also found this kind of exchange to be most irritating. "Captain Miceli frequently pressed us for written statements corroborating their results which, of course, we were never able to do."

When the FBI lab people failed to find evidence of an electronic initiator, Nimmich said that Captain Miceli became short and impatient with them, which only exacerbated the already poor working relationship. Shortly after that, Captain Miceli called Nimmich and abruptly terminated the interaction with the FBI. According to Nimmich, the captain said, "The Crane facility has much better equipment to explore the possible presence of a chemical initiator." Nimmich said he was dumbfounded when the captain mentioned a chemical device. He said to Captain Miceli, "Chemical initiator? I thought we were looking for residues of an electronic initiator?"

"No," Miceli replied, "we now have evidence that a chemical initiator was used."

Nimmich was concerned that the FBI's efforts had at least partially been misused, looking for one thing when the Navy's investigation had shifted in another direction. From the information that the captain provided over the phone, Nimmich recommended tests that he thought would be useful:

> I suggested that steel wool soaked in Break-Free be burned in propellant to see if the residual wires might be coated as reported in the Navy findings. I suggested this because Brake-Free contains calcium, chlorine, and other constituents considered by the Navy to be a signature of a chemical ignitor.[1] At that point I was glad we were out of it. As far as I was concerned it was a total fiasco. The first scenario was an accident, the second an electronic detonator, and the third a chemical ignitor. Each of these scenarios had been considered the right answer by Miceli at one time or another. We packaged up the samples of rotating band and sent them back to the Navy.

I noted that we were now in possession of those same rotating band specimens at Sandia and were having trouble identifying the various items.

I thought of the carton we had received a few weeks ago from the Navy after a long delay. The Navy had difficulty locating the specimens and, at one time, were uncertain if any specimens of the *Iowa* rotating band remained. My understanding was that the specimens had eventually been located in a Naval Investigative Service evidence locker, but no clear story of how and where they were found was ever conveyed to me.

The carton contained several small plastic boxes that had opened in the transportation process, spilling loose specimens of the rotating band inside the carton. Each piece of the cannelure had been marked with an identifying marker: Q1, Q2, and so on. All the cannelure specimens had been opened by sectioning, and some of the sectioned pieces were taped to the parent part, while others were loose in the carton. It was a confused jumble. No one would have guessed this was important evidence from a tragic incident in which forty-seven men died.

It was apparent the FBI had no knowledge of what I was talking about regarding the packaging of the specimens in plastic boxes, and I surmised that the specimens must have been repackaged by the Navy. Nimmich said we could probably clear up the specimen identification problem by having Bob Halberstam and Fred Whitehurst join us: "They were my two key people in this work and I'm sure they can straighten out the identifications."

Halberstam and Whitehurst, earnest, serious men, obviously anxious to help, joined us. They asked me a few questions about Sandia, how we happened to be tapped for this job, and how I was getting along with the Navy. I gave them the short version of how Sandia became involved, but didn't say much about interactions that I felt were about as good as one might expect. I was anxious to get their remembrances about the rotating band specimens that we had recently received.

Without any cues from Nimmich, they were outspoken in their disregard for the unprofessional way the Navy had handled the interaction with the FBI. They reiterated experiences from the captain's frequent phone calls, particularly his offer to have "one of the Navy people come out to the FBI to show you how we cracked the code" of materials identification. They smiled and shook their heads at what they considered the arrogant nature of this offer. They said they were kept in the dark and confused by the switch in the Navy's focus from an electronic to chemical initiator without any word to them.

Nimmich interjected, "By the way, I don't want you to associate our laboratory efforts with the FBI people who carried out the Equivocal Death Analysis. That is a different part of the FBI all together. If the FBI has a full-scale investigation, the reports from the various sections are integrated together into an FBI report. The people in my lab had been asked for rather specific corroborating analysis. We supplied that analysis and the Navy chose not to use it. Rather, they chose to say that we had not been helpful, or even worse. However, the Navy did use the FBI's Equivocal Death Analysis."

I appreciated the clarification and had not understood the connection between these two seemingly disconnected efforts within the FBI. I explained the nature of the specimens we had received to Halberstam and Whitehurst. Since the plastic boxes had opened in shipping and handling, the specimens were loose inside the carton and the only identifiers we had were the Q1, Q2 marked on each piece. I asked if these specimens tallied with the ones the FBI had.

"Yes, those are the specimens we examined and returned to the Navy," they replied.

I explained that we needed to know as much as possible about the sectioning process, what solvents may have been used to rinse out the cannelure, the kinds of analyses they had carried out, and any results they could tell me about that were not contained in the very brief report they had written to the Navy. They both said they were a little fuzzy on the various solvents that had been used and would need to refer to their notes. They might not be able to recover the information today, but they'd be glad to send it to me.

"Fine," I said. "Or better yet, why don't you plan to visit Sandia and talk directly with our materials analysis people. I'm sure they'll have other questions and direct communication between all of you would be of great help."

That was agreeable and we made a plan for their visit in two weeks.

With a future meeting already agreed to, I asked more about their results. They had found no evidence of an electronic initiator, but did find small iron wires or fragments of wires in the cannelure that looked like steel wool. They reported this finding to Captain Miceli during one of his phone calls. Captain Miceli had told them, "Ignore the fibers—steel wool is an expected material since it is used to clean the guns."

Interesting. Captain Miceli had given responses to questions on this subject that ranged from steel wool is never used to clean these guns to steel wool is an expected material since it is used to clean the guns. The iron fibers found by the FBI would later became one of the foreign materials that indicated to the Navy that a chemical initiator of a particular kind was present.

It was apparent that Whitehurst and Halberstam had gone through all of the essential information they could provide without reference to their notes. I thanked them and said we looked forward to seeing them in two weeks for more extended discussions. I was impressed with their forthrightness and obvious intent to be cooperate with our investigation.

Nimmich wanted to show me around his labs and I took the opportunity. When we parted at the guard desk he wished me luck and offered the assistance of the FBI in helping Sandia in any way it could.

10 The House Report

5 March 1990

On Monday, 5 March 1990, the House Armed Services Committee issued a news release on the USS *Iowa* investigation by the Navy:[1]

> The House Armed Services Committee today released its report on last year's explosion aboard the battleship *Iowa*, saying the Navy's investigation had failed to prove its assertion that Gunner's Mate Clayton Hartwig set off the blast that killed him and forty-six other crewmen. In releasing the report today, Chairman Les Aspin (D-Wis.) of the Defense Policy Panel and Nicholas Mavroules (D-Mass.) of the Investigation Subcommittee said they found a number of holes in the Navy's investigation of the April 19, 1989, explosion in gun turret number two. Aspin said, "The major problem with the Navy investigation is that it fell into the trap of an excess of certitude. Thin gruel became red meat. Valid theories and hypotheses were converted into hard facts until the head of the investigation told one interviewer he was positive Hartwig would have been convicted in a jury trial." The committee report concluded: "By the standards of the U.S. justice system, the subcommittee does not believe that Clayton Hartwig could be convicted of any crime. By the more subjective standards of history, there will likely always be a case to be made against him. By the standards of this subcommittee—and the standards that we think should have been applied in the Navy's investigation—there is only a hypothesis, and a tenuous one at that."

As I read the news release, I recalled Captain Miceli's opening remarks at Sandia, when the Navy team visited us in January. His remarks implying that the Navy's report had been well received by the House were off the mark.

It was mid-March when the GAO, one of our primary information connections to the Washington scene, forwarded us a copy of the report, "USS *Iowa* Tragedy: An Investigative Failure." The report of the Investigations Subcommittee and the Defense Policy Panel of the Committee on Armed Services, House of Representatives, was dated 5 March 1990, and highlighted several frailties of the Navy's investigation process. Only portions of the Summary and Findings and Conclusions will be highlighted here.

SUMMARY

On April 19, 1989, an explosion in Turret 2 aboard the USS *Iowa* took the lives of forty-seven crewmen. Despite finding a host of policy, procedural, and safety violations that did not contribute to the explosion, a Navy investigation concluded:

> The explosion in center gun, Turret II, USS *Iowa* (BB-61) on 19 April 1989 resulted from a wrongful intentional act. . . . Based on this investigative report and after full review of all Naval Investigative Service's reports to date, the wrongful intentional act that caused this incident was most probably committed by GMG2 Clayton M. Hartwig, USN.

Normally, as the result of such a catastrophe, the Navy initiates two investigations—a Judge Advocate General (JAG) manual investigation which is an administrative inquiry into potential causes for the event, and a Naval Investigative Service (NIS) preliminary criminal inquiry into "unattended deaths," fire, and explosion. Unfortunately, in this case, only the JAG manual investigation was initiated. This conscious decision by the convening authority was the wrong one. This error was compounded when the least comprehensive form of JAG manual inquiry was convened—a one-officer forum without the use of hearings. At the very least, had hearings before a multi-member board been used, evidence and prospective findings could have been discussed and challenged, and perhaps a more balanced perspective would have resulted. The Navy report contained 230 Findings of Fact and fifty-seven Opinions. Many of these Findings of Fact dealt with shipboard deficiencies. The subcommittee feels strongly that the JAG manual investigation is not the proper arena for a finding of criminal wrongdoing. This unfortunate error by the convening authority and Naval officers in the chain of command complicated and nearly made impossible the ability of anyone to discover the true causes for this loss of life.

The Navy JAG manual investigation initially concentrated on a technical probe, which ran thousands of tests in an effort to see if friction, pressure, electromagnetic radiation, or a host of other technical theories could have accounted for the explosion. This probe could find no accidental technical explanation.

The Navy investigative team concluded that because it could find no technical explanation, there was no technical explanation. This requires a leap of logic and has the Navy concluding that it has proven a negative. In his news conference announcing the results of his investigation, the chief investigating officer left no doubts. "We looked at *all* possible ignition sources" (emphasis added), he said. The subcommittee review of the technical investigation validated its processes, procedures, and protocols. It was conducted professionally. It was a complete test series that addressed all reasonable theories—but that is not necessarily the same as addressing all possible theories.

Modern science knows a great deal about ignition. It doesn't necessarily know everything, however. While the likelihood that some unknown accidental source of ignition caused the *Iowa* explosion is remote, the subcommittee cannot share the Navy's certitude.

The investigation took a curious twist on May 8, 1989. Information regarding an insurance policy on Hartwig, with a surviving crew member as beneficiary, brought in the NIS to address the possibility of a criminal act. At this time, nearly three weeks after the explosion, NIS was faced with a contaminated crime scene, no chain of custody for evidence, and a virtual inability to conduct a proper criminal inquiry from an evidentiary standpoint. For example, the projectile that had lodged in the gun barrel as a result of the explosion was subjected to extraordinary removal efforts. Although this was to become the most crucial physical evidence, it was contaminated during this process. With little physical evidence, NIS was left to conduct hundreds of interviews regarding the lifestyle proclivities, sexual preference, and suicidal nature of Hartwig and Kendall Truitt, his shipmate and beneficiary of the life insurance policy.

As the technical investigation became stymied relative to determining an accidental cause, the NIS investigation took another strange twist. Armed with evidence from a seaman interviewed by NIS that Hartwig had possessed a timing detonator, the Navy turned its technical investigation toward tests designed to determine if a commercial timer would leave residue similar to the material found on the unexpended projectile removed from Turret 2. At the time the report was submitted, the Navy concluded that residues in the projectile's rotating band were consistent with a commercial timer. Shortly after the testimony regarding a timing detonator was received, however, it was recanted. Thus, even though there was no evidence to link Hartwig to a timing detonator, the Navy was left with a determination that this device was the cause of the explosion.

And then another curious twist occurred involving the technical investigation. While the Navy report fully supported the finding that a timing detonator was the initiator for the explosion, the chief investigating officer announced at the press conference releasing the report that material from a chemical detonator was the closest match to the residues found on the projectile. The Navy substantiated this finding with a supplemental technical report issued in October, but has never changed the Finding Fact in its original report that supports the timing device theory.

And the final strange twist occurred when the Navy sought independent expert opinion from the FBI. The Navy used the FBI results in one instance and did not in the other. In the technical investigation, the FBI Laboratory was asked to corroborate the findings of the Navy technical team regarding a timing device. The FBI conducted an analysis, but did not find any evidence to corroborate the Navy's theory. The Navy did not use the FBI Laboratory report, describing it as inconclusive, and requested the FBI technicians do no further independent tests to support the Navy.

The Technical Investigating Officer testified he believed that the Navy laboratory at Crane has the best suite of chemical analytical equipment located in one location in both the public and private sectors and analytical capabilities among the most advanced in the country. The Chief Investigating Officer, Technical Investigating Officer, and NIS Director of Criminal Investigations said they welcomed an FBI review of the Crane laboratory's work, but the Navy to date has not officially requested the FBI Laboratory to conduct its own independent analysis to corroborate evidence of a chemical detonator.

On the other hand, the Navy sought through NIS an independent psychological opinion on Hartwig and Truitt from the FBI's National Center for the Analysis of Violent Crime. The Equivocal Death Analysis, as the FBI calls it, concluded that Hartwig died as a result of his own actions, staging his death in such a fashion that he hoped it would appear to be an accident. This analysis was to become a key document in support of the Navy opinion and was cited in the Navy report.

The FBI's psychological autopsy provided something the Navy needed—a theory that now could be backed with seeming scientific support resulting from its technical investigation. The Navy married these two items in support of the Hartwig suicide thesis: the FBI psychological analysis and technical tests on the residues pointing to the conclusion that ignition was achieved by an explosive device.

Unfortunately, if there was a single major fault in this investigation, it was the FBI system for producing the Equivocal Death Analysis. These documents, most commonly generated after orthodox police investigations have reached no conclusion, are invariably unequivocal in reaching a conclusion. The analysis contains no comment on probabilities, no qualifications and no statement of the limitations of a posthumous analysis in which the subject cannot be interviewed.

The Navy appears to have relied heavily on the FBI analysis. For example, it is one of the few documents specifically cited in two of the three endorsements. In contrast, the NIS tasked its own staff psychologist to do just such a psychological autopsy using the identical inputs available to the FBI. His report was heavily qualified. In the first paragraph of his report, the NIS clinical psychologist states:

> Due to the post-dictive nature of this assessment, the results should be regarded as speculative. This inquiry and evaluation is not a substitute for a thorough and well-planned investigation.

This NIS psychological autopsy concludes, however, that "there is a preponderance of circumstantial evidence" pointing to Hartwig as the culprit. It describes the likelihood that someone other than Hartwig deliberately set off the detonation as "another possible (albeit improbable) scenario." The NIS analysis gives serious standing to the Hartwig suicide hypothesis—but it makes clear that it is a hypothesis.

For reasons that are yet unknown, this "speculative" NIS analysis was not included with the hundreds of other NIS documents forwarded to the chief investigating officer.

Just as the FBI psychological analysis was key to the Navy investigation, so it was to the subcommittee inquiry. As a result, the subcommittee, using the professional services of the American Psychological Association, sought the opinions of 11 independent clinical licensed psychologists and one psychiatrist. Additionally, the subcommittee consulted independently with a psychiatrist and a psychologist who had some previous knowledge of this case. Ten of the 14 experts consulted considered the FBI analysis invalid. And even those who believed the analysis to be somewhat credible were critical of procedures, methodology, and the lack of a statement of the limitations of a retrospective analysis of this nature.

The subcommittee's investigation was not an investigation into the causes of the explosion aboard the *Iowa*. It was an examination of the Navy procedures in the conduct of this investigation and a review of the findings that supported the opinion rendered by the Navy in this case.

The subcommittee finds the Navy's opinion regarding Hartwig unconvincing. The Navy used an investigative format that clearly was not designed for matters of such significance. While the technical investigation found some foreign material on the rotating band of the projectile, the subcommittee does not accept the certitude of the Navy conclusion that this material fingerprints a chemical detonating device as the cause of the explosion. The NIS criminal inquiry was too narrowly focused. Its only value was to serve as the basis for the FBI's Equivocal Death Analysis. Finally, while this served as the key document in support of the Navy's theory on Hartwig, the FBI's analysis failed the peer review requested by the subcommittee.

As a result, the subcommittee believes the evidentiary materials are simply not present to permit the Navy to accuse the late GMG2 Clayton M. Hartwig of being a suicidal mass-murderer.

By the standards of the U.S. justice system, the subcommittee does not believe that Clayton Hartwig could be convicted of any crime. By the more subjective standards of history, there will likely always be a case to be made against him. By the standards of this subcommittee—and the standards that we think should have applied in the Navy's investigation—there is only a hypothesis, and a tenuous one at that.

Findings and Conclusions

The Investigations Subcommittee and Defense Policy Panel find that: The Navy's determination attributing the April 19, 1989, *Iowa* explosion to Clayton Hartwig is based on evidence inadequate to support the conclusion. The Navy's use of evidence in support of its opinions was often selective and presented an unbalanced view of the facts. The Navy should more properly have left the issue unresolved and the investigation open rather than attach its name to a conclusion grounded in evidence that is both limited and questionable. By the standards of the U.S. justice system, we do not believe Hartwig could be convicted of any crime. By the more subjective standards of history, the Navy report guarantees there will always be a case to be made against him. By the standards of this subcommittee—and the standards we think should have been applied in the Navy's investigation—the Hartwig hypothesis was and remains a theory, and a tenuous one at that.

The Investigations Subcommittee and Defense Policy Panel further find that:

1. The investigation got off to a wrong start—in part because the Navy thought it was dealing with a technical problem—and the Navy's leadership never upgraded the character of the investigation when it developed that the cause might be criminal.

(A) Naval authorities convened an inappropriate form of the JAG Manual investigation at the outset, i.e., a one-officer inquiry without hearings. Given the magnitude of the issues, the Navy should have used the more formalized hearing process in conjunction with a Board of Investigation. A board of several members would have subjected the investigation and its evolving theories to more rigorous tests than happened with a one-man operation.

(B) Naval authorities assigned an officer with inadequate investigative experience to conduct an inquiry of this magnitude, especially in view of the investigation's criminal nature.

(C) Naval authorities violated their own Navy instruction by not involving the Naval Investigative Service (NIS) from the outset. NIS's entry into the investigation three weeks after the explosion exacerbated investigative procedural problems, such as crime scene and evidence preservation mistakes. Partly as a result of this decision, potentially significant evidence was literally thrown overboard with the concurrence of the JAG Manual investigator.

(D) Premature signing of the JAG Manual report and its endorsements destroyed the credibility of the Navy's overall findings. Naval authorities issued and endorsed a report prior to the completion of all investigative actions. As a consequence, a key Finding of Fact that subsequently proved to be an error was endorsed—namely, the assertion that a timer was the likely ignitor of the explosion.

(E) The Navy failed to include key evidence in its report. The FBI Laboratory analysis, which did not support the Navy technical conclusion, and the NIS psychological analysis, which labeled a conclusion that Clayton Hartwig set off the explosion as "speculative," were two significant documents not included in the released report.

2. The technical aspects of the investigation were handled admirably—up to a point.

(A) The subcommittee applauds the painstaking efforts of the Navy technical team to reconstruct the explosive event. A review of the test protocols and execution reveals no serious flaws. The technical team set about to test every known potential cause. The tests eliminated one theory after another. The tests can be said to have eliminated all known, reasonable theories; they cannot, however, be said to have eliminated any technical explanation whatsoever. To do so, as the Navy did, requires an assertion that the Navy has succeeded in proving a negative.

(B) The technical examination of evidence failed to confirm conclusively the Navy's theory that a detonating device was used to initiate the explosion. The conclusion of the technical analysis is, at most, that foreign material was found during post-incident examination. It cannot be said conclusively what the source was of much of this foreign material.

(C) The Navy erred in its first identification of an electronic timer as the cause of the *Iowa* explosion. Even after altering its conclusion to a chemical detonator, Navy officials failed or were unable to explain the presence or relevance of other foreign materials found by their examination. We conclude from the incorrect identification of certain materials that the Navy too hastily interpreted ambiguous or inadequately analyzed data to find the type of residue that supported the then-prevailing hypothesis of an electronic timing device as cause for the explosion.

3. The NIS investigation itself was flawed.

(A) Although hundreds of persons had access to the gun turret before the explosion, the NIS focused almost exclusively on Clayton Hartwig, without adequately investigating other crew members or persuasively detailing why other suspects were not credible.

(B) The quality of interviewing could have been higher and more professional. A number of witnesses complained of interviews that were suggestive and leading. The fact that some key information was later recanted provides evidence in support of this contention.

4. The FBI psychological analysis procedures are of doubtful professionalism. The false air of certainty generated by the FBI analysis was probably the single major factor inducing the Navy to single out Clayton Hartwig as the likely guilty party. The FBI should consider revamping its entire Equivocal Death Analysis system.

(A) The procedures the FBI used in preparing the Equivocal Death Analysis were inadequate and unprofessional. As a matter of policy, the analysts do not state the speculative nature of their analyses. Moreover, the parameters that the FBI agents used, either provided to them or chosen by them, biased their results toward only one of three deleterious conclusions. Further biasing their conclusions, the agents relied on insufficient, and sometimes suspect evidence. As a panel of psychologists and psychiatrists noted, the value of material provided to the FBI agents was limited, as was the exhaustiveness of the NIS investigation for the purposes of preparing a psychological profile. The FBI agents' Equivocal

Death Analysis was invalidated by ten of fourteen professional psychologists and psychiatrists, and heavily criticized even by those professionals who found the Hartwig possibility plausible.

(B) The FBI analysis—drafted without caveats or any reference to probability—gave the Navy a false confidence in the validity of the FBI's work. The Navy should have used multiple sources of qualified psychological support for its investigation, rather than relying only on the opinion of two FBI agents. If the Navy had relied solely on the work of NIS's own staff psychologist—which emphasized that such psychological autopsies are by definition "speculative"—the Navy would likely not have found itself so committed to the Hartwig thesis. But the NIS psychological profile mysteriously was never included in the investigation's long list of exhibits.

(C) The FBI should review its procedures and revise its Equivocal Death Analysis format to address probabilities and make clear to consumers of such reports their limitations and speculative nature.

I regarded the House report to be an insightful perspective of the four areas that were discussed in the Findings and Conclusions section. Particularly important in my view was the perspective that "the technical aspects of the investigation [by the Navy team] were handled admirably—up to a point," and that "the technical team set about to test every known potential cause." While the Navy's tests eliminated one theory after another for the explosion, there was essentially no search for previously unknown and accidental causes of the explosion. The failure to find a reasonable accidental basis for the explosion did not logically lead to the conclusion that there was no accidental cause.

11 GMG1 Dale E. Mortensen

15–16 March 1990

WE HAD received several voluminous packages of materials from the Navy related to their investigation. These materials began to arrive in the fall of 1989 and continued through March 1990. Included among them were transcripts of interviews that Admiral Milligan's team had with several officers and crewmen of the USS *Iowa* in the days immediately following the explosion. These descriptions, fresh in the minds of these men, were arresting. One was compelled to read and reread them, not just for their technical content or additional insights but also because of their gripping nature.

Mark Davis and I combed through these interviews trying to better understand the sequence of events, searching for avenues we should pursue in our investigation. The entire team was continually searching for unexpected causes of the explosion, sifting through a mountain of material that might suggest new areas of exploration. These interviews were yet another source of ideas, and we were deeply impressed with the extensive knowledge and courage of these men, with their understanding and the stark directness of their statements.

The testimony of GMG1 Dale E. Mortensen was particularly informative. It was apparent that he had extensive knowledge and experience with 16-inch-gun systems. He had been aboard the *Iowa* more than five years and was qualified in all eighteen positions in the 16-inch turrets. In addition, he had much earlier become concerned that training of the gun crews was inadequate and personally initiated an effort to improve the training program. He had helped write the new 16-inch PQS.

Mortensen had also been involved in critical efforts to minimize further damage to the ship in the hours following the explosion. He took a lead role in removing the propellant from both the two loaded but unfired guns in Turret II and the gun in Turret I that had misfired. Unloading the left and right guns in Turret II after the explosion was particularly important and especially hazardous. It is difficult to imagine the scene that he and the others must have faced in taking on this crucial task. All the men in the turret had been killed, in some cases with severe trauma. There was carnage and extensive damage throughout the turret complicating the working conditions.

GMG1 Dale Mortensen and GMG2 John R. Keerl worked out the details of opening the breeches of the two guns in Turret II. Mortensen, Keerl, GMGC John C. Cable, and GMGC J. C. Miller entered the turret to carry out the hazardous task of opening and unloading these two guns. Power and lights had to be rigged; then because the breeches of the two guns could not be operated with hydraulic power, a winch had to be attached to the top of the turret to lower the breech block of each gun. With the breech open, the five bags of propellant in each gun could then be removed. With the winch in position and ready to lower the breech, Mortensen and the other courageous sailors used a hose to play a steady stream of water on the breech area and then slowly unsealed the massive breech block. The intent was to quench any residual spark or ember that might ignite the propellant bags as they were first exposed to air and precipitate a repeat of the terrible explosion that morning. Mortensen said in his testimony, "I mean it was scary. It was a god damn scary thing."

Sure that there were no residual embers, the breech was fully lowered and the soaked propellant bags were removed and thrown overboard. The procedure was repeated in the other gun of Turret II. Mortensen and the others succeeded in returning the ship to a normal level of safety after many uninterrupted hours of work.

Mark Davis and I believed it would be invaluable to speak directly with Mortensen. I asked Captain Miceli if he could arrange for him to visit Sandia. The captain's initial response was that he doubted that this could be arranged, but he'd check with his superiors. It turned out that the meeting could take place and arrangements were made for Mortensen to be with us on 15 and 16 March.

Captain Miceli insisted on being present throughout the discussion, and while I would have preferred to talk with Mortensen without the inhibition of the captain's presence, I felt it was important to go ahead. I wondered how the insistence of brass being present at such gatherings, no matter how minor, affected the petty officers. It couldn't have reflected either confidence or trust in these fine men.

I met Captain Miceli and Dale Mortensen at visitor control early on the morning of 15 March. Mortensen was very quiet as we completed the badging process, and I was concerned that he might be hesitant to speak openly to us. I wondered what the captain might have said to him about this meeting, how he may have characterized us, and if there were areas Mortensen was asked to not discuss. As we walked to my office, I talked about Sandia and tried to relieve undue hesitancy on Mortensen's part to be forthcoming, trying to convey to him that we were not the enemy, but people trying to understand what had happened.

Paul Cooper, Mark Davis, and Karl Schuler were waiting in my office. I had worried about the intimidation factor of having too many people present and had shared my concern with the three of them. They were sensitive to the issue, and we agreed to keep the meeting as nonthreatening as possible. Once together, I explained the three general thrusts of our investigation to Mortensen. First, we were reexamining the foreign materials and associated work by the Navy as it related to the possible presence of an ignition device. Second, we were examining the sensitivity of the propellant and black powder as a potential cause of the explosion. Third, we were assessing the general methodology used by the Navy in their investigation. I said it was our perception that his knowledge and experience could help us in further focusing our efforts. My comments evolved into a discussion, and Mortensen seemed comfortable with the open interchange and the obvious respect that we had for him.

Mortensen was very knowledgeable, as we had surmised from his interview, and he remembered many things that enlarged our view of what had happened. On the morning of 19 April he was in the booth of Turret I, serving as turret officer so that Ens. Effren S. Garrett IV could observe the process and learn the ropes. It was Ensign Garrett's first shoot. Normally Lt. Dan Meyer would have been turret officer, but he was on the bridge that morning. Davis and I had talked with Meyer on our first visit to the *Iowa*.

Mortensen said that the morning was routine as they began the gunnery exercise. The order came to load the guns in Turret I and, shortly thereafter, fire them. There was a misfire in the left gun. That is, ignition of the primer failed to ignite the powder bags. There was a misfire procedure that required a wait of several minutes, then the spent primer was replaced in the breech and a new attempt made to fire the gun. This too failed.

Mortensen continued, "I saw light indicators in Turret I that showed that Turret II was being readied for firing. This concerned me because I felt the situation in Turret I should be cleared up first. Going on to the firing of Turret II with a misfire in Turret I was not a part of the firing plan for the day. I certainly didn't want anyone to forget that we had a loaded and unfired gun in Turret I."

As the acting turret officer, Mortensen was wearing sound-powered headphones. These phones were connected to the X102 circuit, so he could hear the words of the three gun captains and/or cradle operators in Turret I. The phones also had a connection to the JD circuit, which was linked to Lt. Phillip E. Buch, the turret officer in Turret II, and to Main Plot. Through this JD circuit link, Mortensen was able to hear some of the conversation in the booth of Turret II prior to the explosion.

Mortensen heard the reference to "a problem" in the center gun in Turret II over the JD circuit. About fifteen seconds later there was a second comment about a problem in the loading of the center gun of Turret II. Just moments after this, Mortensen heard GMG1 Ernie Hanyecz call his name, "Mort, Mort," in a louder than normal voice—and then the explosion took place. Hanyecz was not wearing phones, but Mortensen heard him call his name in the background over Lieutenant Buch's phones.

Mortensen spoke of these events with obvious feeling. He'd lost many close friends in that instant of time. It was difficult for him to continue and we all sat silently for several moments before asking him why he thought Hanyecz may have called his name. He said the only thing he could think of was that Hanyecz was taking note that there was still a misfire in progress in Turret I, that Hanyecz was also concerned about the resolution of that situation before proceeded with firing from Turret II. Could he have been confused about what Hanyecz was saying? Mortensen was positive. "No," he declared, "Ernie was calling my name just before the explosion."

We asked him about the typical things that might have been the problem that had interrupted the crew in the center gun room. "A typical problem was closing the powder door," he said. "Sometimes it hangs up, or the rammerman becomes confused because of the strange way the door control operates. This wasn't an unusual problem."

We mentioned testimony that indicated that the powder hoist was not operating properly—could that have had an effect on the operation of the powder door? Mortensen cleared up this issue. "No, it wasn't a powder hoist in Turret II that was not operating properly, but a powder hoist in Turret III.

I'd seen this same thing in the testimony of other crewmen, but I'm positive it was a Turret III hoist that was malfunctioning, not one in Turret II."

We asked about the gas ejection air that flushes the gun barrel when the breech is opened. Could the air valve have been closed in the equipment room and, when the crew discovered this during the loading, one of the crew had to go down and open it? Mortensen nodded. "I'd wondered about that same question shortly after the explosion and went to the gun room to see if the valve was in the open position. It was open, but that didn't mean it was open when the gun crew began its loading process. If the valve was not opened, that would have caused a delay. But, of course, there was no way to tell whether the valve had been open or not when the loading process began."

Could the crew have been confused by the powder car only containing five bags instead of the usual six? "No," he replied, "that seems unlikely to me. I would have thought the gun crew would have just queried the powder flats or the booth, and not just said they had a problem." He briefly paused. "Going back to the powder door, one thing that seemed strange to me was that the powder car was in the up position. It should have been lowered. Since the powder door was closed and dogged, the upper powder hoist operator should have lowered the powder car right away."

Mortensen had anticipated one of our questions. It was the general procedure aboard *Iowa* to lower the powder car as soon as the powder door was closed. If, as the Navy investigators asserted, a sustained overram was held for thirty seconds or so (to initiate the ignition device in their view), the upper hoist operator would have had more than enough time to send the powder car down to the powder flats. But the powder hoist was in the upper position—a clear inconsistency with the Navy routine. On the other hand, Fisk, the upper powder hoist operator, was also performing his job for the first time and may simply have failed to carry out this part of his job. Lowering of the powder car was, however, one of the simplest tasks of the upper powder hoist operator.

It became apparent during the conversation with Dale Mortensen that many ominous things could have, but fortunately did not, happen following the initial explosions. The most obvious possibility was spread of the fire into the magazines. If this had occurred, the survival of the ship and crew would have been in serious jeopardy. The crew's quick and effective response in dealing with the turret fire and flooding various areas saved the ship and many lives. Another possibility was that the high temperatures associated with the fire could have set off the primers in the left and right guns and triggered the guns, possibly injuring men in the fire-fighting teams both inside and outside the turret. A perhaps even more probable event might have been the later ignition of the propellant bags by "cooking off," the fire raising the temperature of the propellant bags in the breeches of the two guns to such point that they ignited. Since the turret fire had emptied the guns of hydraulic fluid in the recoil mechanisms, the guns would have been recoiled to the stops and produced considerable further damage.

The triggering of the huge guns in this uncontrolled manner could also have had deleterious effects down range. The ship turned about 65 degrees to starboard after the explosion (to a heading of approximately 225 degrees true) to help carry smoke off the deck and facilitate fire fighting. The guns were then pointing approximately 300 degrees, and it is not clear that this zone was assured to be clear in advance of this maneuvering of the ship. Fortunately, none of these possibilities came to pass, largely because of the prompt action of the crew with knowledgeable leaders like Dale Mortensen. The crew, acting on their own, had interrupted the cascade of unfortunate events that frequently characterizes major incidents and confined the terrible loss to Turret II.

The discussion went on at length, and Mortensen was the knowledgeable expert we thought he would be. It was refreshing to get responsive answers to direct questions, to sense the authenticity of what he had to say, the significance of talking with someone who was directly involved in the incident.

12 The Sandia Investigation

March and April 1990

THE SANDIA investigation made impressive strides in the new year and several important studies were underway by the beginning of March. The weekly team meetings brought together a core group that would share all aspects of every investigative effort, a group that would remain essentially constant through the rest of Sandia's involvement in the investigation.

Three groups of outstanding individuals, recruited with the full support of management and coming from a variety of organizations at Sandia, were established at the outset.[1] One of these groups focused on materials analysis and addressed all questions related to the "foreign materials" the Navy found on the projectile. The Navy had not addressed the possible presence of these same materials elsewhere on these and other projectiles, guns, or turrets. Jim Borders, a supervisor in the materials area, was the leader of a group, which included Jerry Nelson, Dave Tallant, Bill Chambers, Bess Campbell-Domme, Paul Hlava, and Suzanne Weissman. In addition, Sam Myers and Bill Wampler carried out special ion-beam profiling analysis of various critical surfaces early in the materials studies.

Overram of the propellant by the rammer was the focus of the second key group. Recall that the extent of the overram as determined by the Navy was such that the propellant bags were pushed too far into the breech, but not far enough to push the forward-most bag against the projectile. This was fundamentally inconsistent with the Navy's scenario, since the hypothetical ignitor would not have been initiated under these circumstances. The Sandia thrust in this area was to reexamine the extent of the overram and, more generally, to model rammer operation and the overram. This would include an examination of the static and dynamic effects on the bag charges and, later on, the detailed effects of overramming on individual propellant pellets. Karl Schuler was the key lead in this area. Others working in related areas included Ken Gwinn and Kathleen Diegert.

The third group's focus was on propellants and explosives; it performed analyses of the black powder and stability of the bag charges. The possibility of propellant ignition in the overram process became of particular interest, and Paul Cooper was the primary investigator of this possibility. In addition, Mel Baer carried out interior ballistics computer modeling of the open-breech explosion to determine the site of the ignition along the propellant train. Other key people working in the propellant and explosive area included Dennis Mitchell and Steve Harris.

Rounding out the team were Mark Davis, a materials expert I had asked to examine a variety of special issues; Marv Morris, who performed special studies related to the possible ignition of the propellant by high levels of RF radiation from a new radar on the ship; and John Holovka, who provided administrative support for the team. Jim Mitchell served as our public relations contact for the many external queries about the Sandia investigation. Judy Jewell and Eva Wilcox were my able secretaries, and Susan Compton and Linda Vigil Lopez served as my administrative assistants. Carmen Drebing was the coordinator for our two technical reports.

These studies were yielding important results, but more progress was needed before we could begin to formulate valid conclusions. I was preoccupied with thoughts of presenting an understandable summary of the Sandia studies before the Senate Armed Services Committee sometime within the next few months. Following are some of the principal findings during these few months prior to the Senate hearing.

Materials Analysis

Jim Borders and the materials people detected calcium and chlorine on all the swipe samples that Mark Davis and I had taken in Turret I of the *Iowa* during our visit before Christmas. The distribution of these elements throughout the turret was indicative of the exposure of the ship to a maritime environment, and it now appeared that there was little if any basis for the Navy's association of these elements with the presence of a chemical ignitor.

Four iron fibers were found on the section of projectile's rotating band that had first been examined by the FBI. The Navy had asserted that these fibers were again indicative of the presence of a chemical ignition device. Our analyses showed that the composition of these fibers was that of low-carbon steel, typical of steel wool. We corroborated the surface concentrations of chlorine on these iron fibers by the Navy, but there were substantially higher chlorine concentrations on fibers from a full-scale experiment in which a chemical ignitor was used to initiate an explosion in a 16-inch gun. This raised further questions about the Navy's hypothesis. Jerry Nelson, one of our top surface analysts, spent several days at Crane to have a firsthand look at the "encrusted fibers" cited by the Navy in their technical report as a "fingerprint" of a chemical ignitor.

Nelson found that the high calcium encrustation reported by the Navy was observed on only a single fiber. His telephone call was memorable: "The encrustation was found on only one fiber—and that fiber couldn't be located, even after a two-day search of all their fiber samples." Nelson's work had revealed a serious flaw in this part of the Navy's "foreign materials" investigation. The encrusted fiber was not representative of the fibers the Navy had found on the projectile. Their claim that encrusted fibers were indicative of the presence of a chemical ignitor was based on a single specimen that now could not be found.

In yet another materials study, preliminary information on Break-Free, a complex liquid used to clean and lubricate 16-inch guns, was now coming forward. Break-Free was found to contain glycol, another key constituent of the chemical ignitor proposed by the Navy. In other words, the presence of glycol on the projectile should have been expected since Break-Free was liberally used to free the projectile from the gun after the explosion.

These several results suggested that the materials analytical work by the Navy was seriously flawed, something that was not evident from simply reading the Navy's technical report.

Overram

The Navy's analysis of the overram relied on observations of fire-damaged sections of the rammer, on identifying sections that were partially protected from the fire by bulkheads around the rammer. This qualitative approach indicated that the forward most propellant bag was pushed beyond its normal position but not against the projectile when fire damage occurred to the rammer. As noted before, this was inconsistent with the Navy's scenario in which the gun captain presumably had ordered a sustained overram to activate the chemical ignition device.

Karl Schuler developed an insightful approach to determining the extent of the overram by examining gouges on the spanning tray caused when the explosion blew the heavy rammer chain back into the gun room (fig. 12-1). Schuler correlated the position of those gouges with specific links in the rammer chain. From this exacting analysis he concluded that the rammer was approximately 4 inches further into the breech at the time of the explosion than the Navy had said. That is, the five propellant bags were actually compressed by slightly more than an inch against the rear of the projectile at the time of the explosion (fig. 12-2).

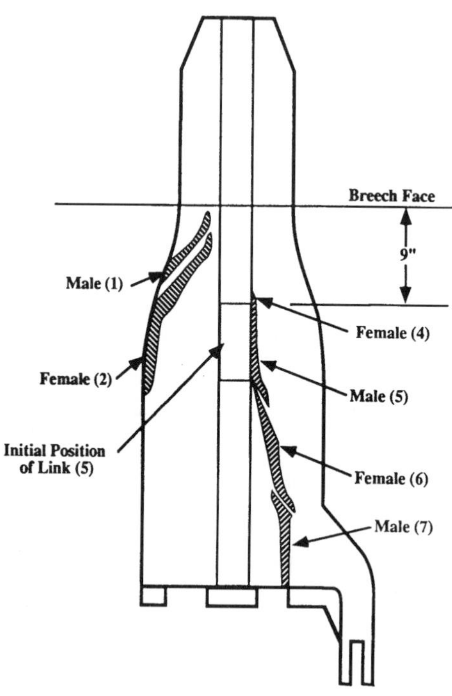

Figure 12-1. The explosion in the open breech of the center gun occurred when the rammer was extended to such an extent that it forced the propellant against the projectile. The blast blew the rammer head and segmented rammer chain backward across the spanning tray and into the gun room. The heavy steel links of the rammer chain gouged the aluminum spanning tray as illustrated in this figure. Sandia's Karl Schuler was able to associate the two different kinds of links (male and female) and their relative location in the rammer chain with the gouge marks to determine the rammer position at the time of the explosion. This analysis showed that the rammer was compressing the propellant against the projectile at the time of the explosion. This key observation stimulated a reexamination of the release of burning particles from fractured propellant pellets.

The Navy eagerly accepted Schuler's analysis because it resolved the (unacknowledged) inconsistency in their scenario, an inconsistency they had not mentioned in their various testimonies. Captain Miceli was particularly pleased and called when he heard of Schuler's analysis. "This is very significant information," he said. "It's the single thing that leads directly to the gun captain. You know, it's impossible to inadvertently overram if you have any experience at all with rammer operation. I assume your group will conclude this, too."

His qualification was an important one: "If you have any experience at all with rammer operation." The rammerman in the center gun room on the morning of the explosion was serving in this position for his first live firing.

Schuler's conclusion that the propellant was actually compressed against the projectile raised the possibility that some of the propellant pellets may have been fractured in the process. This was of immense importance to the experiments Paul Cooper was conducting.

Propellant Ignition

Late in March and early in April, Paul Cooper conducted intriguing experiments dealing with effects related to the fracture of propellant pellets. He presented the fascinating results at the team meeting on 6 April. Cooper had found that fractured propellant pellets emitted burning fragments, fragments that burned through his overalls when single pellets were crushed by metal weights. He then set up an experiment that replicated the configuration of pellets at the rear of the propellant bag and examined the effects of overramming these pellets (fig. 12-3). When the pellets fractured in his drop fixture as a result of the simulated overram, burning fragments were emitted just as before (fig. 12-4). While the burning fragments did not ignite adjacent propellant material, they would sometimes burn through the simulated bag material and ignite the adjacent black powder pouch. Ignition of the rapidly burning black powder then assured that the entire powder train would be ignited.

Cooper's video tapes of his experiments left little to the imagination as to what might have happened in the *Iowa* incident. An overram resulting in propellant pellet fracture could ignite a nearby black power pouch, and if this occurred, the entire series of propellant bags would be ignited in an explosion.

Cooper had discovered a form of propellant ignition that was previously unknown. He and his assistants pursued these reduced-scale experiments at a frantic pace through April and into May. Their investigation centered on pel-

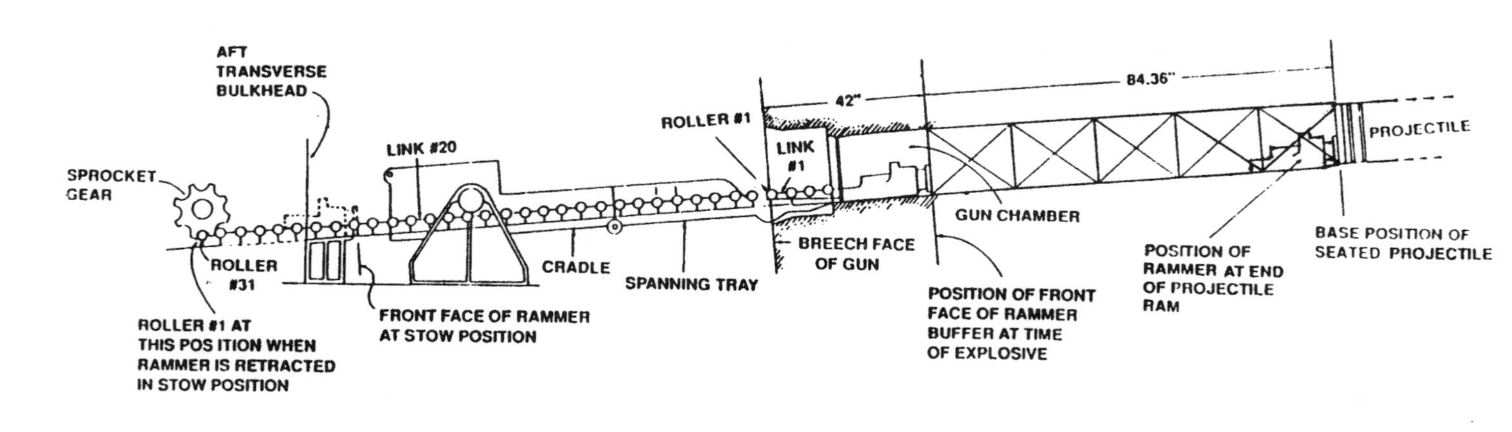
AFT TRANSVERSE BULKHEAD
SPROCKET GEAR
LINK #20
ROLLER #31
ROLLER #1 AT THIS POSITION WHEN RAMMER IS RETRACTED IN STOW POSITION
FRONT FACE OF RAMMER AT STOW POSITION
CRADLE
SPANNING TRAY
ROLLER #1
LINK #1
42"
84.36"
BREECH FACE OF GUN
GUN CHAMBER
POSITION OF FRONT FACE OF RAMMER BUFFER AT TIME OF EXPLOSIVE
POSITION OF RAMMER AT END OF PROJECTILE RAM
BASE POSITION OF SEATED PROJECTILE
PROJECTILE

Figure 12-2. The overram at the time of ignition is illustrated in this drawing. Normally the front face of the rammer head is extended just beyond the end of the cradle and would have left a gap between the forward-most bag and the projectile. In the center gun overram the rammer head was extended so far into the gun, approximately 42 inches beyond the breech face, that the five propellant bags were compressed against the projectile. The projectile base position is established by (high-speed) ramming of the projectile and the rotating band engaging the rifling of the barrel.

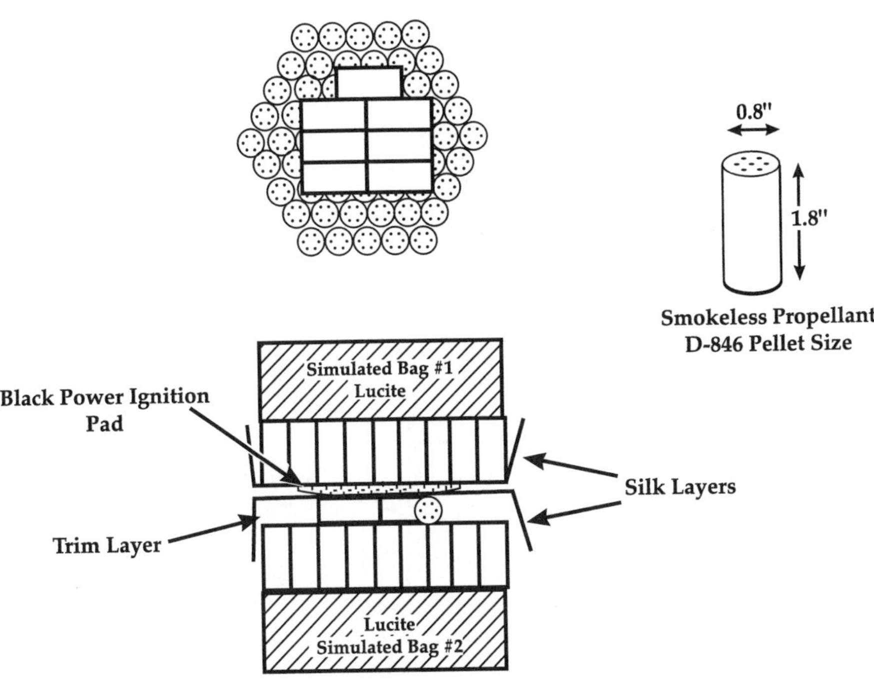

Figure 12-3. Sandia's Paul Cooper simulated the configuration of both longitudinal and transverse pellets in the trim layer in subscale tests. The 8-inch array simulated a single layer of pellets in each of two adjacent propellant bags and the intervening trim layer. The transverse pellets in the trim layer are more easily fractured by compressive forces in an overram and give off burning particles from the fractured surfaces. This array was used in drop tests to demonstrate that fractured pellets in the trim layer of one bag can ignite the black powder ignition pad of the adjacent bag and result in an explosion. The drop fixture is shown in figure 12-4.

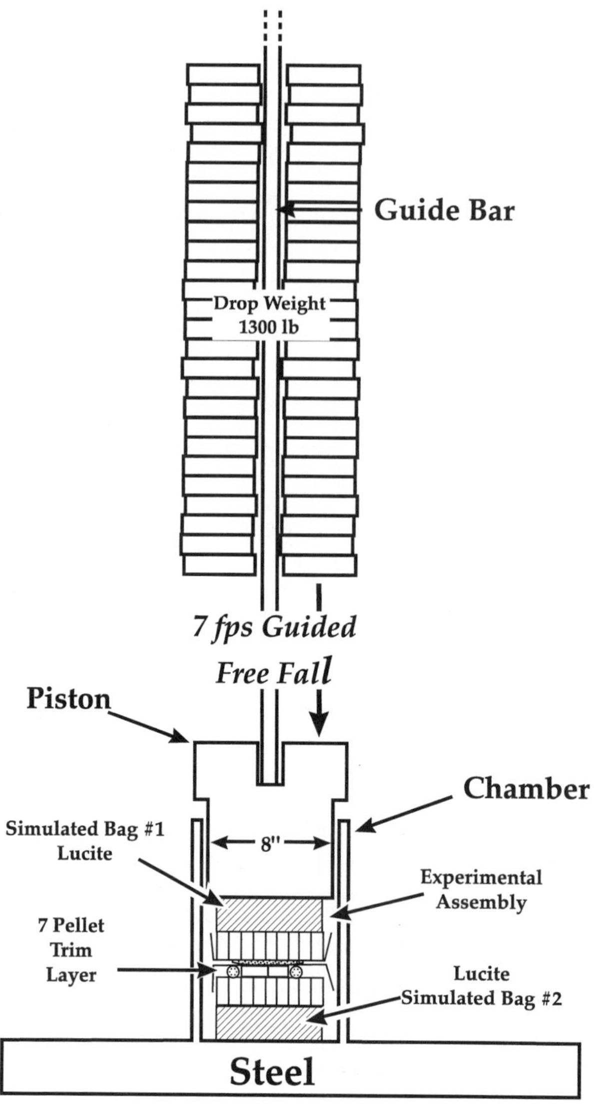

Figure 12-4. The array of propellant pellets of two adjacent bags (described in figure 12-3) was placed in this drop fixture to simulate a high-speed overram in a 16-inch gun. Fracture of trim-layer pellets by the dropping weight caused ignition of the black powder and small explosions in these experiments. These subscale experiments first demonstrated that an overram could cause an explosion and revealed an important but unrecognized safety problem in 16-inch gun systems. Videos of these experiments were shown to the Senate Armed Services Committee during the hearing on 25 May 1990.

lets located in what we called the trim layer, a partial layer of pellets at the forward end of the propellant bag that brings the bag up to the correct weight. A key question was whether these reduced scale experiments accurately simulated conditions in a 16-inch gun.

Interior Ballistics

Mel Baer was deeply involved in a study of the interior ballistics of the explosion in the center gun. This was a computer modeling effort in which the open breech of the 16-inch gun containing the bags of propellant was modeled to determine, among other things, how the point of ignition influenced the nature of the propellant burn.

Baer found that if the ignition point was toward the open-breech end of the propellant train, the propellant bags burned in an intense flarelike mode. If the ignition point was further forward in the breech, the increased pressure in the closed end accelerated the burning rate to such an extent that a rapid deflagration or explosion occurred. He concluded that the ignition point must have been in the vicinity of the first (most forward) or second bag of propellant, essentially what the Navy team had surmised. Baer also concluded that the projectile would move about 30 inches forward in this open-breech explosion in excellent agreement with actual motion of the projectile.

Propellant Stabilizer

Steve Harris reported that studies were in progress to assess the stabilizer level in the propellant at the Pantex plant in Amarillo, Texas. Pantex is a part of the nuclear weapons complex, and we had worked extensively with their explosives experts for many years. They had ideal facilities for the measurement of propellant stability levels. Harris noted that there were several subtleties in the measurements and their interpretation. Decomposition products of the DPA stabilizer were also effective stabilizers and had to be included in the assessment of propellant stability. Harris reported that a few pellets provided to us by the Navy had no detectable level of DPA, but the vast majority had DPA levels within the acceptable range. Further studies were progressing well.

Washington Visitors

The team meeting on 30 March included two distinguished visitors, Richard D. DeBobes, a top staffer and counsel with the Senate Armed Services Committee, and Marty Ferber, the GAO's director for Navy Issues.

I was glad to meet Rick DeBobes and thank him personally for resolving in a single day a funding problem that had threatened to stop our investigation. He was a graying, bespectacled man of medium height and rather quiet in nature. He was intensely interested in what we had learned and wanted to hear all the details. DeBobes was an attorney by training and had retired from the Navy as a captain. He had been commanding officer of the Naval Legal Service Office in Norfolk, and also served as legal adviser and legislative assistant to the chairman of the Joint Chiefs of Staff for the Department of Defense. He had some special thoughts for us: "Your open exchange of information with the Navy has been excellent and I applaud you for this, but as we near the hearing I'm concerned about telegraphing conclusions from your important work to the Navy. It's apparent to me that your conclusions will be substantially different from the Navy's and I don't want to make them known to the Navy before the hearing. I want you to limit communications with the Navy from here on to the extent that they are necessary."

As I thought about DeBobes's remarks, it seemed to me that we could not in good conscience wholly abide by his request. We had allowed Captain Miceli and his people essentially complete access to our work, and this policy had been advantageous to us. It had probably helped engender more Navy cooperation. If we took another tack now, it could jeopardize the current situation and possibly compromise our work. We were dependent on the Navy for information, information that we often didn't know we needed until our investigation led us into new areas.

I believed that we must continue to exchange technical information, but agreed with DeBobes that we needed to avoid discussions relevant to conclusions that might be presented at the Senate Armed Services hearing. Keeping the Navy informed of technical details would not seriously jeopardize the case that seemed to be developing. Jerry Herley of the GAO appreciated this perspective and agreed with the guidelines I developed for the Sandia investigators in interactions with the Navy.

Early April 1990: Discussion with Admiral J. M. Barr, DASMA

Admiral "Mike" Barr, deputy assistant secretary of energy for military applications and a key DOE contact for Sandia, was in Albuquerque and requested an update on Sandia's *Iowa* investigation. I walked to the DOE facilities near Sandia, and the two of us sat alone in an empty conference room talking about the early results of our investigation, beyond the technical details, discussing other issues of the involvement in this complex investigation.

I told Barr of the vulnerabilities of the Navy's assertions regarding "foreign materials," that some of the materials were not foreign but normal to the turret environment. I reviewed the overram studies and the new observation that overramming could lead to an explosion. He listened thoughtfully to these and other aspects of our work. "It sounds like the Navy investigative team may have been hasty in reaching its conclusions," he said, "and that's too bad for them and everyone else. I urge you to continue to do as much as you can to understand what happened aboard the *Iowa*, to pursue all avenues to bring forward as much evidence as possible relevant to the cause of the explosion. But I also urge you to conclude your investigation as quickly as possible. My experience is that there will be those in the Navy and elsewhere who, for various reasons, will want to prolong the investigation. The longer you are involved, the greater will be the tendency for Sandia to become immersed in other aspects of the investigation, aspects in which you perhaps have less expertise or where more qualitative judgments will be involved. Any involvement in these qualitative issues may compromise your technical work and judgments, which are your strength. Start thinking about a logical stopping point for your investigation, and how you can reach that point in the shortest possible time."

I often thought about Admiral Barr's perspective, such as when we were urged to examine the coroner's evidence that the Navy believed to be strongly supportive of their scenario. I consistently maintained the obvious—we had no relevant expertise and could not make valid judgments about such evidence. Fortunately we did not go down this path, at least in part because of Admiral Barr's thoughtful caution.

The conversation with Admiral Barr helped me to better understand that the Navy was comprised of many organizations with different responsibilities and, therefore, different perspectives. Just as I had experienced at Sandia, people of good judgment could come to distinctly different and conflicting conclusions.

23 April 1990: A Call from Captain Miceli

Captain Miceli called to talk about his concerns, concerns that may have not found a ready audience in his office. He recalled the memorial service for the *Iowa* crewmen and how he had been moved by the talk given by the ship's captain. He said that he was deeply concerned about the feeling of many survivors that the Navy was not being forthright: "The survivors have joined together, questioning what we tell them, and even have a newsletter to share information with one another. I find this incredible after the tremendous effort the Navy team has made to find the cause of the explosion."

I said that the Navy team had made a very important effort to find the cause, but added that I believed the survivors sensed the implausibility and unfairness of the Navy's conclusions and allegations, particularly since convincing proof was missing. "Joe," I continued, "I would be hard pressed to take the Navy's position, particularly without convincing evidence to support the two main conclusions. It's difficult for me to understand how the top Navy brass assembled the information available to them and decided to assert that it was a deliberate act, and that a particular individual was responsible." Captain Miceli didn't like this—he felt the Navy had proven the case. I didn't go on to cite the obvious weaknesses in the "proof." This was a topic on which the captain and I would never share a common view.

I went on to another subject, one that I wanted him to be aware of since he was our primary point of contact with the Navy. Sandia had no direct contact with the chief of Naval Operations or other key Navy people. "The SASC people want us to be less forthcoming with the Navy in what we're doing in our investigation," I told him. "Their concern is that our conclusions will be discussed at the team meetings, and the SASC people understandably want to see those conclusions in advance of the Navy."

"I'm opposed to any gag rule, Dick," Miceli replied. "We've been open with Sandia and so have you with the Navy. I'd like to keep it that way."

In spite of our substantial differences, I agreed with him. "I've discussed this with two of our VPs. We've gained a great deal by discussing the details of our investigation to the Navy. I suggested that we continue the exchanges of technical information, but that we stop at any point where we might be discussing Sandia positions that would be included in our report. Both of the VPs agreed with this suggestion. You are welcome to continue direct contacts with our team members so that you're fully aware of what we're doing on a technical level."

The captain appreciated this position.

I went on to mention that Jerry Nelson of our materials group had spent considerable time at Crane looking at iron fibers, and that Dave File and his people at Crane were unable to locate the encrusted fiber featured in the Navy's technical report. I said we were surprised to learn that there was only a single encrusted fiber.

The captain was obviously upset. "I'll have to talk with Dave File about this." It appeared from his response that he was also unaware of the uniqueness of that fiber. He went on to inquire about our measurements of stabilizer levels. I told him that the early measurements were just beginning to be reported and gave him some of the details. Some levels in individual pellets were very low, but others indicated satisfactory concentrations. Perhaps of even more importance, our early results did not show a strong relationship between stabilizer level and sensitivity. He thanked me for the update and the conversation ended.

26–27 April 1990: Captain Miceli's Visit

I briefly met with Captain Miceli on Thursday, 26 April. He was at Sandia to talk with various team members and there was a team meeting scheduled for the next morning that he wanted to attend. We agreed to meet at visitor control early the next morning before the team gathered.

I met the captain about 7:30 the following morning. He was buoyant and full of energy—quite a change from what I had sensed during our phone conversation just a few days earlier. After walking about two blocks, I noticed he was having trouble breathing, and he asked that we stop for a few minutes. I was concerned. He was struggling, and his distress came on very quickly. I thought again of the stress of this program on all the people involved. While recovering in my office, he told me of his preretirement physicals. His retirement had been postponed because of the *Iowa* investigation, and it was now important to document any condition for his upcoming retirement.

Our conversation touched on several subjects relevant to the investigation. The captain asked again about the stabilizer study, a subject that preoccupied him. His concern was that Sandia would find a problem that would counter the Navy's results and shut down the battleship's 16-inch guns. He had authorized the restart of 16-inch gun firings after a temporary shutdown following the *Iowa* explosion and wanted to avoid any reversal of that decision.

I told him our propellant work was still in progress, but there were no obvious problems that had been found. He was disturbed that some pellets had been found with a "zero" level of stabilizer, but I told him that we were still sorting out the analysis of not only DPA but also decomposition daughter products, and this was an important consideration. The daughter products had stabilizing properties of their own, but it was not altogether straightforward to both determine what the effective products were and then analyze their concentration. I told him that current indications were that stabilizer levels were not a problem.

Captain Miceli stood and went to the board, picking up some chalk. He wanted to rebut my comments on the phone a few days earlier about the implausibility and lack of hard evidence supporting the Navy's scenario. He sketched the gun room, where each occupant stood, and where each gunner's mate was located in the booth just behind the gun room. It was very clear in his mind. He could picture all the actions. Hartwig giving the sign for a continued ram, waiting for the explosion. Fisk, the upper powder hoist operator, looking through the window into the gun room, wondering what was going on, not lowering the powder car as he should have been doing. The part about Fisk was new to the story—the captain knew we were perplexed about why the powder car had not been lowered.

He then drew a horizontal line, a time line, and wrote "load" at the left-hand end. This was his zero. About midway across he wrote "forty-four seconds," and underneath, "left gun loaded." He intoned Ziegler's comment heard over the sound-powered phone: "Good job left gun." At sixty-one seconds he wrote, "right gun loaded" and intoned Lawrence's comment heard over the phones, "We're not ready yet, we're having a problem." Then at eighty-one to eighty-three seconds he wrote "explodes." It all fit together in his mind. Each time he told this story it had a few more details.

I had little doubt that Captain Miceli believed this was exactly what had happened. I raised the question about whether the ram speed may have been fast or slow, thinking about Cooper's recent experiments on impact initiation. The captain remarked, "I'm convinced that it was a slow ram. According to the forensic information, Hartwig was leaning over the rammer looking into the breech. I don't believe people lean over that kind of machinery. Technically, of course, we can't say whether the ram was fast or slow."

It was time for the team meeting. We shook hands and I reminded him not to ask any of our people for their conclusions. He laughed and left to talk with other members of the Sandia team.

Drafting Our Interim Report

Marty Noland from the tech writing group went through the details of our interim report preparation. It was going to be a big job to bring this together in a month. We established a deadline of mid-May for the final draft, and two team meetings a week to make sure we were all familiar with the latest information.

John Holovka had talked with Captain Miceli a day or so earlier. "Miceli wants our report to follow his time lines and include forensic information."

Schuler said he got the same word from Miceli, that Joe kept coming back to the forensic information that Hartwig was leaning over the rammer, that it was a slow ram held for twenty to fifty seconds, and so on. I said this was Sandia's report and we would assemble it in the way that seemed appropriate from our perspective. "We're reporting to SASC and GAO, not to the Navy. While the Navy might think we're supposed to report to them, that's not the case. I put little stock in the forensic information that we've been exposed to. It seems to me that the forensic work has been overinterpreted, just like some other things."

I had assembled a five-page outline of our final report that consisted of summary statements of our conclusions—how all our work fit together, where our studies differed from those of the Navy, and the implications of those differences. I outlined how our results suggested another perspective on the explosion and its possible cause. I wanted to get the team's reactions to this draft summary and their thoughts on the strong and weak parts of this view.

Assignments were made for various parts of the report. The tempo of our work was picking up, and preparation of drafts was an added task. It was necessary for us to begin writing just as we were gathering momentum and reaping important results in the investigation, and team members were working right to their limits.

13 Impact Ignition

May 1990

MEMBERS OF the Navy team—including Captain Miceli, Frank Tse, and Steve Mitchell from Indian Head and Rob Lieb from the Ballistics Research Laboratory—attended our regular team meeting the week of 7 May. The meeting was devoted to a discussion of Paul Cooper's work regarding impact initiation through the fracture of propellant pellets. It was important to keep the Navy aware of new developments, and since there were no Navy personnel in residence at Sandia, I had invited the captain to attend along with his experts for the presentation.[1]

Cooper described his work on impact ignition using a fixture that simulated a section of the powder bag, one that used a reduced number of propellant pellets, but pellets from actual bags that we had received from the Navy. He had brought the fixtures to the meeting, showing how they contained a smaller number of pellets, but in the same configuration as in an actual bag of propellant. Similarly, he had duplicated the separation of pellets from the black powder pouch with layers of cloth taken from the propellant bags we had received from the Navy. Fixtures of various sizes were used, and the number of transverse trim-layer pellets were adjusted accordingly. (The trim layer is a layer of transverse pellets added to bring the weight of the propellant to the proper level.) The concept retained all the basic features of an actual bag of propellant, except that it was of a such a size that laboratory experiments could be conducted at remote explosive sites operated by Sandia.

Cooper had found that dropping weights on the fixtures to simulate overramming and compression of the propellant bags against the projectile could result in fracture of the trim-layer pellets, and subsequent ignition of the black powder. This resulted in small explosions in experiments at an outdoor explosive site that Cooper had captured on video tape. He had related the probability of such ignitions to the size of the fixture, the number of trim-layer pellets, and other factors.

Extrapolation of Cooper's results to full-scale 16-inch gun conditions suggested that impact ignition was an important discovery, a potentially serious safety problem with 16-inch systems and a possible means by which the explosion aboard *Iowa* may have occurred.

Captain Miceli listened to the discussion with obvious skepticism. Finally, he commented, "This is interesting work, but of course it has no relation to actual 16-inch gun conditions."

I was stunned by his response, that he was minimizing a potentially serious safety problem that endangered gun crews on battleships. Cooper's results required a substantial extrapolation to make the connection to 16-inch-gun conditions, but the principle of the findings was there for any objective observer. The clear implication was that an overram of the propellant bags could lead to an explosion under certain conditions. The question was, Could these conditions be attained in 16-inch guns aboard the battleships? I responded to Captain Miceli's remark: "These are important results and can't be given short shrift or dismissed out of hand. Work on full scale in a 16-inch gun is needed, but this work is an indicator of a safety problem that clearly needs to be pursued."

The captain was unmoved and shook his head in a way that casually dismissed these critical findings. I was dismayed when one of his technical experts voiced agreement with him. I realized again that expertise and judgment are unrelated.

Cooper smiled weakly from the front of the room where he had just described his results, as if his work wasn't all that significant. For one of the few times during the investigation, I was angry. Not only was their attitude arrogant, but they were dismissing work for reasons more connected to face than to fact. More important, they were ignoring the well-being of gun crews on the battleships that had resumed firing of 16-inch guns following the *Iowa* incident. The meeting concluded on this incredible note. I had expected that the Navy would immediately pick up on this crucial finding. I couldn't have been more wrong.

Captain Miceli left for Washington the following day, and as I drove him to the airport, I again suggested full-scale experiments on Cooper's findings using the outside 16-inch gun at the Navy's Dahlgren facility.

“I can see no reason for doing that. These experiments have no relation to full-scale gun conditions.”

I labored with the captain’s attitude as I left the airport. Wouldn’t the Navy welcome a definitive explanation that showed that the explosion could have been an accident? Why was he so determined to stay with the same scenario? Was the deliberate act and device scenario that important to him?

The impact-initiation results were persuasive, and I could not escape the thought that an inadvertent overram could cause yet another explosion on one of the three operational battleships. The implications were so crucial that I could not leave it to the hope that Miceli would reconsider and go to the Navy with a recommendation for a cessation of 16-inch gun firings.

I went in to my office about 6:30 A.M. on Friday, 11 May, and called Captain Miceli, hoping that he might have reconsidered. “In my opinion,” I said, “Paul Cooper’s results suggest the possibility of a serious safety problem that can’t be ignored. It seems prudent to me that the Navy either institute positive control to prevent overrams, or discontinue the firing of 16-inch guns until more information has been obtained with full-scale tests.”

The captain’s response was not altogether unexpected. “I see nothing here that concerns me. I fail to see that your lab-scale experiments have any relation to the full-sized gun situation.”

I said that establishing that relation would be the purpose of the full-scale experiments, but the captain was adamant. Further technical arguments made no impression, and it seemed that he had made a decision to ignore this work on other grounds.

“Joe,” I said, “it would be a tragedy if there were another explosion aboard a battleship when we have positive indication in the laboratory of a safety problem when propellant is overrammed.”

The captain replied, “I’ve fully discussed this with our technical experts and we’re convinced that there is no connection between your lab experiments and actual gun operation. We’ve concluded that there is no reason to halt firing of the 16-inch guns.”

Further conversation with the captain on this subject seemed useless. I returned to the laboratory, and after thinking about it a few hours decided to call Rick DeBobes, Senator Nunn’s counsel for SASC. Fortunately he was in and free to talk. I explained that we had new results that indicated that an overram could indeed initiate an explosion in small-scale tests. Our extrapolations to full scale suggested that an overram in a 16-inch gun could lead to an explosion, and the results had been outlined to the Navy. I told him that conversations with Captain Miceli and his experts had been unsuccessful in persuading the Navy to conduct full-scale tests, and to either develop positive controls on 16-inch guns to avoid overrams or recommend a cessation of 16-inch-gun firing until full-scale tests were carried out. I added that the development of positive controls to preclude overrams might take some time, and that cessation would be the prudent step.

DeBobes listened quietly and said he agreed that there should be a cessation in gun firings on the three active battleships. "I'll support your position on this somehow, and a letter from SASC to the Navy might be appropriate." The letter was sent to the Navy on 14 May, the Monday after our conversation:

U.S. Senate
Committee on Armed Services Washington, D.C., May 14, 1990

Admiral C. A. H. Trost, USN,
Chief of Naval Operations,
The Pentagon, Washington, D.C.

Dear Admiral Trost: I understand that the then Vice Chief of Naval Operations, Admiral Leon A. Edney, USN, was made aware on May 11, 1990 of the recent finding by Sandia National Laboratories that the explosion on board USS *Iowa* may have been caused by a high-speed overram of the bag charges and impact sensitivity of the propellant. Pursuant to this Committee's request, Sandia National Laboratories is performing an analysis of the Navy's technical investigation.

As soon as the Committee staff director, Arnold Punaro, was informed on May 11th of Sandia's findings, he directed Rick DeBobes of the Committee staff to contact Admiral Edney directly to ensure that Admiral Edney was personally aware of Sandia's findings and concerns. This information was initially provided by the Sandia project director, Dr. Richard L. Schwoebel, to Captain Joseph D. Miceli, USN, Director the Technical Support Team for the USS *Iowa* investigation, in view of Dr. Schwoebel's concern with the safety of continued operation of 16-inch guns in the fleet.

I further understand that the Navy's initial reaction, as conveyed to Committee staff, was that Sandia's laboratory tests and findings, since they were not performed on 16-inch guns, were not relevant and that no action need be taken vis-à-vis the deployed battleship USS *Missouri*.

The purpose of this letter is to ensure that the Navy is seriously considering Sandia's findings in making judgments relating to the safety of the crews of the battleships. At a minimum, I want to ensure that the Navy will actively and expeditiously conduct all necessary tests to determine if Sandia's tests can be duplicated on the 16-inch gun and its associated equipment. I strongly recommend that Sandia personnel be involved in these tests in view of their expertise and experience and so they can independently verify any additional Navy tests.

The Committee is not in a position at this time to make a judgment as to the safe operation of 16-inch guns in the fleet. We do intend to hold hearings in the near future to inquire further into this matter. I am sure that you share my concern that the paramount interest is the safety of the crews of the battleships.

Sincerely, Sam Nunn, Chairman.

I later learned that the Navy began to organize full-scale studies of overram initiation shortly after the conversation with DeBobes and after Senator Nunn's letter to Admiral Trost. While Captain Miceli subsequently stated that the Navy began these studies on their own, this was inconsistent with his statements on the phone that denied the importance of such studies. The onset of their full-scale studies was, however, consistent with the Navy's receipt of the letter from Senator Nunn.

It would be only ten days later, on 24 May, that a full-scale drop test simulating an overram would explode and result in a cessation of all further 16-inch gun operations on battleships.

The president of Sandia, Al Narath, contacted me on 14 May. He said he had received a phone call from Vice Adm. Peter M. Hekman Jr., commander of Naval Sea Systems Command (to whom Captain Miceli reported) on Saturday morning, and that the admiral was very critical of Sandia's propellant initiation studies. Admiral Hekman had insisted that such studies weren't relevant to actual gun conditions. "Nevertheless," said Hekman, "the Navy is restarting their studies of impact initiation on full scale." Narath said the Navy wanted Sandia to participate in the studies. I said that initiating full-scale impact tests was the right thing to do, but the Navy's assertion that it was irrelevant was nonsense. If the Navy really believed that, they wouldn't restart the tests.

Sometime later on the morning of the fourteenth, I called Captain Miceli. Yes, he was aware of Admiral Hekman's call to Narath. I didn't press the issue about the Navy's "renewed interest" in impact initiation, or the captain's assertion that there was no connection between the lab scale results and full-scale gun operations. Obviously, the Navy had been convinced, one way or another, that this was an issue that deserved study. DeBobes called late in the day to say that the Senate Armed Services Committee wanted to hold hearings on the Sandia investigation sooner than expected, probably during the 5–7 June interval.

I drafted and redrafted the conclusions in the executive summary, trying to distill as much into each statement as possible. At the same time, I felt it was important to avoid technical jargon and word each conclusion in a way that could be readily understood. Jim Mitchell's writing expertise was most valuable in shaping the summary. We faxed drafts and redrafts to one another. Each version was given not just a date but also the time of day to help distinguish between the slight nuances being considered.

Finally we came to closure on the executive summary, ensuring that the principal technical people agreed with not only the statements of fact but also the implications of what was being said. This process forged a more coherent understanding of what we had done in our work, and as we proceeded it became clearer to me how we should articulate our results to SASC.

This version, over two hundred pages to describe our five months' effort, was just in time for the report deadline. The report included many technical details and would be heavy going for the uninitiated.

The next team meeting was on Thursday, 17 May, and the GAO people, Marty Ferber, Jerry Herley, and Tim Stone, and also Rick DeBobes from SASC were with us. We went through the technical accomplishments with talks by our principals, who described their individual activities and highlighted the primary observations.

The new result that stimulated an extended discussion was, of course, the observation by Paul Cooper that fracture of pellets in the trim layer could ignite the black powder pouch of the adjacent propellant bag. Cooper's results had been obtained from a carefully ordered sequence of experiments of progressively larger size. He had determined the probability of initiation for bags with a reduced number of trim pellets and extrapolated his results to the full-sized bag charge for five pellets in the trim layer. The plot of initiating probability versus rammer speed indicated that the probability of initiation was significant at the highest ram speeds. The key factor, apart from verifying the extrapolation, was to somehow establish the rammer speed for the overram that occurred aboard the *Iowa* on the morning of 19 April.

DeBobes felt that it was important that the Senate Armed Services Committee hear these latest results and that a hearing should be organized soon. After further discussion, it was agreed that a hearing would very likely be scheduled for Friday, 25 May, in one week. I would serve as principal spokesman for Sandia. The die was cast for the first round.

Al Narath received an interesting letter from Admiral Hekman dated 17 May. The admiral expressed concern with reports he was receiving concerning our analysis of foreign materials and that Sandia "had dismissed evidence of a foreign material in the *Iowa* projectile rotating ring." I drafted a response which Dr. Narath signed and sent to Admiral Hekman. The draft included six paragraphs from our interim report detailing, among other things, our observations of iron fibers and associated surface contaminations. The point was that we had devoted a great deal of effort to assess that nature and origin of these materials and certainly had not dismissed evidence of foreign materials in the rotating band.

I found Hekman's letter to be interesting in his reference to reports that he had received from Captain Miceli. This was not the first time that there seemed to be a discrepancy in the information that we were conveying to Captain Miceli and the perception of that information at higher levels in the Navy.

Thinking that a moot court experience might be valuable preparation for the SASC hearing, I arranged an afternoon session early in the week of the twenty-first in which several tough-minded Sandians brought the "worst" questions they could think of to ask me about our investigation. It was a valuable experience, and I was grateful for all the mistreatment and good advice I received that afternoon.

Linda Vigil Lopez, my administrative assistant, met me at the airport just before 5:00 A.M. the morning of 24 May, totally exhausted from the ordeal of preparing large visuals for our presentation but pleased with the efforts of our tech art people. Jim Borders and I sat together on the plane, occasionally sharing comments about various details of the foreign materials work and other technical results while I continued to edit the notes for presenting our work.

On our arrival in Washington, we drove to the GAO, which had arranged funding for the Sandia investigation and was our connection to the Senate Armed Services Committee. The staff was in a high state of excitement, as if the hearing tomorrow were the only issue of importance. The most recent factor in this frantic state was a request from Congresswoman Mary Rose Oakar of Ohio that she be given an advance copy of our report. The GAO demurred, but they were uneasy about not responding to her. The preoccupation of the staff left us to revision of our notes, the phones constantly ringing around us, drawing our attention to the scene of continuing anxiety.

After DeBobes arrived we went through a set of questions that Senator Nunn would very likely ask me in some form. DeBobes urged me to press our points harder, to boldly state conclusions that went a notch or two beyond what I felt was clearly defensible at this incomplete stage of our work. I pointed out that it was important we not press our points beyond what we clearly understood, nor exceed the bounds of what we had stated in the report. I insisted that we be fully credible and able to back up everything we said, that it would be a mistake to put ourselves in the same position as the Navy with their overinterpretation of results.

DeBobes was impatient with this. "Well, surely with all this data on the foreign materials you can completely set aside the Navy's case—"

I said we still had not found a source for the iron fibers found by the Navy; they still represented an unknown.

"But you can clearly say that a detonator was not there—"

"No, at this point we can neither prove nor disprove the existence of the ignitor proposed by the Navy."

DeBobes rolled his eyes and sat back in his chair, disturbed by what he obviously felt was too conservative an approach. "Well, I guess that you have to do what you're comfortable with."

"Exactly right."

At this same time, Paul Cooper and Karl Schuler were viewing important tests taking place at the Navy facility at Dahlgren. The Navy had initiated a series of full-scale vertical drop tests using stacks of five-bag charges (fig. 13-1). This vertical simulation of an overram was organized by Tom Doran at Dahlgren, a dedicated individual determined to elucidate the problem if it existed on a large scale.

The drop studies were being carried out at an intense level in anticipation of the hearings. Several tests had been conducted without any ignitions. The Navy team was using a trim layer of five propellant pellets closely grouped in the center of the top tier of pellets. After drop number seventeen, Cooper and Schuler inspected the trim layer and noted that some of the pellets had indeed fractured and exhibited evidence of combustion on the fractured surfaces.

Schuler asked Captain Miceli if he could rearrange the pellets in the trim layer to spread them out a bit. Miceli, confident that this would have no effect, told him to go ahead. Schuler rearranged the pellets in the trim layer for test number eighteen. Just as test eighteen was being readied, Captain Miceli was interrupted by a courier with a draft press release by the Navy. Presumably this release was to the effect that Navy investigations of the Sandia hypothesis had demonstrated that there was no impact initiation in gun-scale experiments. It was important that Miceli proofread the final version for release prior to the Sandia testimony before the Senate.

The timing of the press release would, of course, blunt the effect of our testimony and imply a lack of credibility of the Sandia effort. Test number eight-

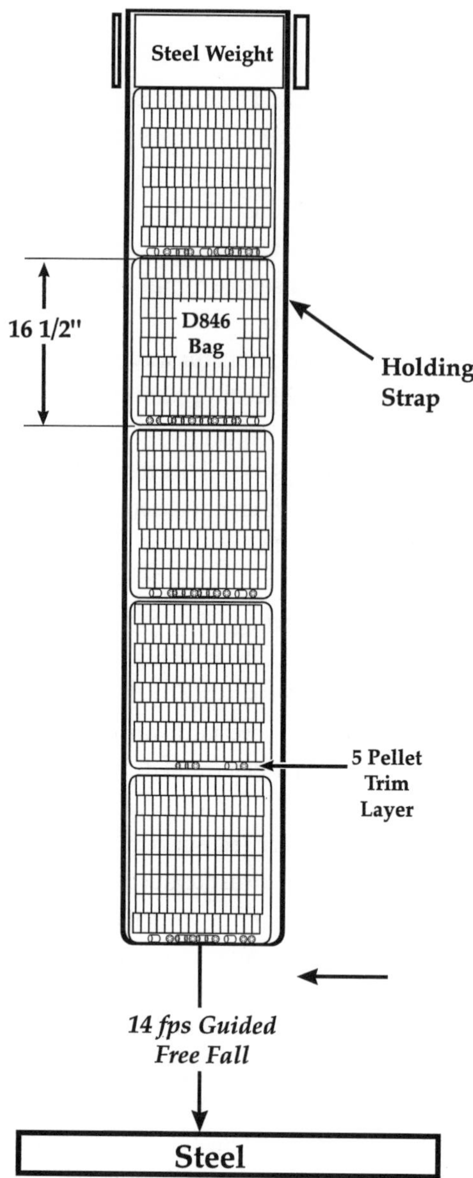

Figure 13-1. The Navy simulated Paul Cooper's small-scale drop test with a series of five full-sized propellant bags like those used on the battleships. The five bags were suspended above an unyielding surface and dropped to simulate the overram situation, the steel weight on top of the bags replicating the kinetic energy of the rammer mechanism. On the eighteenth drop test, some of the trim-layer pellets in the lower bags fractured, and burning particles from the fractured surfaces ignited the black powder at the top end of the lowest bag. The result was a violent deflagration of the entire five-bag array. This explosion caused the Navy to suspend all firings of 16-inch guns aboard the battleships.

een was put on hold while Captain Miceli put the final touches on the draft. His editing was in vain.

Test eighteen was finally readied and dropped. Five aligned propellant bags, just like those involved in the explosion aboard the USS *Iowa*, fell a short distance onto the unyielding concrete surface of the test site. A weight on top of the upper-most bag simulated the added energy of the rammer mechanism in a high-speed overram. The trim-layer pellets in the lower bags were compressed by not only the weight at the top but also the upper bags, each weighing nearly one hundred pounds. Some of the trim layer pellets in the lower bags began to fracture because of the high loads. Fracture of these trim-layer pellets caused them to emit burning particles, just as in Cooper's experiments.

Sensors between the two lowest bags picked up light emitted by burning particles from fractured pellets in the first few milliseconds after impact. The level of energy release was very low and would not be detected by simply looking at the bags during the impact. Some of the burning particles passed through the layers of silk surrounding the black powder patch in the adjacent (lower) bag and ignited the powder.

The energy release increased dramatically as the black powder rapidly burned and ignited the propellant. The multiplication continued swiftly and developed into an all-encompassing fire ball that enlarged and totally filled the video monitors aimed at the test site. To the human eye, it appeared as a sudden and violent explosion at the site of the drop. The explosion was fueled by nearly five hundred pounds of propellant, and in a fraction of a second the shock wave reached the bunker where the Navy crew and the two Sandians sat transfixed before the remote video monitors.

In several seconds the flames began to subside, showing that the test site had been swept clear of surrounding apparatus. After a few more moments of silence, someone murmured, "Holy shit . . ." The implication of the explosion began to register: The explosion aboard the *Iowa* could have been initiated simply by overramming the propellant bags into the breech.

Captain Miceli walked out of the bunker without saying a word. He returned in a few minutes, now convinced. "The firing of the 16-inch guns on the battleships must be halted," he declared.

Borders and I left the GAO offices and went to the hotel. I began again to go through my notes, preparing for testimony the next morning. I spread out the various documents and reports that I would be using during my testimony the next day. I would select just those items I felt were crucial to have at hand for quick reference. I reviewed again the detailed notes that I would use to describe the key points of each visual.

The phone rang. Nigel Hey from Sandia was calling, obviously excited. "Have you heard the news?" he asked. Nigel went on to say that there had been an explosion at Dahlgren. My first thought was that had been an accident of some kind, and Cooper and Schuler were there.

The terse news release reported that an unexpected explosion had occurred at Dahlgren during tests associated with the turret explosion that had taken place aboard the USS *Iowa*. No one had been injured, but the Navy was reconsidering further firing of 16-inch guns aboard battleships. I asked Hey to call me with any new information. It was difficult to fathom that the day before the hearing the Sandia suggestion that an explosion resulting from an overram and impact ignition would literally take on real life.

I turned on the TV and almost immediately viewed an announcement of the explosion at Dahlgren and, shortly thereafter, an announcement of a moratorium on the firing of 16-inch guns aboard battleships. The latter corroborated what seemed unbelievable. I felt a great relief.

I tried to continue preparing for the hearing, but it was impossible not to wonder about the details of what had happened at Dahlgren earlier in the afternoon. Cooper and Schuler had said they would arrive at the hotel about six o'clock. It was almost that time now.

Schuler called from the front desk. I asked, "What's happened? I can hardly wait to hear about your day!"

"What do you mean, it's just been a very ordinary day!"

In a few minutes Cooper and Schuler were in the room describing the day's events. They said Captain Miceli, confident there would be no ignitions from the tests, essentially revealed the Navy's plan to them: to discredit Sandia prior to the SASC hearing with the press release. The release would say that the Navy had conducted numerous full-scale impact-initiation tests at Dahlgren without any ignitions, as the Navy experts had predicted. The competence of Sandia would be openly questioned, it would be stated that we had no expertise in this area. One of the SASC members would articulate the Navy's case at the hearing, emphasizing that there had been no initiations in the full-scale experiments. He would use the Navy's press release as corroboration that the Sandia scenario was invalid.

Schuler described the events in vivid terms, and Cooper nodded his assent as he looked back and forth between Schuler and me. Schuler described the delay of the test so Captain Miceli could once again review the press release excoriating Sandia's hypothesis. He spoke of the captain's offhand approval of his request to rearrange the trim layer by spreading out the pellets. He recalled the shock of the explosion on all of the witnesses, and Miceli's decision to recommend that 16-inch gun operations be curtailed. Unbelievable events.

Our conversation was briefly interrupted by a message from the hotel desk. Jerry Herley of GAO had faxed an Associated Press report with "congratulations" written across the release:

> Associated Press 5/24/90 0605 EST
>
> **Navy Reopens Iowa Investigation,** by Suzanne M. Schafer, AP Military Writer
>
> WASHINGTON (AP)—The Navy on Thursday reopened its investigation into the battleship *Iowa* explosion and ordered a halt to the firing of 16-inch guns aboard all battleships after the "unexplained ignition" of bags of powder during testing. . . . As a safety precaution, the Navy today suspended all live firing of battleship 16-inch, 50 caliber guns, until further notice, the Navy said. . . . Tests on the gunpowder were being conducted there "to evaluate a theory provided by Sandia National Laboratory," the Navy said. The statement did not say what the theory was. . . . The Navy said in its statement that the testing at Dahlgren would continue.

We read and reread the release and continued talking for hours, slowly walking down to the restaurant after Borders joined us. At dinner we repeatedly went over the events of the day, wondering about this turn of fate at the eleventh hour. Incredible luck, not just for us, but perhaps others as well.

In spite of the happenings at Dahlgren, the tension related to the upcoming hearings did not subside. I slept little and was up early going through my notes again, modifying them in accord with the new information. I believed we should go through our presentation essentially as we had planned it, and subsequently go into the implications of the explosion on Thursday. Cooper and Schuler could provide firsthand testimony about events at Dalhgren.

I met the others downstairs for a light breakfast at seven, and we departed in the van about 7:30. A GAO representative had joined us and directed us to the Hart Building, where the hearings would be held. We arrived early and used the time to set up the visuals and the television monitor so the senators could see the video of Cooper's experiments. The video would take on a whole new meaning today.

14 Senate Armed Services Committee Hearing

25 May 1990

WE ARRIVED at the Hart Building at 8:30 A.M. and walked into the large entrance hall, striking in its stark simplicity. The meeting room was directly ahead, a voluminous chamber in which there were a number of press people preparing for the hearing. Others were sitting in a spectator area that would seat about three hundred. A few turned to study us carefully as we entered, and I sensed that some were survivors of men who had died aboard the *Iowa*, wondering if we were the Sandia team, perhaps hoping to better understand, to hear of work that addressed unresolved concerns. A handful of naval officers, none of whom I recognized, were clustered in the spectator area.

Just in front of the spectator area was a long table with microphones for those who would testify. We walked to the table and stood for a moment, glancing back at the spectators and then forward to the front of the room. A raised semicircular dais was located about twenty feet beyond the table and each place was labeled for a member of the Senate Armed Services Committee. Senator Nunn's seat, as chairman of the Senate Armed Services Committee, was at the center of the dais.

In the next few minutes, the senators entered one by one, scanning the interim report that we had put at each of their places. Senator Jeff Bingaman (D-New Mexico) went to his place on the dais to drop off his briefcase and came to our table. He greeted each of us and said he was very proud of the investigative work by Sandia. He thanked us for our efforts and said that the hearing should offer a full opportunity to tell our story, including what had happened at Dahlgren the day before. Senators William S. Cohen of Maine (R) and John Glenn of Ohio (D) also welcomed us and expressed their appreciation for the independent investigation that Sandia had carried out up to this point.

Senator John W. Warner from Virginia (R) took a seat near the chairman's but did not acknowledge us or look in our direction. I understood that the Navy plan prior to the explosion yesterday was that Senator Warner would be the principal critic of Sandia's investigation. He would use the press release that Captain Miceli had carefully edited just before the explosion to minimize our hypothesis of an overram initiation, to question the value of our investigation and expertise. Senator Warner, a former secretary of the Navy, had not contacted us with regard to any aspect of our investigation nor expressed any concerns or hopes—or interest.

The chairman, Senator Sam Nunn (D-Georgia), came to the table and said that the Sandia investigation had brought a great deal of understanding to the incident and he appreciated our contributions. He looked directly at me. "Do you see any problem in continuing your work on impact ignition and working with the Navy?"

I said that continued work was essential and that our working-level relationships with the Navy were good.

"Fine. We'll probably get into this subject later in the hearing."

Other members attending were Senators Carl Levin (D-Michigan) and Albert Gore Jr. (D-Tennessee). Senator Howard M. Metzenbaum (D-Ohio), one of those who called for an independent review of the Navy's investigation, was also in attendance.

Senator Nunn opened the hearing promptly at 9:00 A.M.:

Chairman Nunn: The Armed Services Committee will come to order.

The committee meets this morning for the fourth in a series of hearings on matters associated with the explosion on April 19, 1989 in the center gun of Turret II on board USS *Iowa* which resulted in the death of forty-seven naval personnel.

The committee first heard on November 16, 1989 from Rear Admiral Richard Milligan, the Navy's investigating officer, and from other Navy witnesses who assisted in the investigative effort. We then heard from Captain Fred Moosally, the commanding officer of the USS *Iowa* at the time of the explosion. Finally, the committee heard from three witnesses from the Federal Bureau of Investigation concerning the FBI's "equivocal death analysis." At that last hearing we also heard from the chief of the FBI's laboratory on the FBI's analysis of the rotating band from the projectile that was in the barrel on the day of the explosion.

This morning, the committee will hear from Mr. Frank C. Conahan, Assistant Comptroller General, National Security and International Affairs Division of the General Accounting Office; Dr. Richard L. Schwoebel, Director of Components, Sandia National Laboratories; and Mr. Paul W. Cooper and Dr. Karl W. Schuler, who were both members of Sandia's technical team that conducted the effort that was headed up by Dr. Schwoebel. . . .

In November 1989 Senator Warner, Senator Bingaman, and I then urged Sandia National Laboratories in Albuquerque, New Mexico to assist the General Accounting Office by undertaking a technical analysis of the Navy's tests, since we viewed it as extremely important for the Navy's technical findings to be evaluated by an expert independent source. I ask unanimous consent that our letters to the General Accounting Office and to Sandia National Laboratories be entered in to the record. Without objection, they will be entered into the record.

The purpose of this morning's hearing is to receive testimony as to the results of both GAO and Sandia's efforts to date. I want to emphasize that the Navy has been cooperative throughout this period with our committee, the General Accounting Office and with Sandia. This has been particularly true at the working level of the Navy. It would have been impossible for GAO and Sandia to have accomplished very much without the assistance of the Navy. As will become clearer as the morning goes on, additional action on the part of the Navy will be essential for Sandia's work to be carried to its logical conclusion. In this connection, I would like at this point to enter into the record my letter of May 14, 1990, to the Chief of Naval Operations, Admiral Trost, which I wrote to emphasize the importance I attached to Sandia's findings which were brought to the committee's attention on May 11. Without objection, that letter will also be entered into the record.[1]

On May 11 after receiving this information, the committee immediately notified the Navy. We wanted to make sure that those responsible for the safety of the battleships had access to this information immediately. I stressed the need for the Navy to seriously consider these findings and to expeditiously conduct additional tests with the involvement of the Sandia experts.

The testimony we will hear this morning will expose significant shortcomings in the Navy's investigation into this tragic incident. The testimony also documents serious deficiencies in the Navy's treatment of the battleships, both in terms of officer and enlisted manning and in terms of the training given to the crews who man the 16-inch guns. The testimony will cast grave doubt on the Navy's finding concerning the presence of foreign material in the rotating band of the *Iowa* projectile. As those who followed this matter will recall, this was a key element in the Navy's foundation for finding that the explosion occurred as a result of a wrongful and intentional act. The testimony today will essentially eviscerate the Navy's conclusion that the explosion on the USS *Iowa* was the result of a wrongful intentional act.

Finally, I would note that the effort of this committee has been directed toward finding out what happened so that the appropriate action can be taken to ensure that it will never happen again. In other words, our primary concern has been and is the safety of the crews on our ships.

Gentlemen, we welcome you here today, and we look forward to your testimony. We will hear first from Mr. Frank Conahan, and we will then hear from Dr. Schwoebel.

Before hearing from the witnesses, however, I would ask Senator Warner for any opening remarks he would like to make.

Senator Warner: Mr. Chairman, first I wish to commend you and members of this committee for certain initiatives that you have taken which have led to the production of this evidence which we will consider today. In my judgment, however, it is far too early to jump to any conclusions. The evidence that we will receive today represents certain tests taken first by Sandia and subsequently by the Navy, and we need an additional period of testing.

The Secretary of the Navy has directed at least two more weeks of testing, within which time you have to establish the key fact: Is there a linkage between your discovery that the powder will ignite under certain mechanical pressures and certain geometric orientation of the capsules of powder within the bags, and the operation of this particular gun mount and mounts like it, which have operated in the U.S. Navy since the close of World War II tens of thousands of times without such a problem?

So, Mr. Chairman, I regret that certain elements of the media have used the words that there has been a "cover-up" and that the Navy should apologize. It is far too early to make such pronouncements or reach such conclusions. We must—in the sense of fairness to the families, to the emotions that are evoked by this continuing investigation, to the sorrow they have suffered, to the Navy itself, to the reputation of the Navy—not jump to these conclusions too quickly.

I think the Secretary of the Navy and the senior officers made a prudent decision yesterday to discontinue further training using these 16-inch guns and to reopen the investigation to receive the evidence which you have produced thus far and will continue to produce in the weeks to come.

I commend you for what you have done, but in a sense of fairness let us not leap to conclusions.

Thank you, Mr. Chairman.

Chairman Nunn: Thank you, Senator Warner. Senator Cohen, did you have a statement?

Senator Cohen: Just a few comments, Mr. Chairman.

If I could follow up on what Senator Warner has said. The purpose of this hearing is not to gloat or to try to humiliate the Navy because the Navy, after all, is in the business of protecting our national security and the safety of all of us. I think it will hopefully seek a measure or touch of humility.

In my judgment there clearly was a rush to judgment. A possibility was wrapped up by investigators and psychological architects into probabilities that were then paraded around as certitudes. Faulty equipment was ruled out, and that left only human error. Human error took on the dimensions of a disturbed and unbalanced young man who murdered forty-six of his shipmates.

I must tell you, Mr. Chairman, that I was astonished to listen to the evidence that was presented to justify the conclusion that a sick and twisted soul was in all probability responsible for this disaster. As I sat here during the course of that hearing, the words kept going through my mind—the expression that through jaundiced eyes everything looks yellow. I think that was the situation that I heard during our previous hearing.

Guilt was established, according to one writer, by gestalt, and I think it is important that we take care. We are now debating an anticrime bill with very serious penalties imposed upon individuals who are convicted under that particular legislation. Whenever someone's liberty or life is at stake, we must take great care in arriving at our conclusions

I would like to point out I do not believe that was the case here. As a consequence, at least the lives of other sailors may have been jeopardized as a result. We do not yet know, and we will reserve judgment on that. Certainly reputations were ruined. It was a very famous poet who said that someone who steals your purse from you steals nothing but trash, but when you filch from me my good name you rob me of that which does not enrich you but leaves me poor indeed. This is what occurred, I think, with respect to Mr. Hartwig and certainly Mr. Truitt.

As Senator Warner has indicated, perhaps the most melancholy wounds of all are those that are self-inflicted; indeed, perhaps even to the Navy itself, because if in fact the evidence shows that it was something other than a deliberate act, I think that the Navy will have to do a great deal to rehabilitate itself in terms of its investigative activities.

So I withhold judgment as well, but I must tell you that the case that has been presented to date left a good deal to be desired, in my mind.

Chairman Nunn: Thank you very much, Senator Cohen.

I do think that not jumping to final conclusions as to what caused this are in order here. I do not know that we are going to find today what the cause was. I think that we are going to find that the previous findings are in very serious question.

Any other opening statements? Senator Bingaman.

Senator Bingaman: Mr. Chairman, I do commend you and Senator Warner for continuing to pursue this matter. I think it is very important and a matter which the committee has taken a very responsible role in. I think GAO and Sandia deserve great credit for the work they have done. Obviously the Navy has been very cooperative.

I agree that the purposes of the effort at this point are first to ensure that it does not occur again and, second, to clear the record, correct and clear the record of Seaman Clayton Hartwig. If the evidence is as I understand it to be, I believe that clearing the record is essential as part of this. I am looking forward to the testimony.

Following these and other opening statements, Frank C. Conahan, assistant comptroller general, National Security and International Affairs Division, GAO, presented an extended discussion of the GAO's role in the investigation. He noted that the principal tasks were to (1) conduct an independent investigation of the Navy's technical analysis and the likely causes of the explosion, (2) review the safety aboard the battleships, (3) examine manning and training issues raised by the *Iowa* commanding officer after the explosion, and (4) review the battleship's employment plans and mission.

Chairman Nunn: I suggest to members of the committee we go ahead and hear from our next witness and then come back and ask questions to both of them, including Mr. Cooper and Dr. Schuler. So Dr. Schwoebel, we will hear from you next.

Statement of Dr. Richard L. Schwoebel, Director, Components, Sandia National Laboratories, accompanied by Dr. Karl W. Schuler, Distinguished Member of the Technical Staff, Sandia National Laboratories; Paul W. Cooper, Distinguished Member of the Technical Staff, Sandia National Laboratories; and Dr. James A. Borders, Technical Supervisor, Sandia National Laboratories.

Dr. Schwoebel: Mr. Chairman and members of the committee, as you heard, seated with me are Mr. Paul Cooper and Dr. Karl Schuler of Sandia. Their contributions and important factors in Sandia's study of the explosion on the USS *Iowa* gave rise at least in part to the experiments at Dahlgren. One of those experiments yesterday is germane to the discussion today, and they can provide some insight to that experiment later on.

Our intent today is to go ahead with the presentation as we had originally planned it. It represents, I think, a real background for what has taken place, including yesterday. We agree that the questions that you raise are not settled wholly in the scientific and technical sense. A lot more work needs to be done, and Sandia is very happy to continue to work with the Navy to help resolve this issue. We have had excellent relations with the technical team of the Navy, very open, candid, and they have been extremely helpful to us in every possible way.

I am not going to present a statement about Sandia. That is contained in your handout. I would simply suggest that that [statement] be included in the record for the day. . . .

This visual [following] shows the focus of the Sandia studies, and these are, as you can see, a prescribed list of things that we were asked to review.

Foreign material in the rotating band of the projectile from the USS *Iowa*.
The possible relation of this foreign material to the hypothetical ignitor described by the USN.
Stability and sensitivity of the propellant and black powder in the bag charges used on the USS *Iowa*.

The first of these relates to the foreign material that the Navy identified on the rotating band of the projectile from the USS *Iowa*. The second part of our work is related to the possible relation of this foreign material to the hypothetical or proposed chemical ignitor that was described by the Navy. . . .

We took approximately fifty or sixty samples throughout . . . Turret I of the USS *Iowa*. . . . Note that calcium and chlorine are readily detectable everywhere throughout the turret and could arise from a number of sources. . . . So the existence of calcium and chlorine in the rotating band is not in itself a fingerprint of the presence of . . . the ignitor . . . proposed by the Navy. . . .[2]

In this portion of our testimony, I pointed out that calcium and chlorine were found in many locations within the turrets of the *Iowa*, *Wisconsin*, and *New Jersey*. These elements were found in the magazines, powder flats, projectile deck, gun rooms, and rotating bands of projectiles on the ship. Every sample that we had taken from surfaces within the turrets exhibited the presence of these elements, and the concentrations were not markedly different in any of these locations. In other words, the presence of these elements on the rotating band of the projectile in the center gun was not an anomalous observation but representative of surface constituents found throughout the turret. The fact that these elements were observed on the projectile by the Navy was of no special significance in establishing whether a chemical ignition device was or was not present.

I then continued the foreign materials discussion with our findings related to the presence of glycols on the rotating band, and the Navy's conclusion that these glycols were a part of the hypothetical chemical ignitor:

> In the area dealing with the presence of glycols . . . all [of these materials] are constituents of the fluid that is routinely used to clean and lubricate these 16-inch guns.[3] These glycols, then, are not foreign materials but are altogether expected materials. . . .

I noted that we identified all three of these materials as constituents of Break-Free, which was routinely used to maintain the 16-inch guns.[4] Furthermore, a large amount of Break-Free was used in removing the projectile from the center gun and was known to have penetrated the cannelure of the rotating band. The presence of these three materials on the projectile should have been anticipated because of the extensive use of Break-Free in the gun. Certainly the presence of these three materials was not a definitive indicator of the presence of a chemical ignition device.

The observations with regard to the steel wool–like fibers were more complicated and less complete at this stage of our investigation. The Navy's hypothesis was that steel wool was a part of the chemical ignition device and the fibers found in the cannelure were yet another residue of the device. The concentrations of calcium and chlorine on these fibers as measured by both technical teams were comparable, except for one fiber. That single fiber had been highlighted in the Navy's report as typical of fibers exposed to the combustion of the chemical ignitor. It was hardly typical since it was the only fiber of this kind that had been found. Furthermore, this fiber could not be located for reexamination by the Sandia experts. The Navy was also unable to find other fibers it said had come from other projectiles but were of different diameters. I told the committee that at this point in our investigation we had not identified the source of these fibers and that there were a number of open questions that remained to be answered.

Chairman Nunn: Dr. Schwoebel, let me just ask you this question. I do not know what is routine here and what is unusual. If Sandia had conducted the investigation, when you got through with important fibers, would you have a way of storing them where you could retrieve them?

Dr. Schwoebel: I think that we would obviously work very hard to maintain crucial evidence of that sort.

Chairman Nunn: So if somebody came to you after you had completed an investigation and said where are the fibers, would you expect your people to be able to locate them?

Dr. Schwoebel: I would expect them to be able to locate them.

Chairman Nunn: What would be your reaction if they could not locate them?

Dr. Schwoebel: That would be disconcerting to me.

The last part, the fourth part of the foreign materials area, deals with the polymer films, the PET[5]. . . . It is important to recognize that PET is the polymer from which Mylar is made as the film, or Dacron is made as the fiber. And sources of PET fibers that are normal to the gun environment include, for example, the Dacron cloth, the bore sock that is actually used to clean the gun. . . . That is, there are normal sources of PET that exist in the turret. . . .

Chairman Nunn: Now tell me again how this differs from what the Navy had before you got into this?

Dr. Schwoebel: There was no mention of other sources of this sort of fiber in the turret.

Chairman Nunn: So the Navy had not mentioned other possible sources?

Dr. Schwoebel: That is right.

Chairman Nunn: And they had labeled this foreign material?

Dr. Schwoebel: That is correct. . . . So our first conclusion is . . . we can neither prove nor disprove the presence of a chemical ignitor proposed by the Navy. Prove or disprove in the scientific sense, now, is what I am saying. The interpretation of evidence for a chemical ignitor is complicated by the fact that some chemical constituents of such an ignitor are found throughout 16-inch gun turrets, not only on the USS *Iowa*, but we also did sampling aboard the *Wisconsin* and the *New Jersey*. Forms of the constituents are either commonly used in the turrets or are a part of the maritime environment. . . . We believe evidence for the presence of a chemical ignitor is inconclusive.

Chairman Nunn: Now, let me ask on that point, because I guess that is one of the key findings you made here. If you had access to the other fibers that are not now available to you that we have just enumerated, could that make any difference in your conclusion here?

Dr. Schwoebel: It could. We would have to examine those and understand what is the constituency of those . . . in context with the rest of our observations.

Chairman Nunn: How important were those missing fibers in the Navy's determination that there was unexplained foreign material present?

Dr. Schwoebel: Well, we would like to make that comparison, because that really is a departure from what we have seen. We would like to see these fibers with the high calcium content. . . .

Chairman Nunn: Before we leave that last chart, if you could put it back up there, just so we get this as we go along, because it is complicated. Your finding is "we believe evidence for the presence of a chemical ignitor is inconclusive." Tell us in your own words how that differs from the Navy's finding.

Dr. Schwoebel: Well, I think that our findings are that—and I hesitate to speak for the Navy, but our findings are that if—for example, if the initiator were present, and we looked at the kinds of backgrounds that we would find, we would expect to find calcium and chlorine and the glycols and so on. On the other hand, if the ignition device were not present, we would also expect to find calcium, chlorine, and glycols. So that, in a scientific sense, we can neither prove nor disprove that an ignition device was present.

Chairman Nunn: Right. But you understand what the Navy found. Tell us what your understanding is of what they found.

Dr. Schwoebel: My understanding is that they felt that there was a very high probability of a chemical ignitor being included in the system at the time of the explosion, and that they considered their evidence to be very strong. That is my understanding.

Chairman Nunn: And you do not agree with that?

Dr. Schwoebel: No, we do not agree with that.

Chairman Nunn: What they found to be strong evidence, you found to be inconclusive?

Dr. Schwoebel: That is correct.

I went on to another aspect of our investigation, that dealing with the stability of the propellant and black powder. I said that our analyses indicated that the propellant stabilizer was within acceptable limits in agreement with the Navy's findings. We also found only a very remote possibility that this propellant could be initiated in the breech by friction, electrostatic discharge, or electromagnetic radiation. We also concluded that there was only a remote possibility that the black powder could have been initiated by any of these mechanisms. Our studies indicated that ether/air combustion could not be achieved because minimum necessary concentrations were precluded. Moreover, even if the minimum concentrations could be achieved, our analyses showed that the propellant could not be ignited by ether/air combustion.

The next general area that I discussed dealt with the overram that occurred in the center gun. A schematic of the rammer system (similar to figs. 7-4 and 12-2) was used to describe important aspects of the overram observations. I briefly reviewed Karl Schuler's analysis in which the gouges in the spanning tray were used to calculate the location of the rammer chain, and to determine that the overram was about twenty-four inches beyond the normal position. (Recall that the Navy had estimated the overram to be twenty-one inches beyond the normal position.) Schuler's work implied that the propellant bags were compressed against the base of the projectile and that the compressive load may have been at least twenty-eight hundred pounds at the time of the explosion. I continued my testimony:

Our analyses indicate that the bag charges were under a compressive load of at least twenty-eight hundred pounds at the time of the explosion. There may have been even higher transient forces due to dynamic loading, resulting from a greater than normal ram speed. That is to say, if the ram were moving at some speed it would jam these bags against the projectile and create peak loads that were greater than twenty-eight hundred pounds. . . .

The last major topic deals with impact initiation of the propellant. This ties very directly into this idea of the overram that was just discussed which actually forced the propellant bags into the rear of the projectile. The Navy reported that—and I quote—"Impact and compression of the bag charges were not contributing factors in the *Iowa* incident."

Our results raise some real questions about that statement. We have conducted experiments that indicate that the fracture of pellets of the propellant can lead to initiation.

The arrangement of the pellets in the bag is shown in the left-hand side of this visual. The pellet bag is a right cylinder, as you can see [see fig. 3-3]. Note that most of the roughly eighteen hundred pellets are arranged in eight stacked layers, very neatly arranged in hexagonal, close-packed arrays. Some additional pellets are located in the trim layer at the top of the bag. These trim pellets are used to adjust the total weight of propellant, and these pellets lie on their side at the top of the bag. Note the black powder pouch is at the end of the bag shown here.

Now in an overram situation in which the bags are impacted and compressed against one another, the load can be concentrated into this area of that incomplete layer. Moreover, the pellets that are lying on their side like that are much more easily fractured than those that are standing in the upright orientation. We have done mechanical studies of these pellets to verify that.

In order to assess the effects of impact, Paul Cooper set up the experiment which is shown on the right-hand side of this visual [see figs. 12-3 and 12-4]. If we look at the upper part of that figure, Paul's experiment at the 8-inch size shows an 8-inch array of these pellets, and we are looking down on that 8-inch array. And then on the top of that array is the trim layer—in this case, seven pellets are located in that array.

This array models the forward end of the bag. And this was placed beneath a counterpart of it that models the aft part of the next bag, which includes the black powder pouch. So that you see at that interface the black powder ignition pad and the trim layer adjacent to it.

This assembly was located in a fixture in one of our explosive test sites and a weight was dropped on this combination from various heights to simulate various overram situations. As the height of the weight was gradually increased, one eventually got to the point that these trim layer pellets were fractured. And moreover, they gave off burning particles that ignited the adjacent black powder pouch.

The ignited black powder pouch then rapidly ignited the rest of the pellets in the experiment. That is, there is a kind of important interaction here that occurs, a sort of a synergism that takes place between the fractured trim layer pellets and the adjacent black powder pouch.

We then showed the video of Paul Cooper's experiments. The senators and newsmen crowded around to watch this small-scale example of how impact ignition could occur.

Chairman Nunn: Would you tell us now—are you trying to get as close as you can with this kind of rigging to the—

Dr. Schwoebel: Yes, that is the idea. We are trying to develop as much similarity as we can. However, there are some real questions of how you extrapolate these things, but I will get into that as we go along. . . .

Dr. Schwoebel: In the 16-inch gun situation, the bags would be arranged in this manner. There are five bags there, as you can see [fig. 14-1]. The trim layers are as indicated. The most sensitive interface is the interface between bag one and bag two.[6] The number of pellets in the trim layer is an important factor, as is the rammer speed. That is, the energy that you put into this system.

Now the number of pellets in the trim layer there, [aside to Jim Borders] if

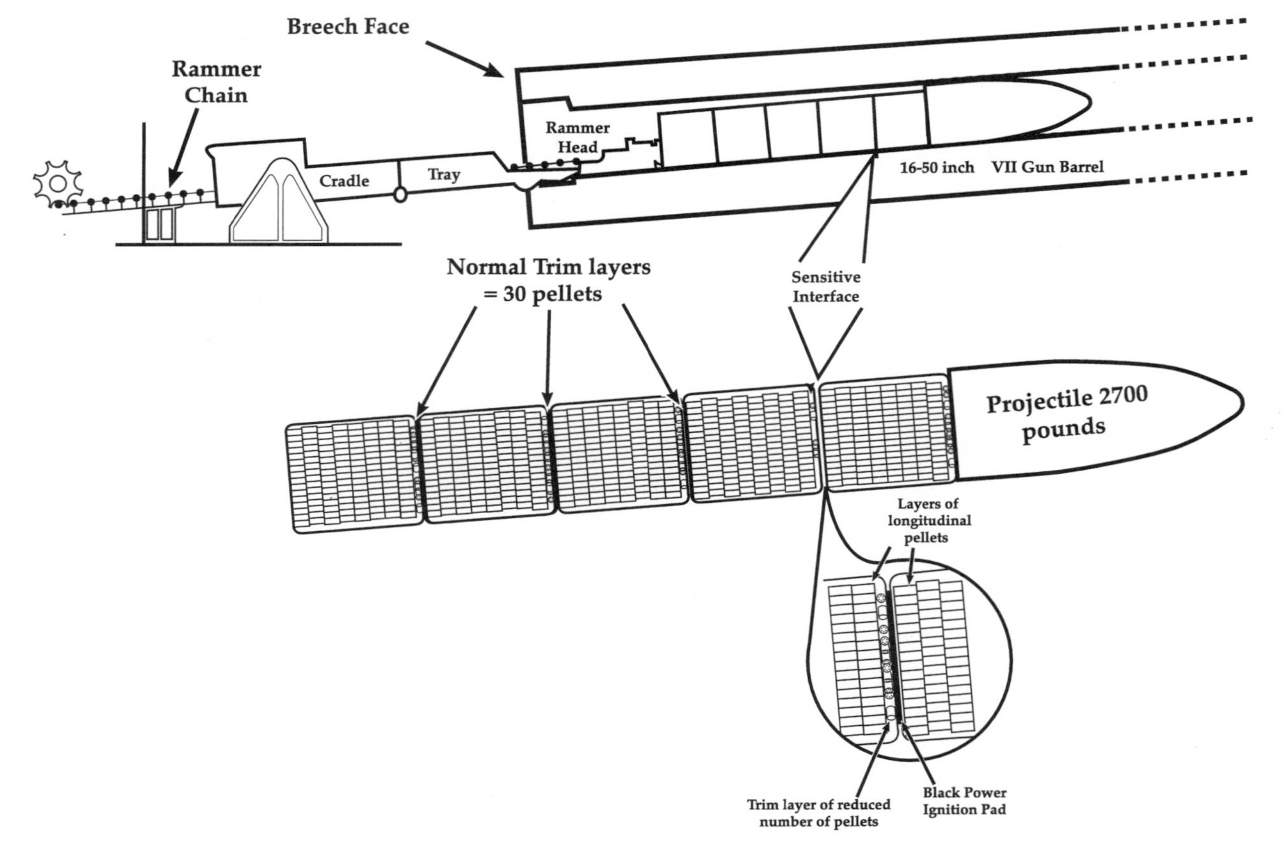
Breech Face
Rammer
Chain
Rammer
Head
Cradle
Tray
16-50 inch VII Gun Barrel
Normal Trim layers
= 30 pellets
Sensitive
Interface
Projectile 2700
pounds
Layers of
longitudinal
pellets
Trim layer of reduced
number of pellets
Black Power
Ignition Pad

you might indicate that in the visual, the number of pellets is not a constant. It varies, because these pellets are not all of the same length. When you adjust the bag weight that number can vary. And we understand from the technical team of the Navy that it varies between roughly twenty and sixty.

We then presented visuals of the extrapolations which illustrated Cooper's estimates of the ignition probability versus rammer speed (impact velocity). The gist of the argument was that the probabilities for initiation could be appreciable at the higher ram speeds, but that these were only preliminary estimates and needed to be determined for actual gun conditions by full-scale experiments. The senators asked perceptive questions about this phenomenon and the significance of the results was apparent to many of them.

Senator Warner: Well, you know, we are in the area of speculation. This gun has operated twenty-thousand plus times, and it is this system that has been utilized, so you said, throughout the history of the use of this gun; you said it provides a rather simple explanation as to how an accident could happen, and I wonder if you want to revisit the word "simple"?

Dr. Schwoebel: Well, I will revisit that as we go along.

Let us then go to the conclusion that we have. The conclusion is that the cause of the explosion was not conclusively determined. However, an important factor may have been the increase in impact sensitivity of a powder bag with a reduced number of pellets in its trim layer. Our half-scale experiments indicate that reducing the number of these pellets lying next to the powder pouch of an adjacent bag increases impact sensitivity enough that an explosion could have been caused by an overram at a higher than normal speed.

Facing page

Figure 14-1. Sandia's analysis of the USS *Iowa* explosion. The rammer was extended well beyond its normal position and compressed the propellant bags against the projectile. Propellant pellets in the trim layer in bag two, just behind the propellant bag in contact with the projectile, were compressed and fractured. The fractured surfaces emitted burning particles which ignited the black powder ignition pad of bag one. This initiated the explosion. The forward-most interface between the propellant bags is the most sensitive because the maximum kinetic energy is delivered to this interface.

Our studies indicate that impact initiation depends on two key factors: the number of pellets in the trim layer and the speed of the overram. However, these experiments must be extended to actual 16-inch gun conditions to establish the validity of this ignition mechanism. A point that I would make in response to your question is that certainly there have been many, many loadings that have been—obviously have gone on without problems. However, in this case, it may have been a situation in which you do have a low number of trim grains.

This case was quite different in that a substantial overram of some kind occurred, and that clearly falls outside the normal procedures that take place in these gun rooms. What happened here, I think, was quite abnormal in terms of the operation.

Now, our experiments on initiation by impact are incomplete and more work needs to be done. Nevertheless, Mr. Chairman, it appears from our present models that the probability of initiation by impact is such that measures should be taken to ensure overrams are precluded at any speed.

Based on our studies of the explosion in the gun turret of the USS *Iowa*, we recommend the following:

1) A mechanism should be added to these guns to control the speed of the rammer and the placement of the powder bags.

2) A new bag charge design should be developed in which the weight of the propellant can be adjusted without the use of a trim layer of pellets. Such a design would be much more robust and less sensitive to impact.

3) Studies of propellant-impact sensitivity should be broadly extended and include both commonly used propellants, D846 and D839. The objective of such studies should be to fully define the safe limits of pellet configuration, bag compression, rammer speed, and other relevant 16-inch gun and turret operations. . . .

Dr. Schwoebel: We can now talk about the tests that took place yesterday.

Chairman Nunn: I think that would be a good procedure. Would you suggest, Dr. Schwoebel, that we have Mr. Cooper and Dr. Schuler go ahead and make their presentation based on the charts, or do you want to get into questions? Are they prepared to tell us what happened yesterday?. That is the general question. . . .

Dr. Schuler: Yesterday's experiment was a drop experiment in which five bags were strapped to a steel plate that provided the weight.

Chairman Nunn: Is that similar to the chart we had up here?

Dr. Schuler: No. I will try to improvise from this chart. The tests at Dahlgren, instead of the rammer head on the top, there was steel plate about four inches thick, and then the five bags were strapped to that steel plate, so initially they were held up against it [see fig. 13-1]. Instead of there being a projectile, there was a gap between the bottom bag and the ground, and then that whole assembly was released, hit the ground, and the kinetic energy of the plate had to be absorbed then by the array of bags.

They had been conducting tests of this nature, I believe, for the last week. The tests yesterday that we witnessed were the seventeenth and eighteenth tests in that series.

Chairman Nunn: The Navy had been conducting those tests?

Dr. Schuler: Yes.

Chairman Nunn: That was basically what you had told them earlier?

Dr. Schuler: Yes. I think they felt this was a very quick way for them to get into full bag testing in a way that they could adjust the kinetic energy that was put into the bag stack and also adjust the number of tare grains [pellets in the trim layer] at the interface between bags one and two. When we got there yesterday we witnessed the tests—

Chairman Nunn: You just arrived yesterday. You were not there for the other seventeen tests?

Dr. Schuler: No. When we arrived yesterday we were shown the videotapes of, I believe, the first twelve or so tests, none of which had any reactions, some of which there were some broken grains observed. We observed one test—I think it was number seventeen—in which five grains were placed in a tare layer, and the five grains were placed very closely packed in the center of the tare layer.

On that test there was no reaction. All the grains were fractured in the tare layer. There appeared to be the possible onset of an event, but there was no event.

In the next test I suggested that the five grains [pellets], instead of being clustered together tightly in the center of the test, be moved out slightly. They were arrayed in an arrangement where there was one grain in the center.

Chairman Nunn: These are the same things we are calling pellets?

Dr. Schuler: Grains or pellets. One in the center and four arranged around it in about a 6-inch diameter circle, 90 degrees apart. That was test number eighteen in which the ignition occurred yesterday.

Chairman Nunn: Tell us about the ignition.

Dr. Schuler: Well, from the high-speed video, what you see is a flash of light that apparently came from the trim layer between bags two and three, and then there was just a cloud or a ball of yellow flame followed by a large cloud of white smoke. The scene was obliterated by the explosion going off.

Chairman Nunn: Could you tell us the significance of this, Dr. Schuler, in your words, and also tell us any shortcomings of it in terms of being conclusive?

Dr. Schuler: Okay. I think it raises the possibility of an event occurring due to this mechanism. However, it clearly was a very severe test in that the trim layer had been depopulated to just five grains. The five grains had been arranged in what I think is a configuration that would tend to put the maximum amount of energy into each of those five grains. The kinetic energy that was delivered due to the drop height was the maximum kinetic energy that could be delivered by the rammer system. So in that sense it represents a severe test. . . .

Dr. Schuler: This test yesterday represented the maximum kinetic energy that the rammer system aboard the USS *Iowa* could deliver.

Senator Warner: Now is there any evidence to show that that maximum energy was in fact utilized in the accident situation?

Dr. Schuler: No.

Senator Warner: Then why was the test conducted outside of the parameters of the likelihood of what transpired on the USS *Iowa*? That is my question.

Dr. Schuler: I believe the reason for conducting the test was to try to extend our results on scale testing to the full-scale situation; and, as such, one of the things one wants to do is establish the probabilities of occurrence. So one has to test at energies that may be over what you could have achieved on the USS *Iowa*.

I point out again, however, that the rammer on the USS *Iowa* could have been going at fourteen feet per second. We just have no evidence that it was going at that speed.

Chairman Nunn: You have no evidence one way or the other, do you? You have no evidence that it was less than that?

Dr. Schuler: That is correct.

Chairman Nunn: You have no evidence where it was?

Dr. Schuler: No.

Chairman Nunn: But you know it could possibly have achieved that.

Dr. Schuler: That may be going a little bit too far. There is evidence that after the incident the stroking piston of the hydraulic drive was in a position that would correspond to, I believe, 1.7 feet per second.

Chairman Nunn: How does that translate into what the kinetic energy—

Dr. Schuler: The kinetic energy at 1.7 feet per second would be very low, probably sixty foot-pounds or something like that.

Senator Warner: Far less that the energy used in the test yesterday.

Dr. Schuler: Far less.

Senator Warner: Let me ask this question. Has the Navy been operating for many years, perhaps since World War II, under the theory that this particular powder would not ignite as a consequence of overpressure and that it required use of an ignitor for detonation? That seems to me to be a very key question.

Dr. Schwoebel: Yes, and I do not think we can really answer that. The Navy training, I think, is rather explicit in specifying the speed and distance of a proper ram operation, but I think that the interaction that Paul and Karl talk about and this mechanism that we are talking about is basically new ground.

Senator Warner: It seems to me that the design of this propellant and the extensive period and number of times that it was operated safely lends support to the hypothesis that probably the Navy operated under the assumption that you could kick these bags around, that the ship could take a direct hit by a 16-inch round from another ship and still there would not be ignition; it would require some type of fusing and, therefore, they did not focus on whatever safety measures were necessary as a consequence of varying the number of pellets or putting a control mechanism for speed of the rammer. There was sufficient operating experience to justify this mode of operation and use of these powder bags. It seems to me that that has to be revisited, Mr. Chairman. . . .

Chairman Nunn: I guess what I would like to find out at this juncture, and then we will open it up, is what was the significance of yesterday's test? Again, what does it tell us and what does it not tell us?

Senator Warner: What does it add to the base of technical data you developed at Sandia?

Mr. Cooper: It gave us two very important pieces of information. One, it is the first indication of how much energy is partitioned to the rest of the system as compared to that which can go into the tare grains, and that piece of information, once it is expanded with more tests, will help us extrapolate this point of data more accurately.

The second piece of information was that it established that within the possible operating envelopes of the gun that with a small number of tare [trim] layer [pellets] and at the maximum ramming speed that is within the envelope of operation of the gun you could get an ignition during an overram. I am not saying that is a probable event— . . .

Chairman Nunn: Could you tell us what scenario comes out of both your previous studies and yesterday? What scenario could we pose, now, as a possible—not a probable—cause of the occurrence on the *Iowa*, the tragedy that took place there? What scenario could have occurred?

Dr. Schwoebel: One that we have thought about is a very simple one that seems consistent with at least several of the facts. During our review and a number of inspections, in conjunction with Navy personnel, we found that the powder hoist, the powder door, the rammer and other mechanisms in the gun room appeared to be in proper operating condition at the time of the explosion. That is, there was no malfunction that we could find in the system.

Now, as established by the Navy investigation, the door to the powder hoist was closed and locked, but the powder car had not been lowered at the time of the explosion. Immediate lowering of the car on closure of the door is the normal procedure. That is the upper powder hoist operator's function. This suggests to us that the ramming occurred soon after closing the powder door, and may have occurred at very high speed. The counter [or alternative] of this is as follows.

Suppose that a very slow ram occurred, as postulated by the Navy. A slow ram of, say, one to two feet per second, followed by this extended period of fifteen to perhaps thirty seconds of sustained overram while the ignitor is activated. That means that the upper powder hoist operator would have had on the order of maybe twenty to thirty seconds to begin lowering this powder car. His job is to do that right away. However, on the contrary, if a high-speed ram occurred, there would have been little opportunity for the operator to begin lowering the powder car. So it occurs to us that another way of thinking about this is a very simple way in which a high-speed overram occurs, and the explosion takes place so fast that the upper powder hoist operator has no opportunity to lower the car.

A factor that might contribute to an overram was an unidentified problem in the loading operation. This unidentified problem was reported through the ship's phone system by a member of the gun crew. It led to a delay in loading the center gun relative to both the left and right guns in Turret II, and this undefined problem might have created confusion, for example, during the powder loading phase.

So we conclude that a plausible cause of the explosion aboard the USS *Iowa* was a higher than normal speed overram of the bag charges into the rear of the projectile, initiating one of the forward bag charges that contained a reduced number of pellets in the trim layer. The fact that the bags were moved to a position substantially beyond the normal position is evidence to us, is an indication to us, that it may have taken place at a higher than normal speed, so that in some sense it was not fully controlled.

This is a very simple view that seems to us to be consistent with the facts.

Chairman Nunn: Is it fair to say this is a possible scenario at this stage?

Dr. Schwoebel: We think it is a possible scenario.

Chairman Nunn: Would you say it would be fair to say it is a probable scenario?

Dr. Schwoebel: I do not think we can say that.

Chairman Nunn: You do not have enough evidence to say it is a probable scenario?

Dr. Schwoebel: That is exactly right.

Chairman Nunn: What else do we need to do now? What else do you believe needs to be done to complete the investigation that you have underway?

Dr. Schwoebel: What I would like to see happen is for technical teams from both Sandia and the Navy to come together again to discuss all of these results and continue studies that explore this range of impact sensitivity and what the key factors are, and explore those in much more detail. We have only in some sense a beginning of this process, and that needs to go on.

Chairman Nunn: Is it fair to say, though, at this stage, that you know enough now on probabilities that you believe your recommendations should be taken seriously by the Navy in terms of changing and eliminating even the possibility of this recurring?

Dr. Schwoebel: We do.

Chairman Nunn: You believe the recommendations you have made, if carried out, would eliminate the possibility of this recurring in this type scenario?

Dr. Schwoebel: We think these are steps clearly in the right direction. . . .

Senator Bingaman: Well, let me ask this in maybe a little less technical jargon. My understanding is that the Navy concluded that something was present there which could not be explained other than by some intentional act of one of the personnel involved. And they concluded that there was some type of homemade explosive device which caused this occurrence.

Did you find any evidence to support the claim that there was a homemade explosive device that caused this?

Dr. Schwoebel: We have concluded that we can neither prove nor disprove the existence of a chemical ignitor.

Senator Bingaman: So you found no evidence to prove it?

Dr. Schwoebel: That is correct.

Senator Bingaman: And you found no evidence to disprove it?

Dr. Schwoebel: That is correct.

Senator Bingaman: And then the obvious chain of logic that the Navy used was since there was not an accident, in their opinion, and there was not a malfunction, that this must have been—I think on page sixty-one of their report they said "the explosion in center gun turret II of the USS *Iowa* resulted from a wrongful, intentional act. And based on this investigative report, and after full review of all Naval Investigative Services reports to date, the wrongful, intentional act which caused this accident was most probably committed by Gunnersmate, Clayton Hartwig."

You are saying that you found no evidence to support the conclusion that there was an intentional act by Gunner's Mate Hartwig or anybody else?

Dr. Schwoebel: Our investigation was, as I have said, circumscribed. We looked at the technical aspects of this. A full investigation, of course, would include many other factors that you are aware of.

Senator Bingaman: Right.

Senator Warner: You were not looking for evidence of the type suggested by the Senator from New Mexico, were you?

Dr. Schwoebel: As I said, we can neither prove nor disprove the existence of an ignitor.

Senator Bingaman: I guess the point that I am just trying to nail down here, first of all, is that you have no evidence that you uncovered in your investigation to support the conclusion that this occurrence was the result of an intentional act?

Dr. Schwoebel: We have no evidence of that nature.

Senator Bingaman: And second, you do have, you believe, a plausible alternative explanation for the accident—or for the occurrence?

Dr. Schwoebel: We believe that there is a plausible explanation. To determine the extent of that plausibility depends very much on continued studies that would be done. . . .

Senator Levin: Thank you, Mr. Chairman. I would like to focus on the foreign materials question for a minute, because it seems to me that what the testimony this morning highlights is, number one, that there is an innocent alternative explanation for what happened which the Navy did not consider. But it also highlights that the Navy's explanation that there were unique foreign materials—and that was the basis of their report—is not accurate. . . .

The report concluded: This foreign residue, unique to the *Iowa* projectile, could not be duplicated by simple contamination of the gun chamber with steel wool and other chemicals that might remotely be present in a gun firing. You are telling us, as I understand it today, that these other chemicals are indeed commonly present, putting aside the steel wires for a moment?

Dr. Schwoebel: The other chemicals are common to that environment.

Senator Levin: So there is a very sharp disagreement on this point, that the other chemicals that were present there were not unique. In other words, these were common chemicals commonly found either in a turret or on a ship; correct?

Dr. Schwoebel: That is correct. . . .

Chairman Nunn: I want to thank all of our witnesses this morning; and I want to thank the numerous personnel of both the General Accounting Office and Sandia who contributed to this effort.

At the outset of this hearing, I stated that I anticipated that the testimony we would receive this morning would expose significant shortcomings in the Navy's investigation and would cast grave doubt on the conclusions the Navy drew as a result of their investigation. I believe that the testimony we have heard this morning has done that. Moreover, this morning's testimony identified a plausible explanation for the explosion.

I note with approval that the Secretary of the Navy has now directed that the firing of the 16-inch guns be suspended indefinitely and that the Navy's investigation be reopened. I also urge him to ensure that the reopened investigation considers all the matters brought out here today or any other matters that have come to the attention of the Navy.

I would like to summarize some of my thinking on this matter, based not only on the hearing this morning, but all the hearings the committee has had thus far. I want to emphasize very strongly that these are my first personal views, they are not committee views and should not be categorized as such. And they certainly do not necessarily reflect the views of any other member of the committee.

First, in terms of personnel. There are significant problems relating to the assignment of key officer and enlisted personnel to the battleships, in terms of adequate numbers, quality and experience. These problems are exacerbated by a lack of advancement opportunity for battleship personnel

Second, in terms of training. There are significant training problems relating to the 16-inch guns. This is demonstrated by the inadequate oversight inspections, the lack of a training plan for the battleship class, and the significant weaknesses in the Navy's formal training program.

Third, as to the cause of the explosion. The Navy's conclusion that the explosion was the result of a wrongful, intentional act is not supported by reliable, probative and substantial evidence. Sandia's alternative scenario of a high-speed overram of a powder bag with a reduced number of pellets in its trim layer is a plausible explanation, although more testing needs to be done in this area. And certainly we cannot draw any definitive conclusions as to the likelihood of that scenario this morning. We will have to get further information.

I think the Navy should continue to conduct serious exploration of the Sandia alternative with the active participation of Sandia experts, plus any other alternative that may come to the mind of the experts.

I also want to make one comment about the process that was involved here. I think the Navy's investigative effort itself was flawed. The Navy chose to use an informal, one-officer format, rather than the type of administrative hearing that is often used to investigate tragedies of this magnitude when individual responsibility may be at issue.

If a hearing procedure had been used, the Navy would have designated persons with a direct interest in the matter as parties, who would have had the right to representation by counsel, and a formal opportunity to present evidence, cross-examine witnesses, and ensure that the proceedings were conducted in a manner structured to seek the truth. There were many people I think that could have been named as parties and given that opportunity.

Adversarial relationships in this kind of investigation always take longer, but in the long run, they may take a shorter time, and certainly there is a real search for truth that is possible in an adversarial relationship with other people being represented with cross-examination and so forth, that was not present here.

I think the Navy, in light of this, should conduct a thorough review of its guidelines for investigations to (1) clarify when formal hearings should be required, certainly that does not mean they have to be done in every instance; and (2) also establish a clear standard of proof, particularly when an individual who is deceased has been pointed to as the likely perpetrator of a terrible tragedy of this nature; (3) provide representation for persons who are unable to represent their interests or reputation due to death or disability.

So I think the Navy needs to look at the process as well as the substance.

Any other comments?

I thank all the witnesses for being here.

Senator Bingaman has been bragging on your laboratory out there a long time, and we know now that he has been telling us a great deal of truth here. We appreciate your being here. [Whereupon, at 11:33 A.M., the hearing was adjourned.]

Following the conclusion of the hearing, the press intercepted us with inquiries, but we soon found ourselves alone in a side corridor and near an exit.

Schuler, Cooper, and Borders exchanged comments along the lines that they thought things had gone well. I walked along silently, commiserating with myself, enormously relieved to have the hearing behind us, now realizing what a strain these last six months had been. There were important issues at stake. It wasn't just a matter of getting all the technical issues straight, although that was crucial. It was a matter of bringing resolution to questionable conclusions and accusations with hard evidence.

I wondered why the Navy was not represented at the hearing by some of their investigating officers. Had Sandia's work really "eviscerated" the Navy's report as Senator Nunn had said? We had convincingly questioned the foreign materials work and presented a credible basis for an accident, but there were other issues that remained open and needed further work. Impact ignition was a viable accident mode—and the full-scale 16-inch gun studies would be the acid test.

Going into work on Monday morning, 28 May, was a special pleasure. Judy Jewell and Linda Vigil Lopez had decorated the office with flowers and balloon bouquets attached to notes of congratulation. A video tape of the hearing was running in the outer office. A number of the team members were enjoying the festive occasion. Several colleagues came by to express their congratulations for a job well done, and to say how happy they were to have Sandia take a key role in the investigation.

Rick DeBobes called and said that Sandia had really done an excellent job at the hearing. He said that he'd heard favorable comments from many different quarters including Senator Nunn and others who had watched the proceeding with great interest. He thanked me and asked that his congratulations be expressed to the entire team. A similar call came from the GAO.

The team members heard many expressions of pride in Sandia during the days after the hearing. It wasn't just that other Sandians believed that the results of our investigation were of good technical value, but that they felt that the Laboratories had stuck to the technical issues and had not deviated into speculation. These expressions of support by our colleagues were gratifying to all of us.

The urgencies of the continuing investigation concluded the brief respite, the pleasant retreat from what at times seemed like insurmountable problems and difficulties. I scheduled a team meeting for the next day to discuss our plans for the next phase of the investigation, and the tempo returned to a quickly paced investigation in just a few days.

Sandia would participate in yet another hearing before the end of the year. Congresswoman Mary Rose Oakar (D-Ohio), chairperson of the House Banking, Finance, Urban Affairs, Economic Stabilization Subcommittee, convened a hearing on the *Iowa* investigation on 8 November 1990. Those who would testify included Frank C. Conahan of the GAO, Vice Adm. Peter M. Hekman Jr., USN, and myself. This hearing (an abbreviated account is in Appendix F) would essentially reiterate salient portions of the testimony presented before the Senate Armed Services Committee.

15 Overdue Contacts

Early Summer 1990

THE TECHNICAL studies and preparations for our testimony before the Senate Armed Services Committee had required our total energy in the earlier months of Sandia's independent investigation. Completion of that phase allowed us an opportunity to draw a breath, to consider again the course of our efforts, to look beyond the important full-scale gun tests of impact ignition and its possible role in the explosion aboard the *Iowa*.

Indeed, preparation of the testimony reminded me again of how Sandia became involved in this investigation, and how we either overlooked or simply neglected to have substantive preliminary conversations with individuals and groups about this potentially significant study. These concerns were reinforced during the hearing by the tenor of comments and questions from Senator John Warner and underscored the diverse interests, motives, and perspectives of people and organizations connected with this investigation.

The letter requesting Sandia's participation in the *Iowa* investigation was signed by Senators Sam Nunn, chairman, Jeff Bingaman of New Mexico, and John Warner, all members of the Senate Armed Services Committee. The primary overseer of DOE national laboratories, including Sandia, was James Watkins, secretary of energy and a retired admiral. The nuclear weapons program for which Sandia was responsible was directed by Admiral J. M. "Mike" Barr, the DOE deputy assistant secretary for Military Applications.

These individuals with their committee and Navy connections might have provided valuable insight regarding Sandia's participation in the *Iowa* investigation, but none was substantively consulted about our involvement or progress with the exception of my informal talk with Admiral Barr. A discussion with our own Senator Bingaman, for example, would have been a simple matter and provided a direct perspective of the Senate Armed Services Committee's view of the Navy's investigation, the role that was envisioned for Sandia, and, perhaps, a few caution signs.

We indirectly came to understand that Senator Warner broadly accepted the Navy's scenario and would be a source of critical questions and inferences at the SASC hearing. This plan had been dramatically set aside by the explosion at Dahlgren the day before the hearing, an event that vindicated our concern about impact initiation.

The House of Representatives had made its position clear. They found the Navy investigation to be "flawed," as they noted in their understated way. Representative Mary Rose Oakar of Ohio had been a vocal critic of the Navy's investigation and frequently asked for information from the GAO during the course of Sandia's study. She would later call a hearing on the *Iowa* investigation in which Sandia would participate.

Our GAO contacts indicated that the outcome of this investigation was of interest to both the GAO and SASC for reasons that included the high cost of battleship operations when compared to the perceived benefit. The reasoning was, if the battleships were not only expensive but also unsafe, perhaps they should be decommissioned, particularly if Navy planning was not supporting them with appropriate manning and training. A thoughtful tactical and strategic plan for the battleships seemed to be absent, at least that was the deeper implication of the testimony by the commander of the USS *Iowa* at the time of the incident, Captain Fred P. Moosally Jr. (appendix D).[1]

The GAO occasionally provided us with useful information on the Washington scene, but we did not have official or formal contacts that steeped us in the innermost thoughts and motivations of the various groups. Preparation of our testimony in the absence of an understanding of these diverse views had a certain advantage, but I would rather have been aware of the various perspectives and orientations.

I had a free hand in preparing testimony for the Senate Armed Services Committee hearing, and I was fortunate to have excellent council from a few Sandians. Glen Cheney, a particularly able vice president and my immediate supervisor, was helpful in clearly defining the key issues. Cheney was interested in all aspects of the investigation and regularly dropped in to catch up on the latest. I frequently called on him to discuss complex problems and always found him to be a valuable source of advice and counsel.

Jim Mitchell, manager of Public Relations, was another valuable resource regarding larger issues and in articulating our work in ways that would be better understood. Beside serving as press officer for our investigation, I frequently sought his insightful judgment to discuss the complex issues that accompanied the *Iowa* investigation. His sense of how Congress and the public would view issues was usually on target, and he was invaluable in preparing testimony and other communications.

Mitchell devoted an enormous effort to the review of our reports, letters, and other documents. His crisp insights and wording of our positions brought clarity to an audience that would not abide the technical detail we customarily included. He sensitized us to the particular questions that were uppermost in the minds of both the media and the public, and his role was as important as that of any member of the technical team. In his laconic way, he frequently reminded me of his basic view of this investigation: "There are a hundred ways the perception of our independent investigation can be negative and we'll get a black eye—and just a few ways that we can do it right and be perceived as having made some contribution. Unfortunately, it's not possible to identify the right ways in advance." His way of voicing my innermost fear was disturbing and irritating, but the admixture of his cynicism served us well.

I talked with Cheney and Mitchell about the lack of intersection and interchange with the key groups. Wouldn't Sandia be in a stronger and more knowledgeable position if we established contact with at least our own senators? Wouldn't it be worth our time to update Senator Nunn's staff on our efforts, concerns, questions? How about updating Admiral Barr and the GAO at the same time, and hearing their perceptions of the key issues?

Both Cheney and Mitchell agreed that Sandia had not been astute in these interactions. Mitchell recounted other recent examples of insensitivity in the public relations area, soberly concluding, "We're not a very mature organization in some ways."

I thought that, since there had been no effort on the part of Sandia in establishing such contacts, we should take the initiative in redressing this situation. Cheney agreed and thought this was the time to rectify the situation by opening regular conversations and making key people aware of our current work.

It was in the early summer of 1990 that I made arrangements for Cheney and me to visit Senators Domenici and Bingaman, Rick DeBobes, the GAO, and Admiral Barr at DOE. We would apprise them of our work since the SASC hearing and discuss prospects for completing the investigation by the end of 1990. We would address questions or concerns they might have, and ask for comments, suggestions, or perspectives they would offer as we continued our work.

Our first stop was with Rick DeBobes at the Senate Armed Services Committee office. We went through the main points, the key investigative steps now taking place, and the prospect for completion of our work. DeBobes encouraged us to be thinking about a conclusion to our investigation, just as Admiral Barr had suggested some months earlier. He asked that we periodically inform him of progress and said he would keep us aware of any information that might be of value to us. This was the kind of informative contact that should have been developed at the outset.

Senator Domenici of New Mexico listened thoughtfully to our discussion, greatly appreciated the update, and noted his appreciation of the fine work Sandia had done in the investigation. Senator Bingaman was unavailable, but his chief staffer, Ed McGaffigan, provided a similar response.

The meeting with Admiral Barr took place in his office in Germantown. He had watched the testimony before SASC and listened carefully to what we had to say. He again emphasized the need to complete our investigation soon in keeping with his earlier advice. "The longer Sandia is involved, the more you will become immersed in areas outside your expertise. I advise you to complete your work as soon as possible."

We had established a few contacts that were long overdue, and I was gratified with the general outcome. It had been a worthwhile endeavor, not only in informing important and interested parties of our latest work but also in getting their perspectives and establishing an avenue for them to keep us informed as we proceeded with the investigation.

16 Gun-Scale Testing at Dahlgren

June–July 1990

GUN-SCALE testing of the overram-initiation concept was a critical area of investigation following the drop test explosion at Dahlgren. One of the directives from the Senate Armed Forces Committee hearing was that joint Navy and Sandia studies of impact initiation in 16-inch guns should go forward.

The explosion just before the SASC hearing had taken place in a drop test that simulated overram in a 16-inch gun and ended the Navy's argument that small-scale tests at Sandia were irrelevant. The Navy prepared to conduct full-scale overram field tests using the rammer that had been removed from the center gun room of Turret II of the *Iowa*, and a simulated breech that could withstand any explosion that might occur. There were two fundamental questions that needed to be examined in these experiments. Would impact ignition occur in the 16-inch gun configuration, and if so, how was ignition dependent on rammer speed and the number of trim-layer pellets?

On 1 June we requested that the Navy begin a statistical survey of the number of propellant bags with various numbers of trim-layer pellets. This would provide basic information needed to calculate the probabilities of impact ignition in the existing stockpile of propellant bags. On the same date, Captain Miceli forwarded the test plan for full-scale impact-initiation tests at Dahlgren. Judy Jewell, my secretary, left me a note: "Captain Miceli called to make sure you had a chance to review this material. Says they haven't made any drops yet, still working with the instruments and photography equipment. He's interested in your quick review of the test plan, especially as regards instrumentation and photo coverage."

The Navy was devoting substantial resources to setting up the full-scale experiments.

Paul Cooper and Karl Schuler went to Dahlgren to observe preparations in mid-June. On the twenty-first, I met with them to get their reactions to preparations at the test site. Even before Schuler began, I could see that he was not pleased with everything at Dahlgren. "I got to Dahlgren Wednesday night and found that the Navy team had planned six phases of tests," he said. "They've included lots of instrumentation on the rammer control linkage to observe how the linkage reacts when an explosion occurs, which all sounds good. My perception is that Captain Miceli's objective is not to broadly explore impact ignition, but to disprove the Sandia scenario and go back to the Navy's idea of an improvised chemical device as the cause of the explosion. He's convinced that the ram speed was only two feet/second and may do the majority of testing at low rammer speeds. Of course there may not be an ignition event under these circumstances. I was also concerned when Miceli briefed four admirals at Dahlgren on impact ignition while we were there, but didn't invite Paul and me to participate in the discussion."

That was disappointing, of course, but there was no reason to expect a new perspective from the captain. Cooper and Schuler obviously should have been included, just as we had included the captain in our salient discussions of this subject.

"Captain Miceli had to tell the brass his story about how the explosion took place," I said. "The same one we've all heard several times. And he had to tell them without any Sandians being around to point out the shortcomings. If the four admirals were worth their salt they would have insisted that you both be a part of that briefing."

Schuler nodded and continued: "The Navy troops were really impressed by the drop test explosion and now believe that the Sandia inadvertent overram scenario is probably the correct explanation for the explosion.[1] They have lots of scenarios based on overram initiation, but Miceli won't let them carry out any work on those ideas."

Unfortunately, the captain and those at higher levels of the Navy were still completely wedded to the suicide-murder scenario, incapable of openly exploring inadvertent accident pathways.

Cooper recounted his perceptions of things at Dahlgren: "Miceli is the only one in the picture who still wants to show that the incident aboard the *Iowa* was an intentional act. Fortunately, as Karl said, the workers at Dahlgren are trying to find out what actually happened. My impression was that the four Admirals are basically technical people. They expressed views quite different from those of the captain's and asked me a lot of technical questions about our impact ignition work. However, I think the tone of the Dahlgren investigation is not right. Miceli wants Sandia completely out of live full-scale testing in terms of what tests are done. He wants total control."

In spite of Captain Miceli's desire to control the testing, the thrust of the experiments at Dahlgren was to determine whether overram ignition could occur in a 16-inch gun. I believed that, one way or another, we could require that a reasonable number of high-speed overram tests be done.

Another unresolved part of our scenario was determination of the rammer speed at the time of the explosion, and if the rammer control handle could have been moved to a lower speed position by the force of the explosion. Instrumentation of the rammer linkage would help resolve that issue.

We talked further about the rammer mechanism. The Navy technical people at Dahlgren had told Schuler and Cooper that they found a very dirty oil filter in the *Iowa* rammer after the explosion. On the other hand, the Louisville people said the rammer ran perfectly after the explosion, more undocumented and possibly conflicting information that seemed all too normal for this investigation.

Cooper and Schuler spoke about the possibility of a fouled rammer mechanism and its possible relation to the explosion. Could a sticking valve have lulled an inexperienced rammerman into pushing the control lever more and more forward since the rammer wasn't responding—and suddenly getting a high-speed response from the system? There were, of course, undocumented reports of erratic operation of rammers, including testimony at one of the hearings.

Cooper and Schuler had learned a lot during their trip, both of a technical and nontechnical nature. They would return to Dahlgren in a few days.

On 28 June I spoke with Orval Jones, the executive vice president for weapon and other programs at Sandia. I reviewed the current technical studies and how we hoped to close the investigation and end Sandia's involvement as soon as possible. I also mentioned my concerns regarding Captain Miceli's perspective for testing at Dahlgren—that the thrust was oriented toward proving that the Sandia scenario was wrong rather than trying to understand what could have happened. It appeared that the Dahlgren tests were being structured to show that overram initiation could not occur, rather than to find the conditions under which it could occur. I wondered aloud if we should try to approach the Navy through people who might be more open to other perspectives.

Jones talked about his views of interactions with others during such conflicts and our approach of full disclosure to the Navy. He felt we should not escalate the conflict but continue to work closely with the naval officers as we had been. In general, the interaction had produced good results and served our investigation well.

That same day I received one of many letters from outside parties regarding the Sandia investigation: "I am a mother of one of the forty-seven young men killed aboard the USS *Iowa*. . . . I wondered if this . . . could have been a factor in the explosion."

It was difficult to read these letters and sense the deep pain and sincere desire to understand what had happened. I did my best to respond to such letters, going beyond the technical detail, trying to convey a sense that dedicated people were doing their utmost to find the cause, sure that my response always fell far short. I often wished that all those connected with the investigation would focus on possible causes of the explosion as thoughtfully as some of the survivors.

Cooper and Schuler called from Dahlgren on 3 July, excited about a recent test. Full-scale impact-initiation tests at rammer speeds of 2, 4, 8, and 14 feet per second had taken place in the field-mounted 16-inch gun. One of the tests at 14 feet per second, the highest speed the rammer could attain, had exploded! In addition, load cell studies had shown that compression in the lower region of the bags, where the rammer head pushes the aft bag, was consistently higher. In other words, this was a particularly sensitive region for pellet damage to occur. The loads in this region could go as high as twenty-three thousand pounds at 14 feet per second. Gratifying results! It had now been demonstrated that an explosion could be caused by overramming the propellant into a 16-inch gun at high rammer speeds.

Captain Miceli called on 11 July to give me a rundown on recent studies at Dahlgren. "We've now run twenty of the phase three [overram] tests in the 16-inch gun simulator without an initiation [explosion]," he said. "We did, however, have an initiation in a bag compression test at 14 feet per second in the simulator earlier in the month."

The latter was the test that Cooper and Schuler had described to me earlier. I sensed that the captain wanted to minimize the fact that an initiation had occurred, to leave the Navy's scenario unchanged, to ignore the fact that the explosion might have been the result of an inadvertent action and an unknown safety problem. I couldn't resist a smile at his reference to an initiation in a "bag compression test," as though that was different from an overram test. I arranged my schedule so I could be at Dahlgren on 19–20 July to review the work firsthand. I was anxious to see the experimental setup and talk face to face with the Navy working-level people.

I arrived in Washington late on the afternoon of 18 July and drove south to Waldorf. The motel was located on the highway about an hour from Dahlgren. Captain Miceli had left a note at the desk that he'd be at the motel at 8:00 A.M. and we would leave for Dahlgren shortly thereafter. Tim Stone from the GAO had also left a note that he and Jerry Herley were staying at the motel across the street and would join us at 8:00 A.M.

I found Tim Stone in the modest coffee room the next morning, and Captain Miceli joined us in a few minutes, impeccably dressed in his whites. He was consistently in uniform and took justifiable pride in being a captain in the U.S. Navy. It was the first time I'd seen him since the SASC hearing. Our eyes met in a different way this time, his casual arrogance slightly diminished but his gregarious nature unchanged.

The captain suggested I leave my car and ride with him to Dahlgren. This would give us some one-on-one time, probably the only opportunity we would have during the day. The drive to Dahlgren was scenic, and the captain preferred lighter conversation than usual on such occasions. He made a few passing comments about things he thought I'd said at the SASC hearing that "surprised" him, but he followed each such comment with an unrelated thought. He seemed to want to acknowledge the hearing, but not talk about it in any depth. I could understand that, and I listened to his continuing light talk without saying much.

He mentioned that he was surprised that I'd testified that Sandia had been told that the cleanup operation aboard the *Iowa* involved the use of steel wool. "I was thunderstruck to hear you say that—it certainly didn't come from me." He quickly followed up with another subject, as though he wanted to make a point without me contesting it in some way, nodding and gesturing in his usual way. Of course, I had not testified that steel wool was used in the cleanup, but that we hadn't received a conclusive response from the Navy about the use of steel wool. I found his remark to be all the more strange since he had earlier reported the use of steel wool in a memo to Admiral Carter, and subsequently said the memo was incorrect.

As the captain continued with his low-key remarks, I sensed that there had been a number of conversations between him and his superiors since the hearing, that he was reiterating some of the discussions they had about the Sandia testimony. He seemed to be intoning questions that must have been put to him by the senior officers. I thought it must have been hard for the captain to speak to those questions, to defend serious technical oversights in the Navy's investigation, and to have his investigation described by the chairman of the Senate Armed Services Committee as being "eviscerated."

The Sandia testimony had raised serious questions and refuted some of the basic information the captain and his team had presented. It must have been difficult and embarrassing for a man like Captain Miceli. I felt that the edge of his personality had been changed in a way, but I never thought for a moment that he had given up on his concept of what had happened to cause the tragedy aboard the *Iowa*.

Captain Miceli mentioned a recent incident aboard the *Iowa* when one of our materials experts, Bill Chambers, along with other Sandians made a visit for additional information. The captain said that a sailor approached and offered Bill some propellant pellets that he claimed were left over after the explosion. Miceli witnessed the offer and all hell broke loose. It stimulated a full search of the ship that turned up several sailors with propellant pellets in their possession, probably souvenirs collected during the cleanup process. I felt sorry for the crewman who had made the well-intentioned offer. He should have been thanked for coming forward.

While I was thinking about the search that Captain Miceli had just mentioned, he went on to say that more incriminating evidence of Hartwig's sexual deviations had also been uncovered. I glanced in his direction and waited for him to continue, but he didn't elaborate. I took that to mean that the evidence was fragmentary or simply rumor. If it had been anything substantive he would have told me about it in detail to further support his views. His demeanor took on a darker tone when he spoke of homosexuality. It was obviously something he deeply detested.

The captain raced along the highway well above the posted speed, his normal style. He relished his Cadillac and enjoyed classical music, one or two of the presets on the radio. We came to the guard gate and were motioned through without stopping, the captain crisply returning the guard's salute.

Immediately south of the gate was an access to the bridge, a long span that led to the field experimental area now visible on the other side of the bridge. The big guns mounted outside on the range fired test shots to the southeast, down the long bay. The day was clear and the impressive view as we crossed the bridge is still with me. There were several tall towers marking the site of the gun mounts and the primary instrumentation facilities.

I asked Captain Miceli about the name Dahlgren, and he related the interesting story of the man for whom this base was named. Ironically, the story centered on a tragic explosion and loss of life. The captain was interested in and knew a great deal about naval heroes and men of great accomplishment. As we drove into the gun mount area, he pointed out the cast 16-inch gun barrels that were stored outside by the score, many from the 1940s. They were neatly stacked in geometric arrays, huge blank barrels that would probably never be machined for their original purpose.

We drove to the same building we had held a conference in once before. The conference room was on the second deck and overlooked the impressive gunnery range on the bay. We entered the back door of the building and climbed up the open steel steps. The first deck appeared to be a storage area for aging electronic gear that probably was used for gun tests in earlier days. The stairs offered a vantage point for viewing much of that interesting old equipment.

The conference room was filled with men, several civilian technical people from the Dahlgren facility that were new to me, a uniformed technical advisor to the admiral's Technical Oversight Board that had been formed in response to the SASC hearing, the Navy team with Chief Tonahill, the GAO people, a scientist from the Army's Ballistic Research Lab at Aberdeen, and Cooper and Schuler from Sandia.

Apparently they had been waiting for our arrival. I introduced myself and shook hands with those I didn't know and greeted the others. It was good to see Cooper and Schuler again. The group took their seats and the meeting began with a series of talks about recent overram tests by several working-level Navy people.

Frank Tse, NOS Indian Head, began the session. His studies were closely related to Cooper's earlier subscale studies at Sandia: "I've extended the subscale data of Sandia, including studies of fewer numbers of trim pellets. This work has shown that ignition energy (energy delivered by the falling weight) was lowest if there were five to ten pellets in the trim layer, and in that case, the minimum energy required was about one thousand foot-pounds (a measure of energy) to cause initiation."

Tse had set up an experimental apparatus very similar to the one used by Paul Cooper in his studies at Sandia. He had found a minimum in the energy required to cause initiation of the black powder pouch by the fracture of the pellets in an overram.

It later became apparent that humidity was a factor in ignition energy—and that the Navy and Sandia results could be brought into agreement with the proper corrections for humidity variations between arid New Mexico and humid Indianhead. I was impressed with the thoroughness of Tse's work, as were Cooper and Schuler.

Steve Coffey, of the Naval Surface Weapons Center, was the next speaker. He had examined the ignition energy of pellets in various fracture orientations and was primarily interested in determining the threshold for ignition, that is, the minimum energy required to produce ignition. His studies demonstrated that initiation could occur at very low energies, much lower than we had imagined. An inescapable conclusion from Coffey's work was that any overram that forced the propellant against the projectile was a roll of the dice and could result in an explosion.

I thought of the words of Lt. Daniel Meyer and GMG Steve Brooks as we talked with them in the center gun room of Turret I last December: "The deck plate lore is that overramming is dangerous. . . . We know about the Navy's experiments and we don't believe them" (speaking of the earlier experiments by the Navy's Technical Review Team in which overramming was eliminated as a potential cause of the explosion).

In another interesting and well-organized study, Bob Lieb of Aberdeen Proving Ground had studied fracture and crack propagation in the pellets. The next speaker was Tom Doran of NSWC. We had known Doran since the first meeting of the two teams in January. He was an able and very competent person—a key member of the Navy Technical Review Team, dedicated to bringing as much understanding to the cause of the explosion as possible. He had fashioned the special milling device that enabled the removal of the projectile from the center gun aboard the *Iowa* following the explosion.

Doran talked about his exhaustive studies of drop tests, including test eighteen that exploded the day before the Sandia testimony at SASC. In the tests that had taken place since then, there had been five more explosions. The captain had not told me about five explosions. Doran presented the data and talked about each explosion in detail, then went on to talk about open field tests in which the rammer from the *Iowa* was used to overram powder bags into a simulated breech causing explosions at ram speeds near the maximum of 14 feet per second.

Doran had also tested an intriguing configuration in which a single propellant pellet was mislocated in the lower quadrant of the bag, just ahead of the ignition pad. This was right where the highest loads are delivered by the rammer. There had been an explosion on the very first overram.

While Doran had not repeated this experiment, the three of us thought the result was most meaningful. Doran's insight was that a misoriented pellet just ahead of the ignition pad would be more dangerous because there was less cloth material for the hot particles to penetrate to ignite the black powder. It made sense. The configuration he used involved just one bag, not two as in our scheme.

Doran's work was very insightful and was just the kind of work that was needed. Perhaps there were other, even more dangerous pellet configurations that no one had yet considered. His talk stirred a great deal of discussion. It was a fine piece of work and an excellent contribution to better understanding this important safety vulnerability in 16-inch gun systems.

We took a break in the meeting and I privately offered congratulations to Doran for his fine work as we had a cup of coffee. He said he wanted to further explore this avenue, but Captain Miceli had given him explicit instructions to not conduct any more experiments of that kind. Tom said that Captain Miceli wanted to clear personally all experiments in advance. No more off-the-cuff stuff.

Doran had clearly identified an important pellet misorientation, one that was apparently more sensitive to impact ignition than any configuration considered so far. His results were the most significant thing we had heard all day. Captain Miceli's instruction to him was one of those disconnects in logic that defied any rationale, that had no place in an open investigation.

After the break, Sam Burnley of NAVSWC talked about the Sandia extrapolation to full gun conditions from Cooper's earlier studies, and the actual data at full scale. It was apparent that the gun experiments involved energy losses that displaced the ignition to higher energy levels. His excellent analysis established the magnitude of energy losses in the 16-inch gun.

The Navy working-level investigators had put on a great set of talks and stimulated valuable discussion. I wondered if the captain knew in advance what they were going to say to the Sandia visitors, if he was aware that the talks might have been a little too forthcoming for his taste. He hadn't said a word during the presentations.

I expressed my appreciation to all the investigators for the fine presentations. It was refreshing to have a technical exchange!

Captain Miceli stood before the group and began a discussion that went on for some time: "I've got a problem and I need your advice. The USS *Wisconsin* deploys to the Mediterranean on 6 August and the Joint Chiefs of Staff have asked me an important question. 'What will you require to allow the ship to shoot its 16-inch guns?'"

He stopped for a moment, scanning the group as I'd seen him do before.

He seemed to intuitively understand the strength of an appropriate pause. The importance of the question by the Joint Chiefs was, of course, related to heightening tensions with Iraq. The implicit dilemma was, how could the suspension of 16-inch gun firing be maintained if the *Wisconsin* was in a war zone and needed to fire in self-defense or in support of various actions? And the question not only applied to the *Wisconsin*, but all of the battleships.

"We've had a 100 percent inspection of all the powders bags that will be used," the captain continued. "All the Crane 87 [propellant bags with a trim layer] has been removed. We've made sure all the Crane 84 has no misplaced pellets under the pad [referring to Doran's insightful experiments], and the Crane 85 has no trim layer. What controls, if any, are now needed? It would not be sensible to send the ship into this zone with a moratorium on firing. We'll institute special training for the gun crews to assure that proper ram speed and ram distance are strictly adhered to."

There were several comments from the group in response to the JCS question, most acknowledging the conflict between safety of the gun crews and safety of the ship in a region of conflict. The consensus among the Navy team and some of the Dahlgren investigators was to allow firing of the guns. Some of those who had served on battleships said there was no problem, the crews would be careful, the additional training would effectively deal with any rammer control problems, the guns had been fired thousands of times without difficulty, the odds of a problem were remote.

I could not agree with the general sentiment and felt that the Navy was on the threshold of another questionable decision, a decision that could be improperly implemented and endanger crews that could still include poorly trained individuals. "I appreciate the danger of entering a zone of conflict without being able to use an important weapon system," I said, "but there is also danger in using 16-inch guns without controls on the rammers, particularly in view of questionable training of individuals on the gun crews and unresolved questions about erratic rammer operation. In my flight related experiences, I've learned not to fly unless I'm satisfied that everything is right, the weather, the equipment, everything. In the situation we're discussing, there are a number of things that are not right. With the deployment to the Mediterranean this soon, there is inadequate time to properly train the crews on how essential it is that ram speed and ram distance be controlled. We know from the GAO review that crew training on these battleships has been poor, and I don't think anyone can guarantee that the training will be properly implemented. No one can assure that an inexperienced crewman will not be put into the wrong place at the wrong time, someone who missed the extra training. Just this kind of thing may have taken a role in the explosion aboard the *Iowa*. In addition, control of ram distance is needed to assure there are no inadvertent overrams. We've just heard from some of the people at this meeting how low the threshold can be for initiation and I think it's only prudent that speed and distance controls be added to the guns before they are fired again. If there is another incident like the *Iowa*, it would be a tragedy that would be impossible to rationalize or justify. The battleship gun crews would say a 'fix' wasn't implemented, and they would be right. I recommend that the response to the JCS be that rammer controls are required."

Absolute silence, mute testimony to how unwelcome my remarks were to a least a few of those assembled. Since there didn't seem to be anything more to say, I thanked the Navy investigators again and rose to leave. Cooper and Schuler joined me and the three of us bid our farewells and stepped down the stairs to parking area. I was the first out of the building and stood by one of the cars waiting for the others. I wanted to get in the car, to leave, but it was locked. I was concerned that the Navy would decide to go ahead without rammer controls and perhaps I wanted to physically distance myself from what seemed an imprudent risk.

Cooper came up to me. "I'm glad you said that, Dick. That was really important." It meant a lot to me that he thought it was the right position. Even if the Navy didn't adhere to my recommendation, they would now have to proceed with even greater caution with any plan to activate the guns on the *Wisconsin*.

We hadn't heard the last of recertifying the battleships for 16-inch gun firings. The Persian Gulf crisis continued to heat up, and the battleships could play an important role.

On 6 August, Captain Miceli sent a letter outlining the program of propellant impact tests and powder bag inspections he had instituted in preparation for lifting the moratorium on the firing of 16-inch guns. It was a long and detailed plan. They were being careful. He followed this with a letter to me on 16 August with more results, and closed with the following paragraph:

> Based on the results which I have described, the Naval Sea Systems Command has recommended to the Chief of Naval Operations that the restriction on firing of the 16"/50 gun systems with the D839 and D846 be lifted. Your comments on these results and support for the recommendation are urgently requested. On behalf of Vice Adm. Peter M. Hekman, Commander, Naval Sea Systems Com-

mand, I would like to express the Navy's appreciation for all the efforts which you and your team, particularly Mr. Paul Cooper and Dr. Karl Schuler, have given to help the Navy in this matter.

Respectfully, Joseph D. Miceli, Captain, USN

The Navy wanted to assure that specific lots of propellant could be safely used aboard the *Wisconsin*. Special lots of bag charges had been configured so that there was no trim layer. This was in accord with one of our recommendations before SASC and the discussion we had had at Dahlgren.

The Navy also began screening other lots to remove all bags with less than approximately twenty pellets in the trim layer.[2] They tested the remaining bags at Dahlgren for susceptibility to initiation by overram. Data of this kind was forwarded to Sandia by Captain Miceli with the request that we put on our stamp of approval for its use aboard the battleships.

My position was that we could approve the statistical treatment of the data obtained by the Navy, but we could not approve use of these propellant bags since that involved operational factors of which we had no knowledge or control. The captain agreed to that caveat, and I forwarded two letters to him to the effect that we agreed with the treatment of the data. From that point on I recommended that the Navy approve, on its own, the use of various lots for the operational battleships.

The full-scale testing at Dahlgren to this point had brought forward several important findings. First, and most important, impact ignition had been demonstrated in 16-inch guns. Second, the Navy working level had demonstrated that the threshold for such ignition was low, and this implied that virtually any overram that jammed the propellant into the projectile could cause an explosion. Third, other configurations of misoriented pellets (at the aft of the bag, just in front of the black powder patch) had been briefly explored and were apparently even more dangerous than the ones we had found involving trim-layer pellets. Unfortunately, this critical finding was not fully explored.

17 Technical Oversight Board

21–22 August 1990

A NEW element of the Navy's reopened investigation following the Senate Armed Services Committee hearing was its creation of the Technical Oversight Board, composed of active-duty and retired Navy admirals. While the purpose of this board was not precisely defined, we assumed the members would review information provided by the two technical teams and make recommendations to the chief of Naval Operations.

Members brought a mixture of technical training and naval gun experience to the board, which consisted of Rear Adm. Donald P. Roane, USN (ret.), Technical Oversight Board chairman; Rear Adm. Roger B. Horne, USN, deputy commander for engineering and ship design and Naval Sea Systems Command chief officer; Rear Adm. George R. Meinig Jr., commander, Naval Sea Systems Command; Rear Adm. Walter H. Cantrell, USN, vice commander, Naval Sea Systems Command; and Rear Adm. Douglas J. Katz, USN, former battleship commanding officer. Rear Adm. Robert H. Ailes, Naval Sea Systems Command, would be participating with the board, but as a nonmember.

The board met several times with the Navy investigating team following the SASC hearing and scheduled a meeting with the Sandia team for 21–22 August 1990. The review at Sandia would also include Captain Miceli of Naval Sea Systems Command and three personnel from the GAO: Martin M. Ferber, director of Navy Issues; Tim Stone; and Brad Hathaway.

On 20 July I sent a note to the Sandia team members with a schedule for the meeting. The meeting would begin at 1:00 P.M. on 21 August in accord with Admiral Roane's request and conclude midafternoon on the twenty-second. Captain Miceli, attentive to the details, sent a letter specifying the shape of the conference table, seating arrangement, and the place card form for each member.

I met the admirals at visitor control. We walked to a conference room in the main administration building and met several Sandians already present. After a brief welcome by Glen Cheney, vice president for Components, I reviewed the schedule and we began what was one of the more definitive discussions of our investigation.

The presentations included talks by Jim Borders and Mark Davis on foreign materials, Karl Schuler on rammer and powder-train mechanics, Mel Baer and Ken Gwinn on interior ballistics and dynamic response of the powder train, Steve Harris on explosive materials analysis, and Paul Cooper on impact-ignition experiments. We also took the admirals on a tour and demonstration at Cooper's explosive test site.

Foreign Materials Analysis: Jim Borders

The charter of our materials analysis group was to perform analysis of the rotating band and other relevant samples for the USS *Iowa* investigation, and supplement and compare their findings with analyses by the Navy.

Borders outlined the three major questions that had been addressed: analysis of "foreign" materials on the rotating band from the *Iowa* projectile, normal battleship background concentrations and other sources of such materials, and whether it could be affirmed that these foreign materials originated from the chemical ignition device postulated by the Navy. He discussed observations of iron fibers in the rotating band by Naval Weapons Support Center–Crane. Crane reported that these fibers had abnormally high surface levels of calcium and chlorine. The Navy hypothesized that steel wool was a constituent of the chemical ignitor and claimed that high surface concentrations of calcium and chlorine on the fibers were only present when they were directly exposed to the chemical reaction between HTH and glycols.

As noted earlier, the Sandia team examined the Crane data and found that only a single fiber had been observed by Crane with high concentrations of calcium. The one encrusted fiber featured in the Navy report was not representative of the thirty or so other fibers found in the cannelure. Moreover, this single encrusted fiber could not be located by Crane for corroborative studies. Other fibers were found to have nominal levels of calcium and chlorine on their surfaces by the Sandia team, not unlike many other surfaces in the gun rooms and turrets of not only the *Iowa* but other battleships as well. Moreover, a commonly used cleaning and lubricating fluid, Break-Free, was also a source of these elements. Our conclusion was that the concentrations of chlorine and calcium on the fibers were typical of those found on many other surfaces in turrets and gun rooms, and were not a indicator of the presence of a chemical ignitor.

Borders went on to discuss NWSC-Crane's identification of three materials on the rotating band as glycols. The Sandia group reexamined Crane's analysis and determined that one of the glycols had been misidentified and was not a glycol but a phenol. Crane agreed with this finding. More important, Sandia found that the remaining two glycols and the phenol were constituents of Break-Free. Large quantities of Break-Free had been used in freeing the projectile from the gun after the explosion and had seeped into the cannelure. We concluded that the presence of glycols in the rotating band was due to residues of Break-Free and unrelated to the presence of the chemical ignitor proposed by the Navy.

Borders noted that Crane had found a single polymeric fragment on the *Iowa*'s rotating band that they had identified as PE/PET laminate, a material essentially identical to that used in Seal-A-Meals and MREs (meals ready-to-eat). The Navy hypothesized that a plastic baggy had been used to contain HTH powder and also a glycol-based liquid in a glass container that was crushed in the overram to cause the ignition.

The Sandia team found other significant sources of PE/PET materials, including the Dacron brush used to clean these guns and various forms of clothing worn by the crew. The instrumental analyses for Dacron plus a constituent of Break-Free were identical to the analyses for PE/PET. It was later confirmed that there was actually no documentation that the polymer fragment found by the Navy came from the cannelure of the center gun projectile, and presence of the polymeric fragment was thereafter ignored.

These were the main points in Border's presentation, and they were powerful counters to assertions and conclusions in the Navy technical report. The implication was that with one exception, the foreign materials identified by the Navy and claimed by Admiral Milligan as evidence of a chemical ignitor were expected contaminations from ordinary sources.

The single exception was the presence of small fragments of steel or steel wool. In the fall of 1990, however, we examined the 16-inch projectiles from the other two guns in Turret II and found similar iron fibers. In fact, there were no statistically discernible differences in the size distributions of the fibers from the center gun, and those from the left and right guns. Since the latter projectiles were sealed in the left and right guns at the time of the explosion, fibers on those projectiles could not have come from the chemical device proposed by the Navy. We concluded that these three projectiles had been subjected to similar environments that produced the fiber contaminations prior to the explosion, and that the iron fibers on the center gun projectile had no connection to the hypothetical chemical ignition device proposed by the Navy investigators.

Rammer and Powder Train Mechanics: Karl W. Schuler

Karl Schuler presented a complete picture of all that was known about this subject at this point in the investigation. He reviewed the process by which gouges on the spanning tray had been correlated with specific links in the rammer chain, and how rammer position had been determined at the time of the explosion. From this analysis it was possible to establish that the propellant bags had been compressed against the projectile when the explosion occurred.

The compression of the propellant bags was estimated to be approximately 1.25 inches, and from the dynamic analysis, a rammer speed of approximately 6.5 feet per second or more would have been required to achieve that level of compression. At 6.5 feet per second the peak load delivered to the trim layer would have been over five thousand pounds about 13 milliseconds after the propellant bags first contacted the projectile. In other words, the analysis indicated that ramming of the propellant occurred at a higher than normal speed and that the rammer went well beyond the normal stopping point and forced the propellant against the projectile. These were characteristics of an uncontrolled and higher than normal speed overram of the propellant.

The conclusion of Schuler's presentation was that the extent of the overram and speed of the rammer would probably have fractured transverse pellets in the trim layer, and this in turn could have initiated an explosion in the propellant train. One important interpretation of this was that the explosion was an accident due to an inadvertent higher than normal speed overram.

Internal Ballistics and Powder Train Response: Mel Baer

Mel Baer presented his work on the interior ballistics and dynamic response of the powder train. Baer and Ken Gwinn had developed a calculational model of the open-breech explosion. This model depicted the ignition, fluidization of the pellets, propagation of the flame, and two-phase flow of the hot gases and pellets out of the open breech. The results of the model calculations were consistent with the ignition site being between the first and second propellant bag in the train. The calculated pressure profile versus time was also consistent with measurements that had been made in two tests by the Navy (numbers twelve and twenty-seven) at Dahlgren.

Using the pressure profile, Baer and Gwinn calculated forward movement of the projectile in the open-breech explosion which was in very good agreement with the actual observation of the projectile movement in the center gun of Turret II. Baer's conclusion was that the most likely ignition point was at the rear of the propellant bag nearest to the projectile. The explosion involved only about 10 percent of the propellant, the rest being ejected out of the open breech. While hot gases from the explosion produced impact on objects behind the breech, the ejected propellant pellets delivered an order of magnitude greater impulse to equipment like the rammer lever. This would have tended to displace the lever to a lower speed position. The implication was that the position of the rammer handle after the explosion was not indicative of its position at the moment of the explosion.

Explosive Materials Analysis: Steve Harris

Harris reviewed work on three subjects: the analysis of chemical stabilizer in the propellant and the initiation properties of both nitrocellulose (propellant) and black powder.

Liquid chromatography had been used to analyze the levels of DPA and three decomposition products of DPA that also contributed to stabilization in propellant pellets. While the mean DPA level was within the acceptable range, there were substantial variations in DPA levels among various pellets.

Initiation of the propellant and black powder was examined for impact, electrostatic discharge, and thermal and shock sensitivity using, in the case of the propellant, pellets that represented both higher and lower concentrations of DPA. None of this extensive testing revealed unusual or unsafe properties of these materials.

Harris's work corroborated earlier work by the Navy technical team with regard to the stability of the propellant.

Ignition Experiments: Paul Cooper

Discussion of the ignition experiments by Paul Cooper was the final talk for the Technical Oversight Board. He began his discussion of the D846 pellet fracture ignition work by describing the subscale fixtures he devised for these experiments. A drop weight weighing thirteen hundred pounds slid along a vertical guide bar and impacted the assembly, simulating the overram situation. The height of the drop weight was simply related to the speed of the rammer.

Cooper had carried out initiation studies for various number of pellets in the trim layer in his 8-inch subscale drop assembly and established the relationship between impact energy per trim pellet versus the number of trim pellets. As might be expected, the energy per pellet required for initiation was greater for larger numbers of trim pellets. In other words, the lowest initiation energies were for those cases in which there were just a few pellets in the trim layer and the drop energy could be concentrated in the fracture of fewer pellets.

Cooper extrapolated these results for his 8-inch fixture to what might be expected in a 16-inch gun. As he carefully pointed out, there were several assumptions in making such an extrapolation. This included the assumption that no energy loss would occur in the actual 16-inch gun situation, which we knew to be incorrect.

Cooper briefly reviewed results of full-scale tests at Dahlgren and the overram initiated explosions that had occurred in 16-inch gun arrangements. The results of these experiments clearly demonstrated that overramming propellant against the projectile could lead to an explosion of the kind that occurred aboard the *Iowa*, and contradicted an earlier conclusion by the Navy that "impact and compression of the bag charges were not contributing factors in the *Iowa* incident."

At the conclusion of the talk, we took the admirals to the remote explosive site and Cooper demonstrated the pellet fracture–initiation effect for them. Captain Miceli seemed tense and ill at ease throughout the proceedings. My impression was that he was uncomfortable with the steady stream of information that convincingly undermined the Navy's scenario. He was visibly disturbed when Mark Davis made an innocuous historical reference to the two turret explosions that occurred aboard the battleship USS *Mississippi* in 1924 and 1943.

Admiral Ailes also became agitated and heatedly said that those events had nothing whatsoever to do with the *Iowa* explosion and "would not be discussed." We were perplexed by the emotion surrounding this brief exchange. The topic was obviously a sensitive one for the Navy, and the complete files on those explosions have never been made available to the public.

The Technical Oversight Board asked many questions and contributed to the discussions throughout the meeting. Their high-level experience with large gun systems was evident, and they were able to understand and discuss several details in the presentations. (About a week later a letter arrived from Vice Admiral Hekman in which he expressed his thanks for the presentations and interchange.)

This was the only meeting with the Technical Oversight Board in which our work was reviewed. I and a few other Sandians attended a meeting of the board with the Navy in the summer of 1991 in which only evidence for the Navy's original scenario was again discussed. I am not aware of any reports of recommendations that the board may have made to the chief of Naval Operations.

An important undercurrent to these discussions was the implication of our findings with regard to the safety of 16-inch guns in overrams and the relation of these findings to lifting restrictions on firing the guns. The Persian Gulf crisis continued to build following the August invasion of Kuwait, and the future battleship role could be important. This was not a topic of conversation with the Technical Oversight Board, but their concerns must have bridged our findings with the possibility of future battleship operations in the Persian Gulf.

Just a few months later, on 26 October, a blustery and rainy day, the USS *Iowa* was decommissioned in a ceremony held aboard the ship at Norfolk. Several relatives of the forty-seven crewman killed in the explosion attended the ceremony. The great ship would eventually be moved to the Philadelphia Naval Yard.

18 Last Words on Foreign Materials

20 November 1990

THE NAVAL Weapons Support Center at Crane, Indiana, is located on a one-hundred-square-mile reservation south of Indianapolis. Employing about five thousand people, it was commissioned on 8 December 1941 to provide ordinance products to the military. This includes the U.S. Navy 16-inch projectiles and propellants used on battleships. By a strange circumstance, the lot of propellant that was being used in the center gun of Turret II of the USS *Iowa* on the morning of 19 April 1989 was manufactured while Captain Miceli was serving as commander of this facility many years earlier.

In addition to ordnance responsibilities, Crane also devotes a significant effort to the design and certification of sophisticated electronic systems used by the Navy. The facility includes a well-equipped analytical group that provides support and failure analysis, and it was this group that carried out analysis of the "foreign materials" in the USS *Iowa* investigation for the Navy team. They contributed heavily to the final Navy report on this subject.

Crane is now under civilian control, and David Reese was in charge of the analytical function. We had several prior discussions with his people, including David File, a principal scientist in Reese's group, during the course of the *Iowa* investigation.

A meeting of the Navy and Sandia teams was scheduled for 19 and 20 November at Crane, the second meeting held at this site. Because of other commitments, the best I could do was to arrive at about 10:00 A.M. on the second day, in time for the last session. The two teams had been discussing the most recent results in the foreign materials area.

Jerry Herley from the GAO walked out to meet me as I parked the car. "The exchange has been a good one," he said, "but there are some clear lines that have been drawn between Sandia and Crane." He gave me an abbreviated rundown on the meeting to this point.

The two teams were taking a break, and I took an empty seat at the meeting table and reviewed handouts used by Crane in their presentations earlier that morning. When they returned, I asked if we could review some the principal materials topics and how the two groups stood in those areas. "For example, do we now agree on the analysis of glycols—that what you observed could be the glycols in Break-Free?"

A Crane analyst responded, "Yes, we now agree that the same glycols are in Break-Free. But the ratio of one of the glycols and the acetate form of that glycol are not the same in Break-Free and the material that was in the cannelure. For that reason we believe the form of the glycol we found in the cannelure is different from that in Break-Free."

Bess Campbell from the Sandia team noted, "The extractions of the material by the two teams differed and this could easily have influenced the ratio measurement. In addition, catalytic effects could have changed the ratio."

The Crane experts would not agree and held firm that the glycols on the projectile must have come from another source since these ratios were different. We went on to the subject of iron fibers on the center gun projectile, fibers that the Navy asserted came from the chemical ignition device.

Not long before this meeting, during this time of exploring impact ignition in full-scale gun tests, Sandia became aware of the existence of the projectiles that were in the left and right guns of Turret II at the time of the explosion. It was an entirely fortuitous circumstance, a remarkable coincidence of a suggestion and the location of the projectiles.

Following one of the several discussions between the Sandia and Navy team at Dahlgren, the conversation turned to the projectiles in the left and right guns of Turret II at the time of the explosion. The Navy team volunteered to show Paul Cooper and Karl Schuler these projectiles. Our team had presumed that these projectiles had simply been returned to the projectile deck on the *Iowa*, that they were mixed in among the other projectiles we had seen during our visits to the ship. The Navy team informed them, however, that the two projectiles had been removed from the ship and were stored in a nearby Navy facility, another revelation.

The group, including Captain Miceli and Frank Tse, went to the facility and found the two projectiles on a loading dock where they were readily identifiable by their unique paint scheme. According to Karl Schuler, Paul Cooper walked up to one of the projectiles and facetiously asked, "Aren't these iron fibers on this projectile?"

His humorous question stimulated a closer look that revealed that there were indeed several very large fibers clearly visible on the projectiles. Cooper wanted to take a few of the large fibers to our materials people, and Frank Tse offered him an empty bank deposit envelope as a container. Captain Miceli became mildly agitated and asked that the projectiles be covered immediately to protect them from the environment. This curious finding stimulated an extensive survey of the iron fibers on the left and right gun projectiles by Crane, and a comparison of these fibers with those found on the center gun projectile that the Navy investigators claimed were from a chemical ignition device.

The existence of these projectiles aroused intense interest among those involved in the analyses of foreign materials. The projectiles' environmental history was similar to that of the projectile in the center gun. For example, they had all been "reconditioned" and repainted in exactly the same unique way. Since these two projectiles were sealed in the left and right guns at the time of the explosion, they represented a unique reference to which we could now compare contaminations on the center gun projectile. Crane was given the responsibility to examine these projectiles for fibers and other materials.

The results of the Crane study of the iron fibers on the two projectiles was reported in some detail at this meeting. They noted that about forty fibers were found in the cannelures and forward slots of the left and right gun projectiles, and at first sight the fibers were remarkably similar to those found on the center gun projectile. Crane charted the size distribution and concluded, however, that it differed from the size distribution of fibers from the center gun projectile. Our uniform reaction was that there were no obvious differences in the two histograms and that Crane may have too quickly decided that the two distributions were different. I suggested that we have our statistician, Kathleen Diegert, examine the size-distribution data for the limited number of fibers and the Crane people agreed.

This analysis showed that there was no statistically discernible difference in the size distribution for fibers recovered from each of the three projectiles. The logical conclusion was, of course, that the fibers on the center gun projectile were the result of some contamination common to all three projectiles and unrelated to the Navy's hypothetical device.

And so it went. Sandia would put forth work to demonstrate that each of the foreign materials identified by the Navy could have originated from a normal source, that there were no clearly identifiable foreign materials. Crane analysts would claim that subtle quantitative differences in materials from the center gun projectile made them unique, unlike any others that had been found. While the original Navy position was that the mere presence of such foreign materials in the cannelure of the center gun projectile was indicative of the chemical ignitor, the Navy was now arguing that subtle quantitative differences in materials from the center gun projectile made them unique.

After an extended series of such discussion topics, I turned to Dave Reese. "Well, Dave, how do you interpret the 'foreign materials' information? What is your bottom line? Is it conclusive in your view that an ignitor was present, or is there ambiguity here?"

He thought for a moment and replied, "We feel quite confident that the case can be made for the presence of an ignitor and we plan to stick by that view."

"Really? You don't even see ambiguity? I think, then, that we'll have to disagree. What we see here ranges from, at worst, no evidence that an ignitor was present to, at best, ambiguity."

We spent about an hour fine-tuning a document that summarized our conclusions, agreements, disagreements, and areas of future work. This had been our practice, and it seemed to work well in focusing our thoughts following such meetings. Dave Reese and I would both sign this as we had before. We picked out a meeting date for January, and agreed to come with our individual conclusions for joint review.

The wear and tear of recent travel had exhausted me, and Paul Hlava, one of the Sandians who had come out for the meeting with Crane, offered to drive my rental to the airport. Hlava was an expert in microprobe analysis with particular interests in mineralogy. He had not interacted with Crane to any great extent before this meeting. As we drove through the gate and off the Crane site, I asked him for his impressions of the meeting. He shook his head. "I was surprised by the strong position the Crane personnel took in the face of what I view as overwhelming evidence that the presence of an ignitor is unproven. Moreover, the Sandia work has found so many holes in the foreign materials case that the Navy story seems even more remote that it did when they first presented it."

We arrived at the airport with only enough time to catch our various flights. I thanked Hlava and wished him a fine Thanksgiving.

19 Naval Research Laboratory

14 December 1990

THE SPEED of the rammer at the time of the explosion was now of considerable interest. If there indeed had been a high-speed overram, impact ignition was a significant possibility, as we had demonstrated in the gun-scale testing at Dahlgren. We thought through the details of rammer operation and searched the drawings of the assembly for some latent indicators of rammer speed. Mark Davis and I reasoned that the damper, a kind of shock absorber built into the head of the rammer, might be a useful source of information.

The badly damaged rammer head and chain links from the center gun were now at the Naval Research Laboratory (NRL) in Washington, on the eastern side of the Potomac, almost directly across from National Airport. The Navy team had sought the services of the NRL on metallurgical matters, and Bob Bayles would be our contact in reexamining the rammer head. Bayles had carried out some new analyses of the rammer assembly.

Davis had brought along a cross-sectional drawing of the rammer head, which we studied during dinner at our hotel, selecting critical areas for examination. We had learned that the damper on the rammer should fully compress in .2 to .3 seconds with the sustained load that the rammer could deliver. If the Navy scenario was correct and there had been a overram of several seconds to activate the chemical ignitor, the damper in the rammer head would have been fully compressed when the explosion occurred. On the other hand, if the explosion occurred as the result of a high-speed overram, the damper would probably not have been fully compressed or closed at the time of the explosion. The full-scale gun tests at Dahlgren indicated that explosions occurred promptly with overram. Delays of even milliseconds had not been observed in studies to date.

We reasoned that if a high-speed overram occurred and the damper was not fully closed at the time of the explosion, the tremendous shock of the explosion might have scored the internal sliding surfaces of the damper. The next day at the Naval Research Lab we would examine particular surfaces that might exhibit scoring due to the explosion. We carefully marked these on the drawing because they were internal surfaces that might require some disassembly or sectioning of the rammer head.

We set the drawing aside and talked about the decreased tempo of the Navy investigation of the *Iowa* explosion, ostensibly because the crisis in Kuwait was demanding more of the Navy's energy. It seemed to us that the crisis argued for more testing of the impact-ignition phenomenon, that it was an incentive to understand as much as possible about this safety vulnerability. For example, no testing had yet taken place with the propellant using a larger pellet, the material that was supposed to be used with the heaviest projectiles.

Davis found other reasons for the slowdown: "I think Captain Miceli is not in any hurry to have either team find more answers in our investigations. Why would he want to rush toward the identification of what might be even more weaknesses in the Navy scenario?"

The next morning we drove to Anacostia and the NRL facility. We arrived about 8:20 A.M. and met Tim Stone from the GAO at the front gate. We signed in and drove toward Building 21, noting Captain Miceli at the entrance of the building as we turned into the parking lot.

Building 21 had been built in the early 1950s and showed all the wear and tear it had been subjected to over the years. Captain Miceli walked over to greet us, and we all followed Bob Bayles as he walked toward the entrance, exchanging notes on the latest results from studies at Sandia and at Dahlgren. Odors from the nearby sewage plant permeated the area and prompted a few comments.

Bayles took us into Building 21, which had its own unique and unidentifiable odors. The building was cluttered with equipment of past projects strewn in disarray. We went down a stairway that led to the basement. Even older unused equipment was everywhere, and it was apparent there had not been an equipment purge or renovation of the building in many years. Stepping around yet more vintage equipment, we entered a storage room with poor lighting and exposed pipes hanging from the ceiling. The headroom in the basement was very low, reminiscent of some spaces in the *Iowa*, and a musty smell filled the dank air.

The rammer head and links were in pieces on top of what appeared to be an old stainless steel food-warming table, illuminated by a single bulb set in a conical metal reflector. The heavy links of the chain had been deformed by the explosion, twisted by powerful forces. It seemed strangely inappropriate to be viewing the rammer parts from a tragic explosion in this dark basement, displayed as if on an autopsy table, darkened as they were by the intense heat of the explosion.

A transverse cut through the rammer head had exposed the damper piston and cylinder in which it moved, just the internal surfaces we had marked on the drawing the night before. We believed this was the key part to examine for any scoring that may have occurred during the explosion. We positioned the cylinder directly under the lamp and examined it with a magnifier, noting that it had been heavily scored about one-quarter to three-eighths of an inch from the fully closed position. We looked at one another, realizing that this was just the kind of evidence we anticipated if the damper was not fully closed at the time of the explosion—suggesting that the explosion took place in the instant that the rammer first compressed the propellant against the projectile.

Captain Miceli had been hovering over us, noting our exchanged glance, impatient with this examination, pacing around the room and then returning to the table, the lower part of his body illuminated by the swinging overhead lamp.

I used a short scale to measure the distance of the scoring from the fully closed position. Bayles had been following our examination and interest in the scored cylinder. Obviously he had noted this same scoring and read our thoughts. "The rammer head might have been blown backward against the bulkhead of the gun room, and impact with the bulkhead could have scored the cylinder back from the fully closed position. The piston head may have moved between the time of the explosion and the impact of the rammer on the rear bulkhead which created the scoring."

Captain Miceli had stopped his pacing and came to the warming table, looking across at us, attempting to underscore Bayles's comment. "Absolutely right." Apparently Bayles had discussed the scoring with Miceli. That is a possible but an unlikely explanation, Davis and I thought to ourselves.

We next examined the broken spring that normally held the damper in the uncompressed position. It was in two pieces, separated by a helical fracture. I looked with a questioning expression at Bayles. He said, "It appears to have a small region of fatigue fracture, but I want to have our expert describe his studies to you. He's ill and at home."

I turned to Captain Miceli with a request. "I'd like to take this section back to Sandia for examination by our fractographer."

"Negative. We need to keep all the evidence here. It's very important that we not let this be separated from the rest of the rammer."

I thought of all the evidence that had been thrown overboard following the explosion, of the misplaced encrusted fibers, and so on. I wondered how Captain Miceli could say things like this with a straight face. "In that case," I said, "I'll plan to have our fractographer come out in the near future and use your equipment to look at these parts."

We looked at everything two or three more times, including a large distinctive mark on the brass face of the rammer that must have occurred in the explosion. The mark was about two inches wide and diagonal to the face, apparently the result of having been blown back against the aft part of the gun room. We reexamined photos of the rear bulkhead of the gun room, looking once more for a piece of equipment that might have left such a mark on impact. Nothing seemed to fit the pattern.

Our attention shifted to the rammer handle and quadrant, the latter being a steel arc that constrained the rammer handle to about 45 degrees of motion. The bend in the quadrant seemed to indicate the position of the rammer handle at the time of the explosion. Bayles told us about his tests of compressing the quadrant with the rammer handle in various positions. For at least the twentieth time we reexamined pictures of the rammer handle and quadrant that were taken following the explosion. The quadrant appeared to have been hit from a direction transverse to the direction of the explosion. Strange.

Captain Miceli walked back over to us. "The quadrant might have been impacted by the steel seat that was used by the rammerman," he said.

"Can we see the seat?"

"It was thrown overboard, but we have a picture of it in a pile of other debris from the turret."

Captain Miceli said he'd send those pictures to us in the near future. We stood silently for several minutes, searching the darkened parts again as they lay before us on the cold steel table. The captain finally gave in to his impatience. "Anything else?"

"No, I guess that's it. Thanks very much."

I went to a sink and washed my hands. They were dark with the same red and black stains as on the rammer parts. I couldn't help but think of this staining material as it circled down the drain. I smelled my hands, an acrid odor filling my nostrils.

We walked back through the door to the hallway, up the stairs, and to the front door of Building 21. We exchanged thanks and walked out to the stench of the sewage plant. We dropped Tim Stone off at the front gate to pick up his car, and Davis and I drove to the airport.

Later in the week Karl Schuler stopped by to say that he had also examined the rammer head and come to the same conclusion—the damper was not closed at the time of the explosion. The sustained overram scenario put forward by the Navy did not appear to be consistent with the facts. He also had recently visited Dahlgren to review the full-scale testing activity. "The impact-ignition work has dramatically slowed," he said, "and the same goes for studies of propellant bag compression under various loads. I was impressed that the Dahlgren people have little knowledge of what Crane or other Navy facilities are doing relative to the *Iowa* investigation. The Navy working-level people are essentially unaware of the larger investigation."

Perhaps Mark Davis was right. Why should the Navy rush toward more evidence that doesn't support their scenario?

I continued the redraft of the Executive Summary for our final report, strengthened some of the conclusions, added suggestions and corrections from earlier drafts that were circulated to the subgroup leaders. Judy Jewell finalized the draft and sent it to our team members for review over the Christmas break.

As Dennis Mitchell and other Sandia teams members remarked, this summary differed from the one we presented to the Senate. The points were stronger, definitively stated, and well supported by the continued studies.

20 Toward a Conclusion

Spring and Summer 1991

THE SPRING and summer of 1991 were occupied with meetings in which the positions of the Sandia and Navy teams were articulated, challenged, and supplemented with further work to resolve various details. Three of these exchanges will be briefly reviewed, more to give the flavor of the meetings than to elaborate on the technical results.

One of these meetings took place on 25 June at the Army's Ballistic Research Laboratory (BRL) at Fort Monmouth, New Jersey, a site that would host another of these exchanges the following week. It was attended by fourteen people representing the BRL, NRL, Indian Head NOS, and Sandia. Karl Schuler, Paul Cooper, Mel Baer, and I represented Sandia.

The primary discussion concentrated on computer models of the open breech explosion. George Keller, BRL, and Mel Baer reviewed "interior" models that could be used to describe the two-phase flow of material (hot gases and propellant pellets) streaming out of the breech after initiation. The goal was a quantitative description of the blast and blast effects in the center gun room.

The description of flow was important to determining, for example, whether particulate material from any chemical device could be carried forward to and deposited in the cannelure of the projectile. The model appeared to be qualitatively correct, but there were complex unresolved issues in which some of the Dahlgren experimental data were not well reproduced. Several questions remained unanswered and the modelers would continue to labor with this subject, eventually using more sophisticated three-dimensional models to accurately describe the explosion.

Also discussed at this meeting was a fairly detailed review of rammer operation by one of the lead engineers from the manufacturer in Minneapolis. The basic questions we wanted to address dealt with undocumented reports by the crew of erratic operation—the rammer not responding properly to movements of the control lever, sudden high-speed operation, or failure to operate. The rammer was a fairly complex hydraulic device, and smooth operation depended on clean fluid, filters, orifices, and other components. While the engineer seemed to clearly understand the way this device was supposed to operate, he was less informed about abnormal operation and the associated causes. We had understood that filters in the rammer of the center gun needed cleaning when it was disassembled following the explosion, but it was very difficult to get clear answers about the various effects of contamination on operation.

The following day, the twenty-sixth, another meeting was held at the Naval Research Laboratory in Washington. Referred to as a "Flag Board" meeting by Captain Miceli, it was a gathering of the Technical Oversight Board of admirals appointed by the Navy and its purpose was to update the board on the status of our studies since the review at Sandia the previous August. In attendance were Rear Adm. Donald P. Roane (ret.), Rear Adm. George R. Meinig Jr., Rear Adm. Roger B. Horne Jr., and Rear Adm. Robert H. Ailes.

Following my brief introduction, we began in our usual way, with Jim Borders discussing the status of analytical work relevant to "foreign materials." Of particular interest were studies of materials found on the projectiles from the left and right guns in Turret II. The key question was, Did these projectiles exhibit any iron fibers or other foreign materials similar to those found on the center gun projectile?

Borders noted that Crane had recently been examining these projectiles. Before he could go on, Captain Miceli interjected that preliminary swab samples of the cannelures of these projectiles had produced no fibers. Since the fibers of interest were nearly microscopic (typically less than a thousandth of an inch in diameter and a small fraction of an inch in length), several questions were raised about these preliminary examinations, but the captain assured everyone that no fibers had been seen. Miceli added that the protective plastic cover over the projectiles had grease and fibers on it, implying that even if fibers were found, the cover was an obvious source of contamination.

No sooner had the captain made these assertions than Borders stated that iron fibers had indeed been found in the cannelures of these two projectiles and, moreover, our preliminary review of these fibers indicated that they were essentially indistinguishable from those found on the center gun projectile. These two widely varying perspectives of the results immediately stimulated a flurry of assertions that led essentially nowhere. It was clear that more information was needed.

Admiral Roane questioned Border's remarks, and Borders detailed his assertions with more information. Admiral Ailes called for a prompt resolution. Were there iron fibers on these projectiles? If so, were they similar to those on the center gun projectile? This was obviously a red-hot investigative area, and I could feel the tension rising in the room as the preliminary and incomplete results, including Crane's disagreements, were bantered about. The Navy's scenario was literally riding on both the existence and the uniqueness of the iron fibers found on the center gun projectile. This part of the meeting concluded with all agreed that a full discussion of Crane's results was essential in the near future.

Paul Cooper summarized the impact-ignition studies, including the results of the investigations at Dahlgren. He also described the very significant test in which a single misplaced pellet was placed at the rear of a bag by Tom Doran, and related that this configuration had led to an explosion on the very first overram.

Captain Miceli nimbly added, "I wanted to see what effect this would have." He nodded toward the admirals as if he had had prior knowledge of Doran's test. I couldn't suppress a smile and vividly recalled that after Doran's test, Captain Miceli had instructed Doran to henceforth clear all tests with him in advance. A number of us had heard the whole story of Doran's experiment at Dahlgren last July and understood that the captain was leaving out important information. But all this was inside stuff, and any attempt at clarification for the admirals would sound too petty and arcane.

The ensuing discussion of impact ignition and the probability of such an event stimulated Admiral Ailes to chastise me for my testimony before the Senate Armed Services Committee. He was visibly angry and went on at some length. "You devastated us with the probabilities you stated—you said it [an explosion] was a 99 percent probability in an overram! And furthermore—"

I told him that the probability curves we displayed at the Senate Armed Services Committee hearing were qualified as rough estimates based on subscale testing, and that the transcript would bear out that I did not state that the probability was 99 percent. I added that the gun-scale testing at Dahlgren had clearly shown that there are conditions of overramming in which none of us would want to stand next to the gun, that a part of our task was to define the safe and the unsafe operating regimes. "However, I'm sensitive to issues of how these and other results are articulated, and I want you to see the conclusions in our draft report and comment on them."

The admiral had regained his composure. "Fair enough."

Karl Schuler began a discussion of the overram and a review of the last results and perspective. He expressed his stark view that it might not be possible from any of the current studies to determine whether a sustained static overram (the Navy's view) or a dynamic overram took place. Again, more questions, discussion, and suggestions.

Mel Bear concluded the meeting with a review of the latest interior-modeling efforts and results, a discussion that helped the admirals better understand the complexities of modeling the open-breech explosion and the excellent understanding that had been developed.

The third meeting took place on 3 July, again at the Ballistics Research Laboratory, and was a day-long review of the Navy's investigation for both the "Flag Board" and Al Narath, the president of Sandia.

Members of the Technical Oversight Committee in attendance included Admirals Roane, Cantrell, Meinig, Horne, and also Admiral Ailes. My innermost thought was that the Navy had probably found the Sandia team, or more likely me, to be as intractable as we, at times, had found some members of the Navy team. The Navy's invitation to have Sandia's president attend was an appeal to a higher authority. This meeting was a Navy show and the Sandians were not invited to rebut or comment.

Captain Miceli opened the meeting with his detailed story of the incident from the Navy's perspective. When he described the cleanup and disposal of equipment overboard the day after the explosion, Admiral Ailes asked him, "Is there any evidence that critical evidence was lost?"

"No, but sailors were allowed in the turret for hours after the explosion without supervision."

As the captain got into the Navy's investigation, several questions were asked by the admirals about the position of the crewmen in the center gun room. Captain Miceli characterized the crewmen's positions in detail: "Hartwig's position doesn't fit the position of a gun captain in a high-speed overram—he's looking into the breech. The upper powder hoist operator [Fisk] was looking at the gun captain—they were all looking at the gun captain."

I wondered if the admirals realized that the medical examiner, by his own admission, could assess the approximate direction that people were facing, but that conclusions about who or what someone was looking at were beyond the ME's capabilities. And even if the men had been looking at the gun captain, the logic of the captain tacitly implying that that necessarily meant something was wrong escaped me. Wasn't the gun captain supposed to be in control? As the conversation continued it appeared that the admirals were not generally acquainted with the qualifications attached to the ME's testimony before the committees.

This was followed by a discussion of a topic now under intense scrutiny by both the Navy and Sandia teams—the motion of the steel rammerman's seat and its relation to the (high- or low-speed) position of the rammer handle following the explosion. The rammer handle had been found in a slow forward position following the blast, fire, flooding, and cleanup operation. This led the Navy to believe that this was the position of the rammer handle at the time of the blast and that the overram had taken place at a slow speed.

The rammer handle moved in a guide ("quadrant") that was pinched by a heavy and/or fast-moving object during the explosion, and the rammer handle was found behind the pinch, in the low-speed area of the quadrant. The Navy used this piece of information to assert that it was a low-speed overram, and that it was the rammerman's seat that had pinched the quadrant. We were not convinced that this was correct.

By careful examination, Karl Schuler had found that the quadrant had been "tack" welded to the bulkhead and that those welds had never been fully filled in as they should have been. Since the quadrant was not well secured to the bulkhead, Schuler wondered if the quadrant may have fallen off the bulkhead during the loading operation and stimulated an uncontrolled overram. As he noted, if this had been the case the pinch in a detached quadrant would not imply anything about rammer speed. Schuler had devoted an extensive effort to computer model the rammerman's seat motion with respect to the pinched quadrant. He concluded that it was not the seat that had pinched the quadrant if, as the Navy assumed, the quadrant was attached to the bulkhead at the time of the explosion. The arguments on this topic were complex and rested heavily on assumptions that went into the computer models. This was another important continuing area of work.

Captain Miceli's lengthy opening talk was followed by a series of thirteen presentations by the Navy's technical experts on virtually every technical subject in their investigation. Late in the afternoon, the captain closed the meeting with comments that reassured the admirals that the Navy's scenario was intact.

The talks by the Navy's investigators were uniformly supportive of the Navy's scenario with very few unknowns or unresolved questions. Everything seemed to be in order, and there just were no open concerns with the Navy's explanation for the explosion. This uniform agreement was, however, based on some assertions that were beyond credence. Some of these assertions dealt with what they considered the improbability of the Sandia suggestion that a high-speed overram initiated explosion. For example, one of the Navy investigators performed calculations of the probability of an overram leading to an explosion. These probabilities ranged from a low of 1 in 200,000 to a high of 1 in 3,000. The implied conclusion was, of course, that an overram-initiated explosion just did not happen.

Lost in the details of the calculations was the fact that an overram simulated by a drop test at Dahlgren produced an explosion on the eighteenth attempt. Similarly, these calculations were at odds with the fact that the single misoriented pellet at the aft end of the bag caused an explosion on the first trial in a full-scale gun experiment. Yet none of the admirals questioned the obvious disparity of these calculations with the hard experimental facts. We summarized our conclusions on ignition statistics shortly after this in a meeting with Adm. Frank B. Kelso, chief of Naval Operations (see chapter 21).

Another important undercurrent in these meetings was qualitative information that dealt with aspects of rammer operations. Rammer speed was an important concern and a great deal of effort was being devoted to establishing the speed of the rammer in the overram that occurred on the morning of the explosion. There were, however, other concerns with rammer operations. One concern dealt with the reliability of rammer operation, that is, the consistent correspondence of rammer control lever position with rammer speed. Another concern was the possibility of an inadvertent overram by an inexperienced rammerman. Our first conversation related to this subject was with Lt. Daniel Meyer during our first visit to the *Iowa* on 7 December (chapter 7). Related discussions took place during other parts of the investigation.

GMG3 Kendall Truitt in his testimony before the House in December 1989 noted that the rammer in the left gun room of Turret II was erratic in operation: "I have been in left gun in Turret II when we had a problem with the rammer. We lost control of it. We would be trying to ram it. Luckily we were using a bullet (and not propellant). We would try and ram, and suddenly it was as if it was a car and you couldn't get it—it was shifting between neutral and drive basically, and it was—you couldn't control it basically. It would take off suddenly, stop without warning. They shut down the whole system. They tore apart the filters. They reworked it."[1]

One of Admiral Milligan's team members, Commander Swanson, had also questioned Truitt about the possibility of an inadvertent high-speed overram the day after the explosion:[2]

Commander Swanson: We know they were having some problems because that was reported over the sound powered phone systems, Petty Officer Lawrence was having some difficulties setting up. Do you think an anxiety to get the center gun loaded, and the fact that the left and right gun were already loaded, that there is a possibility that they [center gun] rammed the powder in at high speed rather than a slower speed?

GMG3 Truitt: That could very well be. It's not that we race; however, there is a competition of bragging to see who got the gun loaded first. They both call through and say, "left center, right gun, load one round." And they do enjoy saying, "I got my gun loaded faster than you did." Lawrence, however, would have been least affected by that than any other gun captains because he doesn't really get off on that or enjoy that quite as much as the others.

Commander Swanson: Plus, he was brand new.

GMG3 Truitt: Yes, sir. Backherms might have noted that they were falling behind, however.

There were also fragmentary reports on variable or erratic operation of rammers from other members of the crew. Larry S. Saunders Jr., rammerman for the right gun of Turret III, noted in his testimony before Admiral Milligan that care was needed in controlling rammer speed. Saunders was not a qualified rammerman, but under instruction:[3]

Admiral Milligan: Did you ever have any trouble controlling your rammer control enough to make sure you don't overram the powder? Is that a tough job, or is that kind of easy, to do that at the right speed and stop it and all that?

Saunders: I'm still learning, now, sir.

Admiral Milligan: Do you have any problems with it?

Saunders: No, no big problems, sir.

Admiral Milligan: Ever run one in there too fast and get the gun captain all excited?

Saunders: Once or twice, sir. But he tells me to slow down and, usually, I get it in there just right but, now, I'm better at it.

Admiral Milligan: But you could run it in there pretty fast if you're not careful, couldn't you?

Saunders: Yes, sir, I could.

GMG3 Murray J. Cunningham, right gun captain in Turret I, also noted that ram speed could be excessive in his testimony before Admiral Milligan:[4]

Admiral Milligan: Have you ever experienced a rammer on a powder stroke that was a little bit faster than you might have wanted?

GMG3 Cunningham: Yes, sir.

Admiral Milligan: And like how fast? Have you ever had— have you ever seen powder rammed at the same speed that a projectile is rammed?

GMG3 Cunningham: Not at the same speed, sir. But I have seen powder rammed too fast, sir. . . .

Commander Swanson: Have you ever had, or observed, or heard of a situation in which the ramming, or the rammer, overrammed the powder to the point where it impacted with the projectile inside the breech, in other words far, so far up?

GMG3 Cunningham: I have never heard where he'd rammed it too hard where it went up against it. But there have been times where you would—to my knowledge it won't even go all the way really against the projectile, because the way the chamber is made. It kind of rounds off, kind of narrows inside, okay, to where your bag will go on to a certain point.

Commander Swanson: So you never really witnessed a severe overramming is what I'm asking?

GMG3 Cunningham: There are different ways you can term overramming and the term, I think that you are saying, is putting the powder up too far into the chamber. I have had a rammerman where he'd taken and put the powder too far up in. Where I had just, after my cradle, my rammer was back and my cradle's back, I reached in and pulled the bag back, but there was an overram of maybe a half inch, an inch, nothing super, nothing really, but there's another way of terming overram and that is ramming too fast.

Admiral Milligan: Does that concern you? Doesn't that scare you?

GMG3 Cunningham: Yes, sir, it does.

Admiral Milligan: Too fast?

GMG3 Cunningham: Yes, sir, it does.

GMG1 Dale Mortensen had also commented on overramming in his testimony before Admiral Milligan's team. The discussion dealt with the ramming process and hand signals from the gun captain:[5]

Admiral Milligan: It's forward and then the speed is the rammerman's decision?

GMG1 Mortensen: Okay. Once he's got the powder in there and we retract, it's forward, retract.

Admiral Milligan: No, no. It's forward and the rammer's pushing the powder in. The speed that he pushes the powder in, is that his decision? He's the one that controls the throttle, so to speak, or—

GMG1 Mortensen: That's at the gun captain. That gun captain should have the say as to how fast.

Admiral Milligan: How does he do that, by fast or slow, or by saying fast or slow?

GMG1 Mortensen: No. I'm sure that—with a good trained gun captain and a good trained crew, they basically know. That's all communications with them in there.

Admiral Milligan: That was from . . . we have a first time ever gun captain and first time ever rammer.[6]

GMG1 Mortensen: Well, I didn't know that.

Lieutenant Roper: Just for clarification, who has direct control over the speed of the rammer?

GMG1 Mortensen: Who has direct—

Lieutenant Roper: Who has direct control over the speed of the rammer?

GMG1 Mortensen: That rammerman is the only—

Admiral Milligan: There are no signals for the rammerman.

GMG1 Mortensen: Backherms was the rammerman? How come I found Backherms at—on lower intercom unless—

Admiral Milligan: Pressure override took it down, I would say, but let me say—

GMG1 Mortensen: Backherms?

Admiral Milligan: Let me say there are no signals concerning speed. There is just forward and aft and stop.

GMG1 Mortensen: Right. Well, you know—okay. But the projectile, it's full stroke until it stops. It's seated. The rammer, you're right. You are correct. There is no set—

Admiral Milligan: Okay. So with the relevance of the inexperienced person as a rammerman unless I get into what his qualifications were, but say relatively inexperienced, he has just rammed the projectile in at full speed, he's pulled the rammer back, he's given credit for guiding the bags down onto the tray—

GMG1 Mortensen: Guiding the powder bags.
Admiral Milligan: —and he rams the powder in full speed.
GMG1 Mortensen: That's what I'm talking about, overramming.

Conclusive evidence was never developed with regard to erratic operation of rammers during the investigation, so a substantial overram due to equipment malfunction remained an unresolved possibility. There was little doubt, however, that the oral tradition among crew was to avoid overramming of propellant bags. It was viewed as a dangerous practice that could lead to an explosion.

Similarly, an inadvertent overram by an inexperienced rammerman also remained as a possibility, as was considered by Admiral Milligan and his team in their questioning of various crewmen.

This series of meetings, information exchanges perhaps, essentially concluded the meetings between the Navy and Sandia. Our efforts were now directed toward completion of our final report in July and August and submitting it to the General Accounting Office and the Senate Armed Services Committee.

21 Reviewing Our Conclusions with Admiral Kelso

August 1991

As we completed our studies and drafted detailed final conclusions to our investigation during the spring and summer of 1991, Adm. Frank B. Kelso, chief of Naval Operations, asked that we present Sandia's findings to him. The meeting was held in Admiral Kelso's office early in August 1991, just as we were finalizing our report to the Senate Armed Services Committee through the GAO. This was an excellent opportunity to present our latest and probably final thoughts on the various points of our investigations. We would conclude each section of our presentation with the actual words of our draft report that summarized our conclusions.

Admiral Kelso had taken over as chief of Naval Operations from Admiral Trost. Kelso, like Trost, was also a submariner, trained in nuclear engineering and technically competent. The meeting in Admiral Kelso's office included several young naval officers who assisted the admiral, Captain Miceli, a few key members of the Navy team, and Paul Cooper, Karl Schuler, Jim Borders, and myself. The Navy personnel, resplendent in their white uniforms, represented a legal branch of the Navy.

As Admiral Kelso welcomed us and spoke about the *Iowa* investigation, my impression was that he wanted to hear about the Sandia investigation firsthand. I wondered if the admiral may have sensed that reports he was getting about our work were not fully informative, if he was searching for facts and objectivity as he contemplated the revised position that the Navy must now take.

We moved from his office to an adjoining conference room and took our seats at a large table that just accommodated all of us. A lectern was at one end of the table, and a projection screen was behind the lectern, adorned with flags on both sides. The admiral invited us to begin, and I presented an introduction and overview of what my three companions would present. I said that we would present summary paragraphs during each talk that duplicated our draft final report and that we welcomed any comments or criticisms. Admiral Kelso asked when we planned to submit the report, and I replied that it would be completed and forwarded later in August. I thought again of the free hand that we had had in formulating and stating our final conclusions, no suggestions or directions from Sandia management, the Department of Energy, the General Accounting Office, or anyone else.

The sequence of talks would be basically the same that we had used in our recent presentations. We would open with foreign materials by Jim Borders, then follow with mechanical modeling of the rammer and related considerations by Karl Schuler, stability of the propellant and impact ignition by Paul Cooper, and I would present the summary conclusions.

Admiral Kelso listened to each presentation with interest and asked thoughtful and perceptive questions. My impression was that he understood the essence of the answers, even in the case of a detailed response. He did not reiterate the Navy's view in these various areas, but rather seemed intent on understanding the basis for our view. The officers from the legal branch remained modestly attentive throughout the presentations but exhibited no deep interest in the subjects or asked any questions.

Jim Borders reviewed the many findings associated with foreign materials and the several discussions we had had with the personnel at Crane. The overwhelming evidence was, in our assessment, that the foreign materials on the center gun projectile were unrelated to any chemical ignition device and simply the result of contaminations from readily identifiable sources within the turret or earlier handling and reconditioning of the projectiles. These same contaminations were found on the projectiles from the left and right guns.

In addition, the previously unexplored forward grooves of the center gun projectile, which were sealed and protected from contamination at the time of the blast, had been opened and found to contain the same contaminations and iron fibers as in the cannelure. This finding was direct evidence that the foreign materials found in the cannelure by the Navy had nothing to do with an ignition device.

We had written the following in a concluding paragraph of our draft final report:[1]

The USN reported that "the residue found in the *Iowa* rotating band cannot be duplicated by simple contamination of the gun chamber with steel wool and other chemicals normally present in a gun firing." This included the presence of calcium, chlorine, various glycols, inorganic particulate, and steel wool fibers found in the cannelure of the center gun projectile and associated by the USN with a hypothetical chemical ignition device. Studies at SNL show that the foreign materials identified by the USN in the cannelure of the projectile of the center gun are indistinguishable from those found in other key locations within Turret II. Chemical constituents and steel wool fibers indistinguishable from those in the cannelure were found in the forward grooves of the rotating band of the projectile in the center gun; that is, in a region of the cannelure that was isolated from the explosion. In addition, the same chemical constituents and steel wool fibers were also found in the cannelures and forward grooves of the rotating bands of projectiles that were in the left and right guns of the turret. These fibers were also indistinguishable from those in the cannelure of the center gun projectile. *These and other facts suggest that the fibers and various chemical constituents found by the USN on the center gun projectile are unrelated to the explosion.*

When we presented the summary conclusions, such as the paragraph above, in our viewgraphs, Admiral Kelso carefully scrutinized the words. He wanted to understand that this paragraph was currently contained in our draft report, and he wanted to know how this statement differed from the Navy investigator's views. Captain Miceli often responded with the Navy's view on these summary paragraphs. I was pleased that the admiral wanted to be sure he understood the Sandia view and how it differed from the Navy's.

Karl Schuler described his work related to the rammer. The overram determination showed that the propellant had been compressed against the projectile, and this finding was accepted by the Navy. The concluding section of the Executive Summary of our report, "USS *Iowa* Explosion, Sandia National Laboratories' Final Technical Report," included the following statement:

A substantial overram of the powder bags occurred for reasons that have not been determined. That is, the powder bags were forced against the base of the projectile by the rammer. This was determined from an analysis of the position of gouges on the spanning tray. Based on the observation that the buffer in the rammerhead was apparently not fully compressed at the time of the explosion, the overram may have occurred at a higher-than-normal-speed. A further observation that tends to support the concept of a high-than-normal-speed overram was the unlowered position of the powder car. The normal procedure aboard the USS *Iowa* was to lower the powder car immediately after closing the

> powder door. If the ramming of the powder bags occurred at high speed, the upper powder hoist operator may not have had time to begin the lowering of the car. If the ramming occurred at low speed, the operator would have had approximately twenty to thirty seconds to begin this process. After the explosion, the rammer control handle was found in the 1.7 feet/second position. However, SNL analyses show that the position of the handle and damage to the quadrant are not definitive indicators of the ramming speed.

We noted again that a key factor in the consideration of impact ignition was the speed of the overram—the higher the speed, the greater the probability of ignition. We noted that there had been an extensive effort by Sandia to determine the overram speed, but that we were unsuccessful in finding a definitive indicator. While impact-initiated explosions in field tests were generally prompt with compression of the propellant, we observed in a single test some compression of the damper prior to the explosion.

This finding called into question our observation of scoring with the damper of the *Iowa* rammer head and the implication that a higher than normal overram speed had taken place the morning of the explosion. Our initial conclusion may have been correct, but the fact that delayed ignition could occur indicated that the scoring we observed could have taken place in another way.

Admiral Kelso seemed to understand the differences in views, and I surmised that this subject had been discussed with him at some length before the meeting. I believe he appreciated our position that we could not definitively conclude that the overram speed was near the maximum, because there had been a single test in which ignition had not been prompt with propellant bag compression as it had been in all other tests. That is, we presented evidence both for and against a high-speed overram.

Schuler also discussed blast effects on the position of the rammer handle. That is, the rammer could have been blown back to a lower rammer speed by the power of the explosion. This led to a discussion of other blast effects, such as what may have occurred to the steel rammerman's seat located in the aft and port side of the center gun room, a subject that is perhaps too abstruse to report here, and some of the complicating factors which precluded a definite conclusion.

Paul Cooper summarized his experiments on impact ignition, the fine corroborating work by the Navy on this subject, and the results of gun-scale studies at Dahlgren from our perspective:

> It has been demonstrated in a full-scale simulator that a high-speed overram can initiate powder bags and result in an open-breech explosion. This previously unrecognized safety problem with 16-in. guns occurs when hot particles from fractured propellant pellets ignite nearby black powder. While impact initiation cannot be proven to have been the cause of the explosion, these results raise serious questions about the USN conclusion that "impact and compression of the bag charges were not contributing factors in the *Iowa* incident." Impact initiation could have been involved since a significant overram occurred.

Cooper went on to note three important conclusions regarding the statistics of initiation in a high-speed overram: "The probability was 16.6 percent (one in six) of selecting a group of five-bag charges from the propellant lot aboard the USS *Iowa* that was sensitive to ignition by overram." This conclusion was based on a count of pellets in the trim layers for propellant bags in this lot, and studies of the sensitivity of trim layers of various counts: "The probability of initiating a five-bag powder train with at least one bag with one to twelve trim pellets is nominally 0.087 (one in eleven) in a high-speed overram."

Combining these two conclusions, we deduced that "the probability of an explosion in a high-speed overram was nominally 0.0144 (one in seventy) for five powder bags randomly selected from the lot aboard the USS *Iowa* at the time of the explosion. Given the statistical uncertainties, the probability could be as high as 0.0639 (one in sixteen)." The inescapable conclusion was that high-speed overramming of propellant was dangerous and could lead to explosions such as had occurred aboard the *Iowa*.

I went through our summary conclusions which went to the heart of the Navy's findings and opinions relevant to the cause of the explosion. One of the summary conclusions was the following:

> A variety of scenarios for this incident have been explored, but they remain unproven for lack of evidence, partially due to the violence of the explosion and fire. Because of this, it may be difficult to ever fully resolve the many unknowns and develop a clear and unambiguous explanation of the events that occurred with the center gun room of Turret 2.
>
> It is concluded that there is no explicit physical evidence that the hypothetical chemical ignition device was present in the center gun of Turret II. It is also concluded that a high-speed overram is a possible cause of the April 19, 1989, explosion aboard the USS *Iowa*.

I felt it was important to say, as the independent investigator, that further work may not be helpful in further resolving these issues, that I believed that within the context of current understanding we had done essentially what could be done. I added that I believed that another independent group would reach the same conclusions as ours regarding the foreign materials issues, the heart of the Navy's scenario.

Admiral Kelso listened to all of this in a sober and reflective way. I was pleased that we had the opportunity to talk directly with him and believed that we had a fair hearing on all the key points of our investigation and draft conclusions.

We returned to Albuquerque and finalized our report, gradually returning to our other duties, closing down an investigation that had taken our total effort for the past eighteen months.

I heard various reports of the development of a new Navy position and some follow-on studies that had been suggested from various quarters. I reiterated during each of the intermittent phone calls from GAO or other groups that we considered our work to be done, that the final report was just that, our last words on the independent assessment activity.

The Navy scenario failed in several respects, from my personal perspective. A few key points are as follows:

The Navy's argument for the existence of foreign materials began with the mere presence of these materials as evidence for an ignition device. As normal sources for all of these materials emerged during the Sandia investigation, the Navy's argument shifted to focus on subtle differences in foreign materials found in the cannelure of the center gun projectile and foreign materials found in the protected grooves of the rotating band a few inches away, and also materials found on the projectiles in the left and right guns. I found the Navy's arguments about these small differences less plausible as the controversy continued and, in the end, unbelievable. The evidence for an ignition device is, in my judgment, nonexistent.

The hypothetical ignition device included steel wool, a novel extension of anything that Hartwig had learned in EOD school. This form of the device was not found, for example, in the FBI bomb data file. Was Hartwig innovative in these ways? Not according to his peers.

The overram-ignition scenario demonstrated by Sandia was initially disregarded by the Navy, and it was only after Senator Nunn sent a letter of caution that it was taken seriously and investigated in tests at Dahlgren. After the explosion in a test on 24 May 1990, the Navy admitted that there was a safety problem associated with overramming propellant. However, Navy investigators eventually concluded that the maximum probability of such an event was no greater than one in three thousand. This assertion, intended to imply that "it just didn't happen," disregarded evidence they had developed in their own gun scale experiments at Dahlgren.

The Navy attempted to support its arguments against an overram-related explosion with an insistence that the overram occurred at low speed. Unfortunately, no definitive indicators of ram speed came out of this investigation.

My belief is that the explosion aboard the USS *Iowa* on 19 April 1989 was caused by an inadvertent overram, and that this tragic event was an accident. It is an established fact that an overram compressing the propellant against the projectile occurred in the center gun. The field tests at Dahlgren clearly confirmed that this could lead to an explosion. There is also evidence that the explosion occurred promptly with the overram, that there was no delay as would have been required in the Navy's scenario. There may have been several factors contributing to this inadvertent overram, including inadequate training of some members of the center gun crew; a poorly conceived, briefed, and executed firing plan that contributed to confusion; and, possibly, a malfunction of the rammer.

22 Admiral Frank B. Kelso II News Conference

17 October 1991

THE FINAL notable event in this long and arduous investigation was the press conference by Admiral Kelso on 17 October 1991 in which he devoted all his remarks to the investigation of the explosion aboard the *Iowa*. He noted that new and more formal procedures had been mandated by the secretary of defense in the case of such major incidents.

First, there would be no more one-officer investigations in such cases, but rather a hearing or formal board of inquiry. While a formal board of inquiry could have been used by the Navy at the time of the *Iowa* incident, the Navy decided to use the less rigorous one-officer investigation, a decision that was roundly criticized in the House report. Second, any accusations against deceased service people must hereafter be accompanied by clear and convincing proof, something that was clearly absent in the Navy's case against Clayton Hartwig.

Admiral Kelso acknowledged that there was no clear and convincing proof that the explosion was the result of "a wrongful intentional act" and that the opinion to that effect, Opinion 55, was "disapproved": "The initial investigation contained a qualified opinion implicat[ing] GM2 Clayton M. Hartwig, USN, and that opinion was interpreted by many as conclusive finding of wrongdoing. For this, on behalf of the U.S. Navy, I extend my sincere regrets to the family of GM2 Hartwig. There is no clear and convincing proof of the cause of the *Iowa* explosion. And the Navy will not imply that a deceased individual is to blame for his own death or the deaths of others without such clear and convincing proof."

Admiral Kelso, however, seriously misrepresented the facts in his subsequent statement regarding the possibility of the incident having been an accident. The carefully worded second sentence implied that no plausible accidental cause was found: "The initial investigation was an honest attempt to weigh impartially all the evidence as it existed at the time. And indeed, despite the Sandia theory and almost two years of subsequent testing, a substantial body of scientific and expert evidence and analysis continue to support the initial investigation finding that no plausible accidental cause can be established."

Perhaps it would have been out of character for the Navy to officially recognize what we had all witnessed in the tests at Dahlgren, and what the Navy officers responsible for battleship safety had acknowledged in the measures that they had carefully instituted aboard the battleships to avoid overrams. All of this attested to the fact that a high-speed overram initiation was an accidental cause that was not only plausible, it had been demonstrated.

Notably absent from Admiral Kelso's presentation were any comments related to the broader issues raised in both Captain Moosally's testimony (see Appendix D) and Admiral Milligan's report to the Senate Armed Services Committee. These issues dealt with systemic management deficiencies that helped create a situation aboard the battleships in which a serious incident could and did occur. This included: a manning policy that resulted in inadequate numbers of trained personnel, both officers and enlisted men, assigned to battleships, the absence of a comprehensive training program for men assigned to these ships and total reliance on shipboard training, an annual turnover rate of 46 percent per year that essentially guaranteed that many men on battleships would not be fully trained, and perhaps most revealing, the void of a clear utilization plan for these ships that might have energized proper support.

Vice Adm. Peter M. Hekman, commander, Naval Sea Systems Command, made a statement to the House Banking Committee (Appendix F) implying that the relatively low level of training as reflected by the absence of E-5s and above on battleships was not unexpected: "Those statistics are not abnormal when one looks at the makeup of the crew. The battleships are not what we would call a high tech ship. . . . These ships were designed in the 1930s for an average education level in the Navy at that time of fifth grade."

This thoughtless remark was not only insensitive for the survivors attending and reading the transcript of the hearing but it suggested that training aboard the battleships was not a priority with the Navy command, that battleship manning, training, and turnover were nonissues to the command structure. It was counter to what Captain Moosally had argued for soon after coming aboard the *Iowa* and was later cited by Admiral Milligan in his investigation.

As is often the case in high-consequence incidents, early warning signals from below were ignored by top management, and underlying deficiencies in the management itself went unrecognized. Certainly the latter were simply ignored in the case of Admiral Kelso's news conference. The Navy, of course, maintained that these issues were entirely unrelated to the incident, and by implication that everything at the top was in good shape. The heart of the problem, the root cause, was well exemplified in what Admiral Kelso failed to even mention.

This news conference brought to an end the investigation of the explosion aboard the USS *Iowa*, one of the most tragic peacetime incidents in the history of our armed services.

Epilogue

ALTHOUGH THIS memoir is primarily concerned with the technical investigation of the tragic explosion aboard the USS *Iowa*, there are other points to be taken from the events surrounding this inquiry.

A high-consequence incident such as the explosion aboard the USS *Iowa* is inevitably followed by an investigation to identify direct and indirect causes of the incident. The depth and objectivity of the investigation depends on a number of factors, one of particular importance being the constituency of the investigating team. The team could be comprised of either members of the organization in which the incident occurred or outside and uninvolved members free of conflicting interests. This will determine whether the investigation is a self-assessment or an independent assessment.

While a self-assessment team may bring more direct understanding to the investigation at the outset, there may also be an inherent subjectivity in which it is assumed that internal management processes, organizational capabilities, resident expertise, and so on are beyond reproach. This may take form in implicit assumptions: we are the experts in this arena and are in full possession of the basic knowledge; we rarely make mistakes, and if there were any problems we would have found them long ago; our processes have stood the test of time; no one could have anticipated this unusual coincidence of circumstances or this irrational act.

Subjectivity can also emanate from top management both before and after an incident. Management may convey tacitly understood messages that they do not welcome discussion of deficiencies or shortcomings in their high-consequence operation, and after an incident, these messages may exert pressure on lower management levels to protect the organization from criticism.

Groupthink and arrogance can lead to diverting the cause (oversight, negligence, malfeasance) anywhere but within the organization.

There are a few notable investigations of high-consequence incidents in recent years that are examples of failed self-assessments, and the explosion aboard the USS *Iowa* is one of these. The Navy's Opinion 55 captures the essence of taking the position of nonresponsibility and going to lengths to divert even minor elements of fault away from the organization.

High-consequence incidents should be addressed by an independent group capable of competently addressing both detailed and root-cause issues. However, it is important to clearly define the assessment task and to conclude the effort when the basic elements of the task are completed—to avoid extension of the assessment role into areas for which the team may not be qualified.

A second general observation is the abuse that results when a powerful organization manipulates the press to promulgate self-serving and fallacious information. Prior to the release of the Navy's report, officials in the Navy and the Defense Department released unverified and sensational information to the media provided that the officials not be identified. These acts contributed little to the state of understanding, appeared as attempts to prepare the public for conclusions in the Navy's report, and in the end these actions by a few had the effect of discrediting the entire Navy. Vice Adm. Joseph S. Donnell III's statement to the Committee on Armed Services of the House of Representatives that "leaks to the media . . . became more than an annoyance and embarrassment and threatened to undermine the investigative effort" was not followed by an effort to identify and deal with the source(s) or, in the longer range, to establish processes to control such actions. Inaction by the Navy to restrain unofficial news releases raised questions about the sincerity of Admiral Donnell's statement and further diminished the integrity of the service by implying that some in the Navy condoned such practices.

A third and related concern is the indiscriminate recitation by the press of sensational material from unidentified sources without reasonable efforts to verify or corroborate. While early reports of the incident were generally informative, subsequent unsubstantiated rumors about *Iowa* crewmen damaged the memory and reputation of these men, wounded their families, disillusioned the survivors, and did little to clarify or to inform. Sensational gossip was published by papers like the *New York Times*. Damaging words of a crewman against those accused by the Navy of crimes were later recanted, but the injury had been done by the omission of thoughtful efforts to authenticate those reports in the first place. The temptation to reveal such "information" outweighed the journalist's integrity to verify or confirm. Writers, editors, and publishers could well reexamine how they deal with reports by those who will not be named, and establish standards for the affirmation of such reports before they are published.

A fourth concern is the absence of due process in military justice as it relates to deceased service personnel. The process by which military servicemen and -women are accused of wrongdoing needs to be reexamined, particularly if the accused are deceased. The accusations and allegations made against Clayton Hartwig were never subjected to a formal process—or one that had a basis in our common law. Clayton Hartwig, a convenient and silent target, was accused of serious crimes by a powerful organization and evidence was authoritatively presented as fact by top Navy officers. In the last analysis, the "evidence" was at best ambiguous—and at worst nonexistent. While inadequacy of the evidence eventually forced the Navy to withdraw its accusations, the damage to the memory of this individual and his family, not to mention the self-inflicted damage to the Navy, should never have occurred in the first place.

If the military chooses to accuse deceased service people of crimes, it should be a formal process in which the evidence is judged to be clear and convincing by an independent review. The formal process should be one in which the deceased service person is represented by an advocate who can cross-examine accusers, call witnesses and present a defense. This would be consistent with our concept of due process, and why should military process be exempt from these principles?

Finally, there is the matter of the crewmen aboard the *Iowa* who struggled and succeeded in bringing the fire under control following the explosion, a fire that could have resulted in a greater loss of life and possible loss of the ship. A number of these men, on their own, took considerable risks, such as unloading the three guns following the explosion. They deserved substantial recognition for their courage and actions in the face of grave threats. While a number of them were awarded medals for their actions, the Navy failed to hold up their accomplishment as an example of the best in military service and to ensure that they received the recognition they deserved. In this, both the Navy and the fourth estate failed miserably.

Appendix A

Elements of the Navy Report

The U.S. Navy report, "Investigation into the 19 April 1989 Explosion in Turret II USS *Iowa* (BB-61)," dated 15 July 1989, was submitted to the commander, Naval Surface Force, U.S. Atlantic Fleet, by Rear Adm. Richard D. Milligan, U.S. Navy, the chief investigating officer. The Navy's technical investigation had been led by Capt. Joseph D. Miceli, Naval Sea Systems Command, who served as director of the Navy's Technical Review Team.

The Technical Review Team was charged with three principal tasks: (1) conduct a comprehensive assessment of the *Iowa*'s Turret II, including determination of reparability, estimated cost, and schedule; (2) conduct such inspection, tests, and analyses as needed to determine the cause (or most probable cause) of the incident; and (3) determine what actions, if any, were necessary to permit lifting the restriction on firing the 16-inch guns.

The Navy's technical investigation developed a Cause and Effects Analysis to provide a guide in methodically investigating all conceivable sources of ignition of the propellant train. This listing of potential sources of ignition related to turret malfunctions, propellant stability, frictional heating (of the propellant), impact and compression (of the propellant bags), electrostatic discharge, electromagnetic radiation, and foreign materials. The Navy team conducted tests in each of these areas in an attempt to determine the cause of the explosion.

Admiral Milligan's report included an Executive Summary, Preliminary Statement, Findings of Fact, Opinions, Recommendations, and Endorsements. The report was accompanied by nearly three hundred enclosures that detailed interviews with the crew, excerpts from various operational manuals, and several other reports relevant to the investigation. Following are entire or abstracted parts of these sections:

Executive Summary

On 19 April 1989 at 0955 local time, as the center gun crew of the USS *IOWA* (BB 61) Turret II loaded five 94-pound bags of smokeless powder from NALC D846 into the gun's open breech, the powder exploded. The force of the explosion drove a 2700 lb Blind Loaded and Plugged (BL&P) projectile about three feet one-inch into the rifling.

Instantaneously, fire and blast of extreme velocity, pressure and temperature spread throughout Turret II. The blast blew back through the gun house into the Turret Officer's booth, into the left and right gun rooms and down through the powder trunks and vents to the lower levels of the turret.

Within seconds, a second explosion occurred when an unknown number of powder bags detonated (low order) and burned in the powder handling flat, filling the turret with smoke. Subsequently, a third detonation (low order) occurred between time GQ plus eight and nine.

All forty-seven (47) servicemen in Turret II at the time of the explosion died instantaneously or nearly instantaneously of either blast, blunt force and/or thermal injuries. All were positively identified by dental records and/or fingerprints. Medical evaluation of the deceased servicemen discloses no evidence of drug or alcohol use. Twelve personnel in Turret II's annular space and magazine at the time of the explosion survived without injury. No personnel outside the turret sustained injuries as a result of the explosions.

At the time of the explosion, *Iowa* was in the North Puerto Rico Operating Area (PROA) participating in FLEETEX 3-89 (ADVANCED). Specifically, *Iowa* was engaged in Open Ocean Naval Gun Fire Support (NGFS) training her Marine detachment in calling missions and spotting rounds, training gunnery personnel in delivering fire against a point target, and verifying operability of the Main Gun Battery.

In commencing the 19 April 1989 NGFS exercise, the firing sequence for the Main Gun Battery was to begin with Turret I firing single round salvos, reduced charge, from each gun. Turret I's firing sequence began with the left gun misfiring. Proper misfire procedures were immediately initiated in the left gun Turret I. The center and right guns both fired two single round salvos with the left gun misfiring again after the first two rounds and the second two rounds. The firing sequence proceeded to Turret II. The misfire in Turret I had no direct relationship to events that followed in Turret II.

Material Condition Zebra had been reported as set in Turret II, yet post-incident inspection indicates Zebra had not been uniformly set throughout the turret. Material Condition Zebra was specifically broken and reset to permit a powderman to exit the powder handling flat and the turret.

Subsequent to this, the order to load was passed. Despite written prohibitions and warnings against using NALC D846 with 2700 lb projectiles, Turret II was scheduled to fire ten rounds using five full charge bags of powder from NALC D846 with 2700 lb projectiles. One round of NALC D846 consists of six bags (nothing more or less). Five bags is an abnormal and unauthorized load configuration.

In preparing to fire multiple rounds, the powdermen in the magazine passed approximately forty-one (41) 94-pound bags of powder into the annular space where other powdermen passed forty (40) of those bags through to the powder handling flat of the turret. Fifteen bags were in the guns and twenty-five (25) on the powder handling flat at the time of the explosion.

In preparing for the 19 April 1989 gunnery exercise, *Iowa* held prefire briefs on 18 April 1989, to cover firing plan specifics. To minimize the number of personnel at any one brief, the ship held two separate briefs, the "pre-prefire" and the "prefire" briefs. The ship, however, did not take musters at either, and approximately half the people required to be present were absent. The Commanding Officer did not attend either of the prefire briefs.

With respect to training and qualification, applicable Personnel Qualification Standard (PQS) directives require the Commanding Officer, Executive Officer, Training Officer, PQS Coordinator, Department Heads, Department PQS Coordinators and Division Officers to establish, maintain, and supervise a formal PQS program for qualifying personnel on various shipboard watch stations. Turret watch stations are not excluded from this program. Training received by *Iowa* gunnery personnel, however, is suspect.

Personnel within the turrets came from two basic sources, the Weapons and Deck Departments. Deck Department personnel assigned to Turret General Quarters or Condition III watch stations were not PQS qualified by either the Deck Department or Weapons Department. Deck Department personnel assigned to turret crews were trained almost exclusively during gun firing evolution, but this training was not documented.

Of the fifty-five (55) watch stations actually manned in Turret I on 19 April 1989 which required formal PQS qualified watch standers, four (4) personnel were PQS qualified. In Turret II, thirteen (13) out of fifty-one (51) personnel were PQS qualified and in Turret III, nine (9) out of sixty-two (62) were PQS qualified. ENS Effren S. Garrett, IV, USN, was the only officer in Turret I after being onboard for only sixteen (16) days. He was not familiar with turret operations, safety or misfire/hangfire procedures.

PQS Boards in all three turret divisions were not reviewed weekly. The Training Officer/PQS Coordinator did not submit monthly PQS progress reports to the Commanding Officer as required. Neither the Commanding Officer, Executive Officer, Weapons Officer nor the Gunnery Officer knew of the large number of watch stations being manned by personnel not qualified under the PQS program.

In contrast to the poor PQS training program, the damage control efforts of the ship's crew were extraordinary. Crew members led by BM2 Charles R. Dickinson, USN, on main deck, and BM1 Mark A. Tonielli, USN, on the 01 level, quickly responded to General Quarters. Charged hoses were spraying Turret II from outside, shooting water through open hatches, around the gun barrels and in through vents within minutes of the explosion. Although many members responding to the mass conflagration were not in full battle dress and were unfamiliar with the physical layout of Turret II, they nevertheless fought the fire valiantly and effectively.

CAPT Jeffery W. Bolander, USMC, and 1ST SGT Bruce W. Richardson, USMC, were quickly on scene and, in an effort to rescue any Turret II survivors, quickly forced open an emergency escape hatch. Within time General Quarters plus eight, FN Brian R. Scanio, USN, ENFA Robert O. Shepherd, USN, FR Ronald G. Robb, USN, and MR3 Thad W. Harms, USN, all members of repair V, entered Turret II gun house and fought the fire from within. Protected from the extreme interior heat by recently delivered one piece fire fighting ensembles and OBS's, their brave efforts quickly brought the fire in the gun house under control.

GMGC J. C. Miller, USN, GMG1 Verlin W. Allen, USN, and HT1 Thomas J. Smith, USN, immediately entered behind the first four servicemen and took control of the fire fighting efforts from within, applying Aqueous Film Forming Foam (AFFF), and setting reflash watches. At great personal risk, these three servicemen stayed in Turret II, almost continuously, until all fires were extinguished. Although too numerous to list in this summary, in helping to save their ship and attempting to rescue their shipmates, many *Iowa* crewmen distinguished themselves.

Many possibilities for the cause of detonation have been investigated. The burning ember theory has been ruled out. The primer was removed and had not fired. Questions of static electricity generated sparks (ESD) or electromagnetic radiation (HERO) as a source of ignition have been tested and available data rules them out.

Although the powder used in Turret II had been temporarily stored at Naval

Weapons Station, Yorktown, Virginia, in barges from April until August 1988 without temperature or humidity records, controlled tests of powder from the same lot number, including powder from the magazines of *Iowa* Turrets I, II, and III, indicate both the black powder and the propellant were stable. Tests showed that any possible static electric spark within the gun turret was too insignificant to ignite either the black powder or propellant. Moreover, after thorough investigation, no mechanical failure in the gun room was found that could have been or served as a source of ignition.

Analysis of the reconstructed rammer places the rammer head about 21 inches past its normal point inside the breech at the time of the explosion. At this position the rammer would have pushed the five powder bags up to the base of the projectile while constricting the opening and defining a confined space. Controlled tests of similar powder explosions indicated detonation occurred in the area of the first and second bags from the projectile in the breech and was a high order explosion generating about a 4,000 psi pressure wave.

The investigation into and the analysis of all potential causes of this tragic explosion have been complicated by the issues of improperly loaded munitions in the center gun (NALC D881 projectile with five full charge bags from NALC D846 vice six), lack of an effective and properly supervised assignment and qualification process, and poor adherence to explosive safety regulations and ordnance safety. While none of these factors have been determined to be the cause of the explosion, or provide an ignition source, they cast the proper operation of gunnery systems in USS *Iowa* (BB 61) in a very poor light and generate doubt.

Despite extensive testing, no anomalies which could have served as an accidental source of ignition have been found in either hardware or ammunition components. There is strong evidence, however, to support an opinion that a wrongful intentional act caused this incident.

Preliminary Statement

1. By 19 April 1989 oral appointing order, VADM J. S. Donnell, U.S. Navy, Commander, Naval Surface Force, U.S. Atlantic Fleet, appointed RADM Richard D. Milligan, U.S. Navy, to conduct a one officer investigation into circumstances related to the explosion in Turret II on board USS *Iowa* (BB 61) in the vicinity of the Puerto Rican operating area (PROA) on 19 April 1989. The original oral appointing order was subsequently confirmed, in writing, on 27 April 1989 by enclosure (1).

2. This investigation commenced in USS *Iowa* (BB 61) on 20 April 1989 and continued on board USS *Iowa* (BB 61), at Naval Legal Service Office, Norfolk,

Virginia, and at Headquarters, Naval Surface Force, U.S. Atlantic Fleet until completion. Assigned counsel for the Investigating Officer was Commander Ronald V. Swanson, JAGC, USN. The following officers assisted the Investigating Officer as required:

Captain Edward F. Messina, USN
Lieutenant Commander Timothy J. Quinn, USN
Lieutenant Jeffrey W. Styron, JAGC, USN
Lieutenant Benjamin F. Roper, USN
Lieutenant James F. Buckley II, USN
Lieutenant Patrick M. Brogan, JAGC, USNR
Lieutenant (junior grade) James T. Black, USN

Additional Navy and Army technical expertise and assistance was provided by activities listed in enclosure (2) pp. 2, 3, Appendix M and Addendum 3 pp. 2, 3 to enclosure (2) under the direction of Captain Joseph D. Miceli, U.S. Navy, Naval Sea Systems Command (SEA-06X).

3. On 8 May 1989, after receiving information that suggested motive for a criminal act that could have caused the 19 April 1989 explosion in Turret II, USS *Iowa* (BB 61), I made a formal oral recommendation to the Convening Authority that he immediately initiate a criminal investigation into circumstances surrounding the incident. Commander, Naval Surface Force, U.S. Atlantic Fleet, on 8 May 1989, directed the Naval Investigative Service (NIS) to commence such an investigation. Although that investigation remains open and is ongoing, I have reviewed the 21 June and 10 July, 1989, NIS interim reports. Certain Findings of Fact and expressed Opinions contained in this report have been formulated after full consideration of the contents of those reports. Section 0212 of reference (a) proscribes inclusion of Naval Investigative Service Reports of Investigation in JAG Manual Investigations. Accordingly, a transcript of testimony taken from Mr. Robert M. Nigro, the NIS case supervisor for the criminal investigation of this incident, has been included in this report to serve as an abbreviated foundation for Facts and Opinions formulated after consideration of the NIS investigation.

Findings of Fact

1. At 0955 on 19 April 1989, while being loaded into the open breech of the center gun of Turret II in USS *Iowa* (BB 61), five 94-pound bags of smokeless powder from NALC D846 ignited. [Enclosures.]

2. The force of the explosion drove a 2700 lb. BL&P projectile about three-feet one-inch into the rifling with the blast blowing back through the gun

house into the Turret Officer's booth, into the left and right gun rooms, and down through the powder trunks and vents to the lower levels of the turret. [Enclosures.] . . .

8. All forty-seven (47) servicemen in Turret II proper at the time of the explosion died instantaneously or nearly instantaneously of either blast, blunt force and/or thermal injuries. All were positively identified by dental records and/or fingerprints. Post-incident medical evaluation disclosed no evidence of drug or alcohol use by deceased servicemen. [Enclosures.] . . .

20. If all personnel assigned to the above positions had attended the 18 April 1989 pre-prefire brief, the actual number of service members in attendance would have been in excess of 100 people. [Enclosures.]

21. *Iowa* procedures did not ensure safety briefs were systematically conducted for all main gun battery personnel before gunnery exercises. [Enclosures.] . . .

24. At the pre-prefire brief, personnel were not mustered, but approximately forty (40) servicemen attended. [Enclosures.] . . .

27. The Commanding Officer was subsequently briefed on the firing plan, while on the bridge . . . immediately before commencing the exercise. [Enclosures.] . . .

30. The Weapons Officer intended to request authorization from the Commanding Officer to fire the right and center guns of Turret III (left gun of Turret III was inoperable due to a broken powder hoist). No request was ever made or received. However, Turret III personnel prepared to fire 2700 projectiles (NACL D881) using four bags of full charge powder from NALC D846 by moving ordnance within the turret. [Enclosures.]

31. On and before 19 April 1989, the Commanding Officer's policy was that no ordnance could be moved in *Iowa* without his direct authorization. [Enclosures.] . . .

33. The Commanding Officer was not advised of the plan to fire right and center guns of Turret III or the load configuration intended to be fired from these guns. [Enclosures.] . . .

41. On 19 April 1989, at morning quarters, both the Turret Officer and Turret Captain advised G-2 division personnel they would be firing 2700 lb projectiles (NALC D881) with five full charge powder bags from NALC D846 that morning. A total of ten rounds were to be fired, two from left and four from both center and right guns, respectively. [Enclosures.] . . .

44. NALC D846 powder cans and the ammunition data cards contained therein state: "WARNING DO NOT USE WITH 2700 LB (AP, BL&P) PROJECTILE." [Enclosures.]

45. Although the Commanding Officer knew Turrets I and II would fire reduced charges on 19 April 1989, he did not know the reduced charge anticipated for firing in Turret II was to be an abnormally configured charge of five full charge bags instead of six reduced charge bags. [Enclosures.] . . .

50. *Iowa* had no authority to fire 1900 lb projectiles with less than six bags of powder on 4 November 1987, nor did *Iowa* have any authority to shoot 2700 lb projectiles NALC D881 with any amount of full powder charge from NALC D846 on 7 November 1987 or on 19 April 1989. [Enclosures.] . . .

54. LTJG Buck ordered all (Turret II) guns one round, load in response to FC2(SW) Colage's communication. Left gun was loaded in forty-four (44) seconds, right gun was loaded in sixty-one (61) seconds, and center gun did not complete loading. (As timed by Investigating Officer from video tape recording submitted with this report as Enclosure [79].) [Enclosures.]

55. LTJG Buck reported, "Left gun loaded" and then "Right gun loaded." Ten seconds later, there was a premature detonation in Turret II, and communications with Turret II ceased. Approximately eighty-six (86) seconds elapsed between placing the gun to load elevation and the explosion. . . . [Enclosures.] . . .

59. GMG3 Mullahy recalls hearing GMG2(SW) Richard E. Lawrence, USN, state over the "XJ" circuit, "I have a problem here, I'm not ready yet." [Enclosure.]

60. Additionally, GMG3 Mullahy recalls that shortly before the explosion, he heard over the "XJ" circuit GMCS(SW) Ziegler shout to LTJG Buch: Tell plot we are not ready yet, there is a problem in center gun, or words to that effect. GMG3 Mullahy also recalls hearing GMG2(SW) Lawrence excitedly restate, "I'm not ready yet. I'm not ready yet." [Enclosure.] . . .

72. At time of detonation the cradle was spanned and the rammer was inside the breech in a forward ramming cycle about 21 inches past the end position of a normal powder ram. This position would place the powder at the base of the projectile. The rammer control mechanism was positioned to produce movement of approximately one foot per second in the ramming direction. . . . After detonation, the force of the explosion shattered the rammer chain, hurling the rammer head against the after bulkhead and blew the door and door frame off center gun room. [Enclosures.] . . .

82. The Ship Manning Document identifies ninety (90) positions to be filled in Turret II during General Quarters. . . . [Note: the following listing is only for the center gun.]

CENTER GUN CAPT	GMG2(SW) Richard E. Lawrence, USN
CENTER CRADLE	BM2 Gary J. Fisk, USN

CENTER RAMMER	GMG3 Robert W. Backherms, USN
CENTER PRIMERMAN	SR Reginald L. Johnson, Jr., USN
CENTER POWDER CAR	SN David Williams, USN. . . .

137. Post-incident tests and analysis disclosed that the center gun, Turret II, rammer system was operating properly up to the time of the explosion. [Enclosures.] . . .

139. On 19 April 1989, remote operation of Turret II hydraulic sprinkler system was not possible from Turret I annular space. Similarly, the center gun Turret II powder hoist had to be stopped manually vice automatically as designed and as possible in both right and left gun powder hoists. Although these discrepancies existed for an indeterminate but lengthy period prior to 19 April 1989, no CASREPs were submitted. [Enclosures.] . . .

151. Capt Jeffery W. Bolander, USMC, and 1st SGT Richardson, USMC, were the first personnel to reach the 01 level outside Turret II. With some difficulty, yet within eight minutes of the explosion, they opened Turret II's emergency escape hatch to rescue any possible survivors. [Enclosures.] . . .

153. Prior to the opening of the escape hatch, a number of crew members led by BM2 Dickinson, right gun captain of Mount 54, had charged hoses and were spraying water into Turret II from port side main deck. [Enclosures.]

154. Simultaneously, a group led by BM1 Tonielli, hooked up a hose on the 01 level and also began spraying Turret II. [Enclosures.]

155. As soon as the escape hatch was opened, FN Scanio, a repair V member, in a recently delivered one-piece fire fighting ensemble and OBA, entered the turret through the opened escape hatch to fight the fire. [Enclosures.] . . .

157. While alone in the turret, a secondary explosion pushed FN Scanio against an interior bulkhead. This explosion occurred between General Quarters plus eight and nine minutes as announced on the 1MC. [Enclosures.]

158. Immediately thereafter, ENFN Shepherd, FR Robb, and MR3 Harms, all from repair V, joined FN Scanio within the turret fighting the fire. All wore the new one-piece fire fighting ensembles. [Enclosures.] . . .

160. GMGC Miller, GMG1 Allen, and HT1 Smith (all wearing flash gear and OBA's) then entered the turret and took charge of fire fighting efforts until all fires were extinguished. [Enclosures.]

161. As repair parties initiated fire fighting efforts on deck, the men stationed in the annular space of Turret II and the men in magazine A-515-M escaped and attacked the fire by other means. Specifics: . . .

a. Upon hearing the explosion, GMG3 Mullahy, a petty officer in the magazine, departed the magazine, and entered the annular space. He opened the watertight door into the powder handling flat and took two steps in. Upon seeing active fire, feeling extreme heat, and receiving no response to his call for survivors, he retreated.

b. The personnel from the magazine and annular space evacuated, redogging all hatches behind them as they departed their spaces.

c. GMG3 Mullahy went to DC central and activated the groups three and four powder magazine sprinkler system and the electrically activated sprinkler system covering the annular space and the outer (nonrotating) portion of the projectile magazines. Then GNG3 Mullahy assisted the Damage Control Assistant (DCA) in setting fire boundaries from DC Central. [Enclosures.] . . .

165. After all fires were out, the presence of unburned ordnance and hydraulic oil continued to present a significant safety hazard. Ordnance disposal and cleanup efforts were quickly initiated and subsequently continued for several days. [Enclosures.] . . .

175. Applicable Personnel Qualification Standard (PQS) directives require the Commanding Officer, Executive Officer, Training Officer, PQS Coordinator, Department Head, Division Officer and the Department PQS Coordinator to establish, maintain, and supervise a formal PQS program for qualifying personnel on various main gun battery watch stations. [Enclosures.] . . .

179. In *Iowa*, watch stations which require formal PQS certification must be manned by personnel qualified through the PQS program. Prior to 19 April 1989, *Iowa*'s Commanding Officer established a policy which stated no person was to be assigned a watch station unless PQS qualified to stand that watch. No one was allowed to stand an under instruction watch unless he was observed by a qualified person. [Enclosures.] . . .

193. Only thirteen (13) of fifty-one (51) watch stations actually manned in Turret II requiring formal PQS qualification were filled with PQS qualified personnel at the time of the 19 April 1989 explosion in Turret II. There were some personnel assigned to watch stations in Turret II whose PQS books could not be obtained. These books were either destroyed by fire, never existed, or have not been located. Accordingly, since no PQS book was found for a deceased service member, findings are based exclusively on service record page four entries. Available Turret II personnel PQS books are enclosures (226–242). The following is a list of personnel by watch station and their PQS qualification status as of 19 April 1989: [Note: Only a portion of the listing in the report is noted below.]

Position	*Person Manning*	*PQS Qualified*
C Gun Captain	GMG2 Hartwig	yes
C Cradle Operator	GMG2(SW) Lawrence	yes
C Rammerman	GMG3 Backherm	no
C Primerman	SN Johnson	no
C Powder Hoist Op	BM2 Fisk	no

201. BM2 Fisk was assigned to Turret II and walked through his duties as upper Powder hoist operator for center gun Turret II a "few" days before the accident. BM2 Fisk was not PQS qualified for this position. [Enclosures.] . . .

203. The Commanding Officer, Executive Officer, the Weapons Officer and the Gunnery Officer were not aware of the current qualification status of personnel assigned to the 16-inch/50 caliber turrets. None were aware of the large number of watch stations being manned by personnel not qualified under the PQS program. [Enclosures.] . . .

216. The following are the most plausible non-intentional causes, in no specific order, for the explosion in center gun Turret II on 19 April 1989.

a. Burning ember

b. Premature primer firing

c. Mechanical failure

d. Hazards of Electromagnetic Radiation to Ordnance (HERO/EMI)

e. Electrostatic discharge (ESD)

f. Propellant instability

g. Friction

h. Personnel error. . . .

226. Friction (related causes)

i. There were inexperienced personnel manning assigned Turret II center gun watch stations, specifically the rammerman and the primerman. [Enclosures.]

j. Although the rammerman in center gun Turret II was not PQS qualified and had never served as rammerman for a live firing, he had observed five live fire exercises (14 rounds) and had practiced operating the rammer prior to filling the position on 19 April 1989. To be qualified under the Navy PQS program in effect on 19 April 1989 (NAVEDTRA 43415) an individual must have demonstrated an ability to ram/retract the rammer once and must have stood two (2) watches under qualified supervision. [Enclosures.]

k. An improper ramming of the powder bags caused the rammer to be extended about 21 inches past the point of a normal ram pushing the powder bags to the base of the projectile. [Enclosures.] . . .

229. No accidental cause for premature ignition of powder located in the center gun, Turret II on 19 April 1989 has been identified. [Enclosures.]

230. An intentional wrongful act as the source of ignition was considered. The following related facts, compiled after review of the interim NIS reports of investigation and enclosures (274) through (278), and as discussed in paragraph 3 of the Preliminary Statement, are germane:

a. GMG2 Clayton M. Hartwig, USN, Turret II center gun captain on 19 April 1989, was a capable Gunner's Mate equipped with a working knowledge of explosives and explosive devices. He graduated from the basic electricity and electronics (Class P) and Gunner's Mate (Class A) schools and possessed literature on how to build explosive devices.

b. GMG2 Clayton M. Hartwig, USN, Turret II center gun captain on 19 April 1989, experimented with, was capable of, and had made explosive and detonation devices prior to 19 April 1989.

c. GMG2 Clayton M. Hartwig, USN, center gun captain, Turret II, on 19 April 1989, was the serviceman closest to the location of premature ignition of powder in the gun. He had full access and opportunity to intentionally cause premature detonation by placement of an ignition source into center gun, Turret II.

d. The rotating band from the projectile in center gun, Turret II on 19 April 1989, was removed and analyzed. Similarly, analysis was conducted on two other rotating bands; A "control" band from a projectile used in a test firing employing a standard propelling charge and a rotating band from a projectile used in a test firing which employed a timer controlled explosive device.

e. Metallurgists at the Norfolk Naval Shipyard determined the rotating band from the projectile in *Iowa*'s center gun, Turret II on 19 April 1989, contains traces of Aluminum, Silicon, Calcium, Barium and Iron Wire, all inorganic materials not found in an uncontaminated propelling charge.

f. All three rotating bands have been examined under a Scanning Electron Microscope (SEM). The overall SEM spectra show a close comparison between the *Iowa* ring and the ring from the test firing employing a timer controlled explosive device and a marked difference in properties between these two rings and the "control" ring.

g. A post-incident "equivocal death analysis" was prepared by qualified psychologists from the National Center for the Analysis of Violent Crime (NCAVC), Federal Bureau of Investigation (FBI) Academy in response to an NIS request and as part of the criminal investigation into this incident. Opinions formulated in that report concern GNG2 Clayton M. Hartwig, USN. . . . After lengthy review, the analysis concludes: "Clayton Hartwig died as a result of his own action, staging his death in such a fashion that he hoped it would appear to be an accident."

Opinions

1. There was not a viable Main Gun Battery PQS program in *Iowa* on 19 April 1989. [Findings.] . . .

7. *Iowa*'s failure to adhere to the formalized PQS qualification process negates structured Navy wide quality control policies designed to ensure uniform and effective training of 16-inch/50 caliber gun battery watch standers. [Findings.]

8. *Iowa*'s turret watch stations were informally assigned at the Division Officer level, and subject to last minute undocumented changes. Such last minute substitutions occurred in Turret II on 19 April 1989. This may have resulted in confusion on the part of some center gun Turret II personnel during loading operations. [Findings.] . . .

13. Ineffective enforcement of safety policy and procedures was the norm within Turret II. Specifically: . . .

e. Standard safety briefs were not given. [Findings.]

14. The complexities of turret operations, when coupled with the relative inexperience of main gun battery turret officers, contributed to poor management and administration of maintenance, safety and training programs. [Findings.]

15. As a result of the efforts of . . . [working informally with employees of NAVSWC Dahlgren], *Iowa* utilized her Main Gun Battery to engage in unauthorized Research and Development. [Findings.] . . .

26. *Iowa*'s turret crews were not properly prepared for the Main Gun Battery gunshoot on 19 April 1989. [Findings.] . . .

50. No musters were taken at either the pre-prefire brief or the prefire brief. Firings conducted were inconsistent with the written prefire plan. Accordingly, it cannot be determined that center gun Turret II personnel were adequately briefed and confusion may have resulted from an abnormal configuration of five vice six powder bags. [Findings.] . . .

52. The investigation into and the analysis of all potential causes of this

tragic explosion have been complicated by the issues of improperly loaded munitions in the center gun (NALC D881 projectile with five full charge bags vice six), lack of effective, properly supervised assignment and qualification processes, and poor adherence to explosive safety regulations and ordnance safety. While these and all other personnel error related issues were not the cause of the explosion and did not provide an ignition source, they cast the proper operation of gunnery systems in USS *Iowa* (BB-61) in a poor light and generate doubt. Further, such a substandard operations and readiness baseline results in systemic deficiencies that can serve as a foundation for disaster. [Findings.]

53. Personnel error could only have caused the rammer to extend about 21 inches past the normal position as the result of an improper signal on the part of the gun captain, miscommunication of signals between the gun captain and rammerman, or improper operation of the rammer by the rammerman. None of these causes are likely in light of the qualifications of the gun captain, the training of the rammerman, and the fact that the rammer was in the proper slow ahead position for a powder ram. The rammer was extended beyond the normal position by the rammerman in response to an overt and intentionally conveyed hand signal on the part of GMG2 Hartwig, Turret II's center gun captain. [Findings.]

54. In the normal course of events, the 19 April 1989 ramming of five powder bags about 21 inches past the standard ram position could not have caused premature ignition. [Findings.]

55. The explosion in center gun, Turret II, USS *Iowa* (BB-61) on 19 April 1989 resulted from a wrongful intentional act. [Findings.]

56. Based on this investigative report and after full review of all Naval Investigative Service's reports to date, the wrongful intentional act that caused this incident was most probably committed by GMG2 Clayton M. Hartwig, USN. [Findings.]

The Recommendations section of the report included twenty-one recommendations related to investigations, procedure changes, manning of battleships, training processes, and personnel actions. The report was signed by Admiral Milligan and endorsed with attached statements by Admiral J. S. Donnell III, Commander, Naval Surface Force, U.S. Atlantic Fleet; Admiral P. F. Carter Jr., Commander in Chief, U.S. Atlantic Fleet; and Admiral C. A. N. Trost, Chief of Naval Operations.

Appendix B

Explosions in Gun Rooms

Explosions in gun rooms of naval vessels are an infrequent but not an unknown phenomena. An incident similar to that which happened on board the *Iowa* occurred on the battleship USS *Mississippi* (BB-41) in 1924. This ship was launched on 25 January 1917, and 14-inch rather than 16-inch guns were the standard at that time. During a gunnery exercise off San Pedro on 12 June 1924, an explosion in Turret II killed forty-eight crewmen. This incident was essentially repeated during World War II. The *Mississippi* had been overhauled in San Francisco and sailed from San Pedro on 19 October 1943 to take part in the invasion of the Gilbert Islands. As the ship was participating in a bombardment of Makin on November 20, an explosion in the same turret killed forty-three crewmen. As in the case of the *Iowa*, these strangely similar explosions took place in Turret II and involved open-breech ignition of the propellant. The causes for these two incidents aboard the *Mississippi* were never definitively established.

The last incident of this kind prior to the *Iowa* took place in 1972 during the Vietnam War, when an explosion occurred in the number two 8-inch gun turret on the heavy cruiser *Newport News*. Twenty of the crew were killed and ten were injured. The cruiser, the largest in the Seventh Fleet at that time and carrying a crew of thirteen hundred, was located near the DMZ, approximately thirteen miles north-northeast of Quangtri City, shelling North Vietnamese positions. The explosion occurred during the shelling at 1:00 A.M. local time on 1 October. Apparently a shell exploded inside the turret, but no definitive report on the incident has ever been released.

Appendix C

Other Testimony before Joint Committees of the House

Following is the testimony of GMG3 Kendall Truitt, GMG2 John Mullahy, Dr. Richard L. Ault and Mr. Robert R. Hazelwood of the FBI, and Dr. Bryant L. Welch of the American Psychological Association before the House Investigations Subcommittee and the Defense Policy Panel of the House Committee on Armed Services on 12, 13, and 21 December 1989.

GMG3 Kendall Truitt

The committee interviewed GMG3 Kendall Truitt, former *Iowa* crew member, on 13 December. Truitt's testimony dealt in part with his perceptions of Clayton Hartwig and personal experiences with rammer operations in Turret II, but primarily with his actions on the morning of 19 April following the explosion.

Truitt believed that Clayton Hartwig was an unlikely person to have planned and initiated such an explosion. He noted that Hartwig was not on the watch bill for the gunnery exercise that morning and was a last-minute replacement as gun captain. He considered Hartwig to be mechanically inept and thought him essentially incapable of assembling a chemical ignitor of the kind proposed by the Navy.

With regard to the overram that occurred in the center gun, Truitt testified: "I have been in left gun in Turret II when we had a problem with the rammer. We lost control of it. We would be trying to ram it. Luckily we were using a bullet [and not propellant]. We would try and ram, and suddenly it was as if it was a car and you couldn't get it—it was shifting between neutral and drive basically, and it was—you couldn't control it basically. It would take off suddenly, stop without warning. They shut down the whole system. They tore apart the filters. They reworked it."

Truitt also testified with regard to his actions on the morning of the explosion:

Mr. Mavroules: Where were you during the explosion on April 19, and what duties were you performing on that particular day?

Mr. Truitt: I was in the magazine. I was the officer in charge along with Gunner's Mate Mullahy.

Mr. Mavroules: Now as a survivor of the explosion in the powder magazine in the gun turret, you are one of the few who had first-hand knowledge of what happened on April 19, 1989. What do you recall happening during the morning before the explosion?

Mr. Truitt: Everything was routine. We were told we would be shooting later that morning. I think it was postponed for an hour or so. I believe everybody was cleaning up as they routinely do. Nothing was out of the ordinary.

Mr. Mavroules: All right. Can you describe for us what occurred in your actions during and immediately after the explosion.

Mr. Truitt: We heard the explosion. We were all sitting down. We had been given the order to stop passing powder. We heard the explosion. The sequence wasn't right. We should have heard salvo signals, but we did not. John Mullahy, John was on the phones. We heard the explosion. We looked at each other, and we said that didn't sound right. He tried to get somebody on the phones. Nobody answered him on the phones. He said he was going to go and investigate. He dropped the phones, and started to walk out the door.

I was at the other end of the magazine. It was a very tight space. I started making my way through the magazine to get to the door. We had ordered our guys to restow the powder. By the time I got to the door, John had returned and said that the powder bags were on fire, and to evacuate the spaces. We ordered everybody to evacuate. We started going up the ladder.

I was going to go to D. C. Central [damage control], but John, below me, said I am going to go flood mags; I am going to go flood them. So I thought there was some smoke. My thoughts were that this could go any time. You better either head topside or you better at least get an OBA [oxygen breathing apparatus]. I went to the berthing, which is the closest space for an OBA. I was donning an OBA. By the time I had it on John came back from D. C. Central. He was kind of staggering, and there was a lot of smoke. He didn't look the best, and he said I think I got them. I hit them all. I think I got them.

There is no way of knowing when you light them off in D. C. Central if you get them or not. He said it is evacuated. I said okay. He helped me finish putting on the OBA. I said I will go check them. I went down to D. C. Central. He had hit all the right switches. They are—there was a lot of smoke in the D. C. Central. I didn't know how long he had stood there and cranked on the switches. They are all hydraulic. It is like cranking up a really old car with the handle on the front, and I set all the switches back to neutral and then back to flood and proceeded to crank as if it had never been done before. I was thinking, I was thinking I know I had just cranked them, but there was no switches, no gauges to tell you if they are actually flooding from D. C. Central.

I then went from D. C. Central back over to the ladder which led down to the magazines. I pulled a guy off from the ladder and said, "Watch me. I have got an OBA on. I don't know if I am going to make it up through the hatches or not." I said, "Basically be aware if I don't come back." I went down to the magazines. The dogs weren't all dogged; the doors weren't closed properly. They were flooding. I redogged all the doors. I walked over to the other magazines. I tightened them, walked up to the fourth deck magazines, inspected them. They were also flooding. I dogged all them properly, came up out of the hole, sat down for a minute to catch my breath. . . . Eventually I made it top side. They had removed, I think, five or six bodies and I went in to go inside and help. I went inside and started helping them remove bodies and identify them. I don't know how graphic you want me to get.

After that, we had removed most of the bodies from the top portion of the turret when they realized that left and right guns were still loaded. . . . I made seven trips with Fireman Glynn and a couple other guys down to the bottom of the turret, and we actually came on top of the water in the powder flats, and gave reports to the XO and CO about how high the water was, the progress of the flooding, the deflooding, where bodies were, who they were, if we could identify them.

On the last trip the water was about five feet deep. We waded across. There were bodies underneath the water. You couldn't really see them. We opened the door out of the powder flats into the annular and met the other deflooding crews on the side. After that I may have made one more trip in there.

GMG2 John Mullahy

GMG2 John Mullahy, former *Iowa* crew member, opened his testimony with a statement that included the circumstances surrounding his reassignment to the *Iowa*. Questioning followed:

Mr. Mavroules: Thank you, sir, for your opening statement. . . . Describe what happened during the time immediately before and after the explosion. In other words, whose voices did you hear, and what did they say?

Mr. Mullahy: When we first got on the lines, when we first started manning up, it was about 7:45. The word had come out . . . to man turrets I, II, III and some of the 5-inch mounts. . . . When I got down below to the magazine, there were a couple of guys already there, so I opened the magazine up, and Seaman Freeman, who is normally on the phones wasn't there either yet so I put on the phones. By the time everybody showed up, we gave our report. . . . Then Petty Officer Lawrence got on the phone and said we have a problem here, we are not ready yet, we have a problem here and that is when the explosion went. At the same time, you could hear Senior Chief Zeigler yelling over to Lieutenant Buch to tell Plot that we are not ready yet they have a problem there. That is when the explosion went.

We really—it was kind of hard to explain because it jolted a little bit. It was different from a normal gun shoot. I tried to reach someone on the intercom in the inner turret. . . . The phone lines were completely dead. So I opened the hatch, going out into the trunk area where the ladder is, and the armored hatch is going into the annular space, and also there is access to another mag[azine], and there was some smoke coming out of the top of the annular space hatch.

I yelled into the guys, into the magazine, to get out that there had been an explosion, and at that time there was some banging on the wall, and so I pounded the doors. A lot of times when you dog a door down they get tight, or they could have gotten jarred by the explosion, we don't really know. But I took the dogging wrench, and beat the door open and that is when the three guys in there came out.

All the lights were gone, communication. Emergency lighting didn't come on. I don't know if I opened the hatch going into the powder flats or if it was already ajar, but when I got inside the powder flats, I went and took a couple of steps.

The entire right side was on fire. There were a couple of bags of powder on fire, the Petty Officer in charge in there was good friend of mine. I had yelled his name out a couple of times. There was no reply, and I could see some of the personnel there, and when I saw the powder burning, I immediately got out of there, closed the hatch up there, closed the armored hatch. . . . I went around, being in the Navy at this present time for almost 19 years—at that time it was about 18, 18 years exactly. I had been a magazine sprinkler inspector before, and I have installed magazine sprinklers and repaired them. I immediately went to Damage Control Central, and even though I had not had permission from the Captain and knowing that only the Captain could give me permission to light off the sprinklers, I went ahead and first I hit the electric sprinkler system, which even Petty Officer Truitt did not know I did to this day. . . . They cover the eight magazines. You have got two groups, groups 3 and 4 are for Turret II. . . . I had no breathing apparatus. . . . I was still on my feet at the time. Then by the time I got up to the berthing part I was on my hands and knees.

Somebody had come by then and said that some of the engineers were still down in the hole, some of the master at arms were there. Petty Officer Melendez, me and him started grabbing the EEBDs, which are the emergency escape breathing devices. I didn't know it at the time, but I know who it is now, it was Petty Officer Maze, who was the electrician, came by, had an OBA on. He was taking the EEBDs down to the guys in the engineering spaces so they could get out.

Then the Damage Control Assistant, the DCA, Lieutenant Blacky, he came by and he grabs me and we went back down to the D. C. Central—the smoke and everything—still neither one of us had breathing devices on.

We started setting fire boundaries and everything else for the turret, and by that time, personnel started coming in with OBAs on, manning the various different positions in D. C. Central, because when I went in there to light off the sprinkler system, it had already been evacuated, it was abandoned.

So then he got overcome by smoke. Both of us were about trashed. We started on our way out to get out of there because there was another officer, there was a relief crew down there, and he passed out, and I carried him up. . . . That is when Captain Moosally was on the bridge. He passed the word for the medical people to go over there and get us. That was the first time I was treated for smoke inhalation. I was treated three times altogether, and I was working in the turret until like 4 in the morning.

Mullahy was questioned about his views of a homosexual relationship between Hartwig and Truitt. Mullahy said he thought there was no such relationship. He knew both Hartwig and Truitt well and saw them daily in the pursuit of their various jobs. Hartwig was his immediate supervisor. Mullahy said, "Petty Officer Hartwig also was a dedicated gunner's mate who knew gunnery and loved the *Iowa* very much. I just can't see him harming it in any way."

Mullahy went on to describe his impressions of some of the crewmen:

Mr. Mullahy: . . . They weren't druggers, none of them were dopers, they weren't incompetent. They were well trained. They were a good crew. Senior Chief Ziegler was probably one of the best Senior Chiefs I have ever met.

Petty Officer Hanyecz was the first class. The only thing he ever served on since he had been in the Navy was battleships. No one knew that turret better than Ernie. . . . There were a lot of people on board that ship that did a lot of things, and there were a lot of guys that aren't getting credit for things. . . . I was ordered to go to bed at four in the morning, and I know for a fact there were a lot of people up—Petty Officer Mortensen must have been up for a good thirty hours.

Mullahy found the Navy's scenario difficult to accept. He couldn't imagine that Hartwig would undertake to kill himself and his shipmates. He said that if Clayton Hartwig would have wanted to take his life, he could have done so in many simple ways, he didn't have to resort to such a scheme. Mullahy believed the explosion must have been an accident, perhaps caused by instability in the black powder.

Dr. Richard L. Ault and Mr. Robert R. Hazelwood, FBI

The hearing before the Joint Committees of the House on 21 December 1989 dealt with the Equivocal Death Analysis of Clayton Hartwig by the FBI psychologists that was a linchpin in the Navy's Opinions 55 and 56. Representing the FBI were Anthony E. Daniels, assistant director, Training Divisions, Dr. Richard L. Ault, and Mr. Robert R. Hazelwood, the latter two having conducted the Equivocal Death Analysis.

Also testifying was Commander Thomas Mountz, clinical psychologist for the Naval Investigative Service Command; Bryant L. Welch, J.D., Ph.D., executive director for professional practice, American Psychological Association; and a panel of psychologists organized by Dr. Welch, who had reviewed the development of a psychological profile of Clayton Hartwig.

The FBI team were the first to be interviewed by the committee. Dr. Richard Ault testified about their analysis and conclusion that Clayton Hartwig had committed suicide and killed forty-six of his comrades:

The reason that we arrived at the conclusion we arrived at, with our opinion, on the amount of evidence available, was that it was more than sufficient to arrive at that conclusion. We found that the quality of this information was excellent, based on our experience, and the emphasis should be placed on that fact, that in the report which Mr. Hazelwood is going to read to you and which I will help supplement, in the report we only used a small amount of information that we had available to us to sustain that report. It is, in fact, not the total of the evidence we felt we needed. We met with members of the Naval Investigative Service, who advised us that the Navy, because of numerous exacting tests, I think at the time they told us they had expended millions of dollars to determine a cause, they had ruled out accident as the cause of explosion. The Navy had received a letter concerning an insurance problem between two individuals who were involved in the explosion, and they also advised us that reliable forensic evidence revealed that Mr. Hartwig, in the turret, was out of position at the time of the explosion, and that as Gun Captain, he was in the best position to sabotage the gun.

Ault then introduced Hazelwood, who read key sections of their report. Hazelwood provided an extensive description of Clayton Hartwig from his perspective. This included details of Hartwig's early life, limited friendships, interpersonal problems, his career in the Navy, what were described as suicidal tendencies and "suicidal ideation," and his preoccupation with death. Hazelwood concluded his report:

In summary, it is our opinion that the victim [Clayton Hartwig] was a very troubled young man who had low self-esteem and coveted the power and authority he felt he could not possess. The real and perceived rejections of significant others emotionally devastated him. This, combined with the inability to verbally express anger and, faced with a multitude of stressors had he returned from the cruise, virtually ensured some type of reaction. In this case, in our opinion, it was in fact suicide. He did so in a place and manner designed to give him the recognition and respect that he felt was denied him.

Several questions by the chairman, Representative Aspin, Representative Mavroules, and Representative Sisisky pursued the point that Ault and Hazelwood had not conducted any interviews in formulating their opinion but had relied wholly on the interviews supplied by the Naval Investigative Service. Representative Aspin quoted from the FBI report: "It is the opinion of Mr. Hazelwood and Dr. Ault that the victim, Clayton Hartwig, died as a result of his own actions, staging his death in the way that would appear to be an accident."

Representative Mavroules asked the following questions:

Mr. Mavroules: Can you tell us here this morning that you are absolutely sure that this is what happened?

Mr. Hazelwood: Yes, sir.

Mr. Mavroules: You can say that?

Mr. Hazelwood: Yes, sir.

Mr. Mavroules: On the reports given to you by the NIS?

Mr. Hazelwood: Yes, sir.

After further discussion, Ault and Hazelwood acknowledged that interviewers other than those from NIS might have elicited different responses and have arrived at different conclusions. Representative McCloskey raised a related series of questions about the documentation sought out by Ault and Hazelwood in forming their conclusion:

Mr. McCloskey: . . . You mentioned that in the previous question as to information from the Naval Investigative Service about his personal records. Psychological, alcohol use, et cetera. You said something about having received them orally. Can you tell me what that means?

Dr. Ault: We asked the NIS about the drug use, alcohol use, about his service record, what they called efficiency ratings in general, and so forth, yes.

Mr. McCloskey: Did they just give you an oral report—it was such and such—or did you read that? Did you study it?

Dr. Ault: By and large it was a summary report, oral. Verbal.

Mr. McCloskey: Why didn't you get his full reports if you are putting this psychological criminal profile together?

Dr. Ault: This isn't a criminal profile.

Mr. Hazelwood: Because we felt the information we obtained from the NIS investigator was sufficient, sir.

Mr. McCloskey: Well, is it not your conclusion that he deliberately set off the explosion?

Dr. Ault: Absolutely.

Mr. Hazelwood: Yes, sir.

Mr. McCloskey: If that isn't criminal activity, what is it? It is criminal activity. You are concluding it is a criminal event.

Mr. Hazelwood: It is an opinion.

Mr. McCloskey: You concluded as a matter of your opinion, which Mr. Aspin said you assert fairly strongly, you are concluding this is a criminal event. Now, it would seem to me, in putting together a report like this, would you not want to get all the direct source material rather than having the NIS saying it was such and such on alcohol, such and such on sex? Why not go to the primary documents?

Mr. Hazelwood: We were satisfied with the information we received from the NIS investigators, sir.

Mr. McCloskey: Well, I for one, Mr. Chairman, Mr. Mavroules, I just find that—I know you are honest law enforcement officers doing your job. I think you might be over-stretched as to the efficacy of your conclusion, but I find that mind-boggling that you are making criminal documentation and assertion of criminal homicidal conduct and don't go to the primary source material in your evaluation. I think it is almost scandalously flawed. I can't believe you could be so confident in your honest assertions.

Dr. Bryant L. Welch, American Psychological Association

Concluding testimony for the House Committee on Armed Services was a panel of psychologists convened at the request of the committee by Bryant L. Welch, J.D., Ph.D., executive director for professional practice, American Psychological Association. This panel was another attempt to bring independent review to the Navy's key findings.

Dr. Welch began by noting that the panel of twelve was selected in consultation with other psychologists and officers of the American Psychological Association and that it included those with expertise in the areas of adolescents and young adulthood, suicidology, testing and neuropsychology, forensic psychology, and peer review.

Dr. Welch summarized the findings for the committee:

The panel was not unanimous in—it was not in unanimous agreement in its conclusions suggesting that competent individuals can disagree in this complex matter. Based on our staff analysis of the report, which you have, and the reasoning process used to arrive at the specific conclusion, there is considerable similarity among eight of the twelve psychologists/panelists in their conclusions. Mr. Chairman, the majority of psychological experts tended not to support the validity of the FBI profile of Clayton Hartwig. Four of the twelve experts were in more substantial agreement with the FBI profile. I should add that all twelve experts discussed the limitations of Equivocal Death Analysis in their statements.

Dr. Welch then introduced a number of these psychologists, who spoke briefly to the committee. Some highlights:

Dr. Ronald S. Ebert, Ph.D., senior forensic psychologist, McLean Hospital: "In brief, my review of the materials that were presented to us enabled me to draw the conclusion that the data collection by NIS was not, in my mind, an objective or thorough analysis. . . . The process by which data was collected, in my opinion, was of question and was not objective. Contradictions that were raised in the materials, in my opinion, were not attended to."

Dr. Norman G. Poythress Jr., Ph.D., professor of psychology, American University: "I would like to make four points in my opening statement. First of all, I believe that the FBI report which has been discussed substantially here this morning is incorrect as to form, as I understand what psychologists are able to do. . . . I think that the FBI report is also flawed in terms of failing to present in a candid fashion the limits of the science. . . . This literature is rather uniform in one particular finding and that is that when we make positive statements that someone will become violent or will behave in a violent fashion based on this kind of data, we are wrong much more often than right."

Dr. Alan L. Berman, psychologist, Washington Psychological Center; professor, American University; former president, American Association of Suicidology: "The psychological autopsy . . . is a procedure designed to arrive at a conclusion based on retrospective date. . . . I think it is practically impossible to be terribly assertive . . . in deriving conclusions from the information. . . . I am comfortable that it is a reasonable hypothesis that Clayton Hartwig did commit suicide, but I am uncomfortable with the procedure that led to the data upon which that conclusion was derived. . . . There are major problems with the way the Naval Investigative Service collected its data leading to tremendously biased sorts of information that were passed on to the FBI, and a number of competing hypotheses appear not to have been investigated."

Dr. Robert L. Greene, Ph.D., professor, Department of Psychology, Texas Tech University: "First, I am really concerned about the unreliability of interview data, a point that numerous people made this morning, and particularly the selective bias, both of the interviewers and the type of information they are looking for and how they ask the questions and also in the interviewees in what they think is being asked of them. . . . Second, the difficulty of predicting any type of infrequent behavior, such as suicide or homicide, has already been pointed out. . . . I am also concerned about the selectivity of the data that was used in the FBI's report and frequently they would ignore data that was directly contradictory to the point they were making and seemingly just said it was not important. Finally, I am concerned about the absence of significant areas of information as to his developmental history, his familial background, his active personnel record in the Navy and so on, that would be needed to complete a picture of Petty Officer Hartwig."

Dr. Robert P. Archer, Ph.D., professor, Department of Psychiatry and Behavioral Sciences, Eastern Virginia Medical School: "My review of the materials provided to me concerning the April 19, 1989, explosion on the USS *Iowa* led me to the following opinions: First, that the linkage between the evidence and the conclusion that the explosion was caused by a suicidal act of Clayton Hartwig is tenuous. I was concerned about possible selectivity or bias in the materials I reviewed and in general felt that I reviewed a range of materials that was too narrow. . . . In summary . . . it is my opinion that the evidence is not sufficient to allow me to conclude that Mr. Hartwig was responsible for the April 19, 1989, explosion on the *Iowa* as a result of a suicidal or homicidal act."

Appendix D

Testimony of Captain Fred P. Moosally Jr.

Following is the testimony of Fred P. Moosally Jr. before the Senate Armed Services Committee on 11 December 1989.

The Senate Armed Services Committee met at 9:08 A.M. in room SH-216, Hart Senate Office Building. Committee members present were: Senators Nunn, Dixon, Warner and Cohen. . . .

Chairman Nunn: The committee will come to order.

The committee meets this morning for the second of a series of hearings on matters associated with the explosion on April 19, 1989 in the center gun of turret II on the USS *Iowa* which resulted in the deaths of forty-seven Navy personnel. . . .

This morning we will receive the testimony of Capt. Fred P. Moosally, Jr. of the U.S. Navy, Commanding Officer, USS *Iowa*. Captain Moosally assumed command of the USS *Iowa* in May 1988. . . .

I outlined in my opening statement at our last hearing the problems found by the investigating officer in the weapons department of the *Iowa*. It must also be noted that testimony was received during the course of the overall Navy investigation that cast doubt on the Navy's support for the USS *Iowa* and, by implication, for the other three battleships. The Navy's investigation did not inquire into these matters, but we will this morning. They include:

First, the priority of officer and enlisted manning and the quality of personnel on board the USS *Iowa*;

Second, the adequacy of training on the 16-inch guns since there is no hands-on training for personnel prior to reporting to the battleships;

Third, the employment plan for battleships, how they will be used tactically and strategically;

Fourth, the responsiveness of the Navy to repair and repair parts requests for battleships, and

Fifth, the adequacy of various inspections and surveys conducted on board the battleships.

As indicated at our last hearing, I have requested the General Accounting Office to look into these matters as well as to review the Navy's investigation as a whole in an attempt to assess its adequacy and to determine whether its conclusions are correct. . . .

This morning we want to give Captain Moosally an opportunity to respond to the finding of the Navy's investigation and to explain his testimony during the investigation as to the lack of support to the USS *Iowa* in connection with manning, training, repair and inspections and surveys as well as his perspective on the Navy's employment plan for battleships.

Captain Moosally is appearing in his individual capacity as the commanding officer of the USS *Iowa*, and the committee will, of course, expect you, Captain, to give your personal views. We not asking for the Navy's views today. We are asking for your views individually.

I should note at this point that the *Iowa* returned just last Tuesday from a five month deployment to the Mediterranean.

Captain Moosally, we certainly appreciate your presence here this morning, particularly in view of the fact that you have just returned from what must have been a very difficult and demanding deployment, since it took place so soon after the tragic explosion of April 19.

I also want to point out at this time that the Navy's investigation found that in the aftermath of the explosion, "the damage control efforts of the ship's crew were extraordinary."

Chairman Nunn: . . . Captain, we are delighted to have you this morning . . . and we look forward to receiving your testimony.

STATEMENT OF FRED P. MOOSALLY, CAPTAIN, U.S. NAVY, COMMANDING OFFICER, USS IOWA.

Captain Moosally: Good morning, Mr. Chairman, Senator Warner, Senator Dixon. I am Captain Moosally, the Commanding Officer of the battleship *Iowa*. I was born and raised in Youngstown, Ohio, and graduated from the U.S. Naval Academy in 1966. For twenty-three years I have dedicated my life to the naval service, serving on six ships and previously commanding the USS *Kidd*.

I want to thank the committee for the opportunity to be here today to discuss with you the battleship *Iowa*.

Mr. Chairman, you have before you a paradox, a tale of two ships. One ship is this *Iowa* you read about in the newspapers, a ship of laid back attitudes, failure and ineptitude. The other *Iowa* is the *Iowa* that I command, an *Iowa* that is well trained, well maintained and professional.

You have heard many things about the other *Iowa*, but the one I command is an *Iowa* to be proud of, with a crew that deserves much more credit than they have been given.

I assumed command of the *Iowa* in May 1988, and over the last 19 months my crew and I have proved that *Iowa* is one of the best ships in our Navy. Mr. Chairman, this is a fact, not because I say so, but because *Iowa*'s track record of proven performance in every area of naval operations prior to April 19, on April 19, and every day since April 19 says so.

We men of the *Iowa* are proud of our ship. I hope that today I can convince the Congress, the American public, and most important, the families of our fallen shipmates, some of whom are here today, that the *Iowa* described in the press never existed.

Having completed a 6-month deployment for America, we ask that America give us the chance to set the record straight. We have earned that right. . . .

I witnessed both the tragedy where forty-seven of our shipmates died, and the birth of hundreds of heroes. I stood with my crew as we rebuilt our ship in the face of overwhelming emotion and grief.

During the weeks that followed, *Iowa* worked with investigators providing hundreds of hours of testimony while rebuilding our ship. At a time normally associated with liberal leave and liberty in preparation for a 6-month deployment, the crew selflessly devoted thousands of additional manhours, working side by side with workers from Norfolk Naval Shipyard, to evaluate the extent of damage and restore vital systems in Turret II. . . .

Iowa was front page news. Speculation, innuendo and out-of-control quotes were rampant. We even had to endure media interviews with Navy deserters, one of whom appeared on television with a pillowcase over his head, claiming to be an expert on our ship. Still, we remained silent and continued our predeployment preparations.

We made the necessary sacrifices under the most stressful, adverse, and unusual conditions ever encountered in a peacetime environment. Just seven weeks after a devastating explosion aboard our ship, we deployed. . . .

I submit that you cannot do these things without good leadership and a well established, effective training program. Exactly two months after our deployment began, just two days prior to its formal release, we got our first chance to look at the official investigation report. Prior to this, we relied on the media and our families for information. . . . When I received the report I was horrified to learn that the explosion was caused by a wrongful, intentional act. It is very difficult for any family to accept that one of its own could do such a thing.

In the days following the release we were dismayed with the report's emphasis on the apparent shortcomings of my command. While these shortcomings had no causal effect on the explosion, they were difficult to separate from the actual conclusion of the report and have become the source of much confusion.

I would thus like to clarify a number of misconceptions by focusing on some critical facts, which appear to have been lost in the shuffle. These facts are based on close inspection not only by myself and my crew, but from competent outside sources, both uniformed and civilian, including fleet commanders, senior Navy civilians, the Navy Inspector General, and the Government Accounting Office.

Fact number one: *Iowa* was and is well trained. Much has been said about *Iowa*'s PQS program. PQS is a list of minimum knowledge and skills required to perform certain duties.

Let me set the record straight. Our men had the skill, training and experience to perform the assigned tasks. Our only deficiency was in maintaining a formal record of these skills. . . .

Fact number two: *Iowa* was and is well maintained. After completing refresher training in November 1988, we successfully completed an extensive operational propulsion plant examination. Then after the first of the year, *Iowa* completed a comprehensive planned Maintenance System inspection which resulted in a recorded accomplishment rate of 99 percent. Within *Iowa*'s turrets, 100 percent of the spot checks done by the inspectors were graded satisfactory. . . .

Fact number three: *Iowa* did not experiment. Let us set the record straight. There was never a shot fired during my command that was not safe and sanctioned by the appropriate authorities. That is, *Iowa* fully supported 16-inch 50 gunnery improvement and worked closely with the Navy's ammunition experts. . . .

Fact number four: *Iowa* was and is well led and well managed. The officers and chief petty officers serving under me are real professionals. They are well disciplined and knowledgeable in their fields. I cannot praise them enough.

After the release of the investigation, my sworn personal testimony was taken apart and used out of context. I described very directly the conditions I found in specific areas when I assumed command. Those conditions do not exist aboard *Iowa* today.

At one point my testimony was used to indicate that I was not happy with my crew. Nothing could be further from the truth. The truth is I was asked specifically why I had certain personnel in turrets who had disciplinary records. In that case I did reply that I had to work with what I got from the Navy. I have little control over the people who come to my command, and, yes, I have an obligation to provide leadership to my men. . . .

Fact number five: *Iowa* was and is ready. Just look at the response to the explosion itself to assess our readiness. On April 19 the crew fought bravely to put out the fire from the explosion. The response was immediate. We were able to contain an explosion and fire which might have destroyed any other vessel. The crew then tirelessly worked throughout the night and the next day to dewater the spaces and recover their fallen shipmates. With that accomplished, we went back to work and made our deployment. We were ready. . . .

Finally, *Iowa* has pride and endurance. It has been painful to watch so-called experts slowly erode the Nation's confidence in our ship and in us. We have worked together to prove to others that we can do the job, and we are here today to tell you that we are the best team on the best strike platform in the Navy.

The fact that *Iowa* had an unmatched capability to deliver ordnance on target was a major factor in the recent approval of a gap in the aircraft carrier presence in the Mediterranean. There is a plaque mounted on our bridge which states, "We are battleship sailors. When it's getting too tough for everyone else, it's just right for us." You can believe it. . . .

Thank you, Mr. Chairman.

Chairman Nunn: Thank you very much, Captain. . . . When was your interview with Admiral Milligan?

Captain Moosally: It was right after we got back, sir. I am not sure of the exact date.

Chairman Nunn: Does May 1st sound about right?

Captain Moosally: Around about that time, about two weeks after the explosion. . . .

Chairman Nunn: Let me just quote a couple of things you said and get your reaction to them or amplifications, see if you recall exactly the context.

You stated, quoting, number one, "When I came here, you know, when I first came on here, you know, we had a NMP." Tell us what NMP means.

Captain Moosally: Navy manning plan.

Chairman Nunn: Continuing, "Of 118 and I was 37 gunner's mates short at the time, I have messages where I sent messages out requesting. I also found out through EPMAC"—could you tell us—

Captain Moosally: That's EPMAC, the enlisted detailers—not detailers, but the enlisted distributors of enlisted personnel.

Chairman Nunn: And BUPERS?

Captain Moosally: Bureau of Personnel.

Chairman Nunn: So, quoting you again, "I also found out through EPMAC and BUPERS that the reason I wasn't getting any more gunner's mates was because I was 37th on the priority list. The basic word I was getting was that, 'Hey, you are not going to get anybody there, Captain, because you are so low on the priority list, you are never going to make it.'"

Did you so testify?

Captain Moosally: Yes, sir. . . .

Chairman Nunn: You went on to say, "So, I felt like we were kind of—if we would go away and hide somewhere, it would be fine with everybody, and I felt that to be thirty-seventh on the priority as the biggest gun ship in the world was kind of incredulous." Are those your words?

Captain Moosally: Yes, sir.

Chairman Nunn: Tell us a little more about that.

Captain Moosally: Well, the first thing I want to say is if we would put this in perspective, it was a very emotional time for me. I just had forty-seven of my men die. I was being called in and given my rights, and I was very emotional about it, and when I say that was going on in the room there—but, as I saw it, coming to the ship once again, looking at our employment schedule, and my general feeling was that we were not being employed the way the battleship should be employed.

I did not feel like manpower-wise we had the priorities we should have. I was talking as the CO of a ship, and my job as CO of a ship is to ensure we get the proper manning that we ought to have, that we are in good materiel condition. So that was my perspective as the CO of the *Iowa*. . . .

Chairman Nunn: You felt like you were not being given priority?

Captain Moosally: I looked at my manning once again. For example, in June 1988, if you take a snapshot, I was supposed to have eight E-7's. I had one, and that was a problem. The problem was in the E-5 and above ratings, and I did not feel like for the scope of the work that the battleship has with all the gun systems we have that we were getting the personnel we should have had in the gunner's mate rating. . . .

Chairman Nunn: So, basically you are saying that as captain of the ship when you came on board you had not nearly enough gunner's mates. You did not have the right billets, and most of the people there had not gone through any kind of formal training, so it was up to you to do all the training, is that right?

Captain Moosally: That is correct, yes, sir.

Chairman Nunn: So, all the training on battleships is having to be done there, on the ship?

Captain Moosally: All except for a C school out in San Diego, which is a paper course, an administrator course, which is given to lower rated personnel, mostly third class petty officers coming our of the gunner's mate A school. They then go to the C school for a few weeks, but there is not hands-on training. It is basically a paper course. There are no mock-ups or visits to the ships.

Chairman Nunn: And you believe that ought to be corrected?

Captain Moosally: Yes, sir. I think that the chief petty officer should have some kind of enroute training. I think myself as the CO and certainly the weapons officer ought to have some enroute training to be introduced to the 16-inch gun. . . .

Chairman Nunn: Senator Cohen.

Senator Cohen: Just a few questions, Mr. Chairman.

Captain, you were asked earlier if you would characterize your earlier testimony, your private statement, differently had you know it would be made public?

Captain Moosally: Yes, sir.

Senator Cohen: The question I have is, was it a question of language or substance that you would change?

Captain Moosally: I would change the language. I would have protected people who I think got hurt by making my statement public. I certainly would have changed my language. Had it not been under the circumstances of my being under a very stressful, emotional period, I think I overstated myself in some areas.

So yes, I would have definitely not said things in the context in which they were said in that statement. If I could have retracted a lot of those things and the hurt they gave some of the people, especially in my wardroom, I would not have said them.

Senator Cohen: Was it a situation in which you were angry perhaps that you were put in charge of a ship on which you saw clear deficiencies?

Captain Moosally: I would state that I felt like the good Lord in the Garden of Gethsemane when I looked around and saw that various problems that I was facing materielwise and some of the standards in training. If you go through my written statement I submitted to the investigating office, I had trouble in the engineering department. I had an engineering officer quit on me. I had to relieve my damage control assistant because of the poor training that I found there. . . .

Senator Cohen: Basically, the language that you used in your statement reflected the obvious sense of, I would say, anger—

Captain Moosally: Yes, sir.

Senator Cohen [continuing]: —that you are put on a ship, you are out there, you are on duty.

Captain Moosally: It was anger and the stress. Like I said, the 47—no commanding officer wants to lose a man on any ship, and to lose 47 men in such a tragic explosion is devastating; and then to be given your Article 31 rights and to be accused of dereliction of duty after all the things that you had done to make this ship one of the best in the Navy really hurts; and you do become angry, yes, sir. . . .

Senator Cohen: Could you list for me the factual differences that you have with the Navy's investigation?

Captain Moosally: I can provide those to you, sir.

Fourteen pages of comments by Captain Moosally were submitted dealing with various Findings of Fact and Opinions contained in Admiral Milligan's report. This document is included in the proceedings. . . .

Chairman Nunn: Thank you. Senator Warner.

Senator Warner: Let me start with a preliminary question, and then I will refer to the findings momentarily. As a follow-on to those series of questions already asked—as I understand it, your personal opinion is that this tragedy was the direct result of a deliberate act?

Captain Moosally: Yes, sir.

Senator Warner: But that you disagree with the finding of the investigating officer which implicated a specific sailor, Hartwig?

Captain Moosally: I do not disagree with that, Senator Warner. What I was saying is I cannot come to the conclusion myself.

Senator Warner: Let me read it. It is opinion number fifty-six—"Based on this investigation report and after full review of all Naval Investigative Service reports to date, the wrongful intentional act that caused this incident was most probably committed by Clayton Hartwig."

Now, do you agree or disagree with that conclusion?

Captain Moosally: I do not agree or disagree. What I am saying is I, as the commanding officer of *Iowa*, from what I have read, I cannot come to that same conclusion.

Chairman Nunn: You are saying, as I understand it, that you do not have the expertise, the knowledge, or the investigative knowledge to come to that conclusion?

Captain Moosally: Yes, sir, that is correct.

Senator Warner: Let me just follow up on it. Do you entertain or consider or have in mind any other plausible or reasonable explanation for what happened?

Captain Moosally: No, sir, I do not.

Senator Warner: Again, I am going to follow up on what the chairman just said. Once again, why is it that you cannot agree with that?

Captain Moosally: I said I do not have the expertise or the knowledge to agree or disagree with it.

Senator Warner: Well, now, you have had twenty-three years of naval service and have commanded other ships. How is it that you lack the expertise to either agree or disagree with that conclusion?

Captain Moosally: Well, I have not had time, Senator Warner, to study all the laboratory results, forensic results, the various tests that were done with regard to this investigation.

Senator Warner: Well, then, you have the expertise, presumably as a professional naval officer—

Captain Moosally: No, sir. I am not a munitions expert. I am not a munitions expert.

Senator Warner: Well, is the admiral who prepared this report an expert?

Captain Moosally: He is an expert certainly in some areas. He is not a munitions expert.

Senator Warner: So, primarily, you have not had the time to go over the body of evidence?

Captain Moosally: Yes, sir, I have not had the time.

Senator Warner: And I am not in any way disputing that you had to press on with your duties for the ship's deployment. You have not had the opportunity to go back over the evidence. What I am trying to bring out is whether or not the reason that you do not agree with this is based on some other plausible explanation.

Captain Moosally: No, it is not, no, sir.

Senator Warner: So there is no mystery out here that we have not penetrated?

Captain Moosally: No, sir. I have no revelations on any of this. If I did, believe me, I would have come forth a long time ago.

Senator Warner: Thank you. . . .

Senator Cohen: I am still not clear in terms of the response because I think what the captain is saying is—let me pose it this way—assuming you had time to read all the evidence, that you read the forensic material, that you looked at the pathology reports, I understand from your testimony you still would not have an opinion as to whether or not a particular individual committed the act or not?

Captain Moosally: Yes, sir.

Senator Cohen: So, it is not a question of not having time. What you are saying is you do not have the expertise to reach a conclusion as to a specific individual?

Captain Moosally: That is correct.

Senator Cohen: And given all the time—take the next 6 months off duty and review the evidence—you would not be in a position to affirm the results or the conclusions reached by the Navy?

Captain Moosally: Yes, sir. . . .

Chairman Nunn: I want to follow up on that. Do you believe Admiral Milligan had that expertise? Do you think he is qualified to make that judgment based on the report? You said he was not a munitions officer, either. What makes him better qualified than you?

Captain Moosally: He has a team, and he has all the inputs.

Chairman Nunn: You are saying maybe his team had that capability?

Captain Moosally: I think his team does, yes, sir. . . .

Senator Warner: Well, then, if I might resume on my time, you agree the team had the capability and they assembled the facts, then reached the conclusion, but you still do not agree with it? I mean, it almost infers that somehow the procedure of putting together these complex facts and drawing this conclusion is faulty.

Captain Moosally: No, sir, I am not saying that it is. I cannot make those judgments. I mean, I just cannot make those judgments.

Senator Warner: Suppose you were given the job of examining this accident, as was the Admiral. What would you have done differently or would you have done anything differently?

Captain Moosally: I would have to look at what has been done and make that decision. I could not answer that. . . .

Senator Warner: Well, do you have any recommendations as to how this committee might broaden or extend these hearings in an effort to try and make certain that nothing is left uncovered, to determine whether or not the Navy acted properly?

Captain Moosally: No, sir. I think that you are doing everything from what I have seen, and in talking to the General Accounting Office personnel who visited the ship, I think that everything that can be done is being done. . . .

Senator Cohen: One further point to try to clarify this. Captain, if you were not a captain but simply a juror, we have jurors who are impaneled every day who have no expertise, certainly, in forensic science or pathology or anything else, and they are called upon to make decisions, the prosecutor gets up, the plaintiff's attorney, whatever, makes a presentation of the evidence.

Under those circumstances if you were just a juror and the evidence presented to you, and you had an opportunity to review all of that evidence, are you saying that you would not be in a position to either come to a conclusion as to a specific individual without looking at your background and saying you are an ordinary lay person looking at the evidence the Navy has assembled and presented to you? Would you be in a position at that point to reach a decision as to whether the Navy points to a specific individual or not?

The question we have is are you afraid of a lawsuit or the Navy?

Captain Moosally: No.

Senator Cohen: So, you can answer the question, then?

Captain Moosally: Probably I could if I was a juror and all of the evidence was brought. Yes, I could make a decision.

Senator Warner: You would have the expertise to do it then?

Captain Moosally: I would have the decision-making expertise to make judgments.

Senator Dixon: What would your decision be then, if my colleagues would yield?

Captain Moosally: I do not know because I have not seen all the evidence.

Senator Warner: Well, Mr. Chairman, one of the reasons you have not seen it—we understand this—is you have been busy.

Captain Moosally: Yes, sir.

Senator Warner: But earlier you said you felt perhaps we ought to go back—not we, the congress, but the Navy Department—and review the procedures for this type of investigation, which are time tested and time honored so as to allow the skipper of a ship to make comments on the findings of fact before the tribunal of the investigation draws its conclusions.

Captain Moosally: Well, I do not think, Senator, I said I wanted to change the procedures other than the fact that I would like to have had the opportunity to comment on the findings.

Senator Warner: I think that is one constructive observation.

Captain Moosally: Yes, sir.

At this point in the proceedings, the entire testimony of Captain Moosally before Admiral Milligan's team was entered into the record.

Chairman Nunn: Captain, let me see if I can summarize your testimony, and you tell me where I go wrong if this is incorrect.

Captain Moosally: Yes, sir.

Chairman Nunn: I am not trying to capture the whole, I am just trying to summarize these particular points.

[Nunn continued:] You still believe that there was no employment plan for the *Iowa?*

Captain Moosally: At the time that I gave the testimony and came on the ship, that is correct.

Chairman Nunn: Second, the ship was not properly supported by the Navy in both officer and enlisted manning?

Captain Moosally: I would put the emphasis on the enlisted area, Mr. Chairman, in the quality area, not numbers, but quality.

Chairman Nunn: Quality?

Captain Moosally: By that I mean the chief petty officer, the first class petty officer and the second class petty officer. That is the area that I was complaining about the most, because that is the area that you need to have what I call deck-plate leadership.

Chairman Nunn: At the time of your testimony, there was a lack of appreciation in the chain of command, at least on the east coast, for the capability and utilization of the battleships?

Captain Moosally: Well, I would say only as reflected in our employment schedule. . . .

Chairman Nunn: I want to say that I am proud of all the men and women on your ship for what you all have been able to do, particularly since this tragedy happened. I think to go back out in those circumstances is most commendable and I congratulate you and your whole crew on that. . . .

Captain Moosally: . . . My biggest concern is the high turnover rate that we have on ships, which approximates 45 percent. In our case it was 46 percent. That concern is only that you have to pay constant attention out there, because training has to go on and on and on. Forty-six percent to us last year equated to over six hundred new faces on the *Iowa.*

So the CO has to be more involved today than at any other time since I have been in the Navy, has to be tremendously involved in every evolution. . . .

But, you cannot be everywhere, all the time, and this is where these leaders that I was talking about before, the E-7, E-6, E-5, and above, become important, because they have got to carry that policy that you have about direct involvement and supervision all over the ship. . . .

Chairman Nunn: I hope you will express our appreciation to all of the men.

Captain Moosally: Thank you, Mr. Chairman.

Appendix E

Testimony of Frank C. Conahan

Following is an extended excerpt of the testimony of Frank C. Conahan before the Senate Armed Services Committee hearing of 25 May 1990.

Statement of Frank C. Conahan, Assistant Comptroller General, National Security and International Affairs Division, General Accounting Office, Accompanied by Martin Ferber, Director, Navy Issues Group, General Accounting Office. . . .

Mr. Conahan: As you mentioned at the outset, Mr. Chairman, we were asked to (1) conduct an independent investigation of the Navy's technical analysis and the likely causes of the explosion; (2) review the safety aboard the battleships; (3) examine manning and training issues raised by the *Iowa* commanding officer after the explosion; and (4) review the battleship's employment plans and mission.

Working with this committee, we arranged for the Department of Energy's Sandia National Laboratories to conduct a technical analysis and review the adequacy of the Navy's technical investigation. Dr. Schwoebel and his colleagues are here today to discuss why Sandia's analysis could not corroborate the Navy's finding and their conclusion of another plausible cause for the explosion.

I will look forward to their discussion on that matter and then briefly discuss the other matters that you asked us to address, Mr. Chairman. First, I would discuss a series of safety issues which indeed do raise concerns about the general safety of the ship. I will then discuss manning and training issues that raise questions concerning general readiness of battleships. I would like to say a few words about the mission of the battleships that you requested us to review, we address particularly in our changing world environment, and finally the utility and supportability of the two remaining battleships after the presently planned retirement of the other two battleships.

First, a few words about safety. The Navy's investigation of the explosion found that safety policies and procedures simply were not being followed aboard the ship. There are a number of examples of that. Perhaps one of the better examples is that although no spark-producing items are allowed in the turrets, items such as cigarette lighters, rings, and keys were found in the remains of the deceased sailors.

The Navy's investigation at the time also noted that *Iowa* personnel had improperly approved and were conducting gunnery experiments. Ship personnel were loading inappropriate projectile and powder combinations when the explosion occurred. The Navy Inspector General subsequently investigated and reported the experiment, and concluded that the firings in question on the *Iowa* were, in fact, improperly authorized and contrary to Navy procedures. His report concluded that the safety hazard posed to the *Iowa*'s crew by the experiments was at best undetermined. I expect that that conclusion needs further exploration, particularly in view of what we will hear a little later on this morning. My prepared statement discusses other safety and serviceability issues, but let me move on to the manning and training issues that you referred to.

We found that battleships, in comparison to other surface ships, were not assigned an equal share of authorized enlisted supervisory personnel or personnel in ratings associated with gun turret operations. Additionally, the personnel assigned on battleships rated lower by several measures than those assigned to other ships.

The battleships, to include the *Iowa*, deployed with significant lower percentages of their authorized enlisted supervisors and turret-related journeymen. The other surface ships which we sampled deployed with an average of 101 percent of their authorization for supervisory enlisted personnel while the *Iowa* and the battleships deployed with 92 and 93 percent respectively.

These differences are more pronounced with respect to gunner's mates and fire control men. The impact of manning for gunner's mates aboard the *Iowa* was highlighted at the time of the explosion. In Turret II, two of the three journeyman-level gun captain positions normally manned by E-5s were filled by E-4 apprentices. The center gun captain was the only journeyman gun captain at the time. All three of the gun captain positions in turret I were filled by E-4 apprentices.

We have been told repeatedly that the Navy has had difficulties in filling billets in battleships. Other surface ships that we sampled had excess gunner's mates and fire control at the journeyman and supervisory levels, primarily because personnel are promoted faster at these ships, or at higher rates. We were also told that personnel request duty elsewhere to enhance their promotion opportunities. Similarly, they prefer to go to schools other than the 16-inch gunnery school so as to get training in more technologically advanced areas to advance their prospects for future promotion and civilian employment.

We found that battleship personnel fare worse in advancement opportunities. This is true for both officers and enlisted personnel. My prepared statement gives the percentages, the comparisons as between the battleships and the other ships that we sampled. The other surface ships that we sampled included destroyers, cruisers, and so on. I do not need to go into those comparisons right now.

Also, there is a higher rate of disciplinary actions among battleship personnel. For example, the battleships' nonjudicial punishment rate per thousand was approximately 25 percent higher than the ship sample rates. I might say that about 70 percent of the battleships' manning consists of personnel in grades E-1 through E-4. Battleships have a lower level of supervisory personnel than the ships in our sample. Navy officials agreed these factors probably have contributed to the higher disciplinary rates aboard the battleships.

Now a few words about training. The adequacy of training on the *Iowa* itself became an issue because the Navy's accident investigation report on the explosion said that unqualified personnel were manning the turret. However, the former commanding officer of the *Iowa* said the crew was trained, just that the records were not up-to-date. Since the training records for the deceased crew were destroyed in the explosion, never existed, or have never been located, we were unable to reconcile this conflict.

We found, however, that oversight inspections which should have assessed the *Iowa*'s personnel qualification standard program failed to do so during the 18 months preceding the explosion. Priorities were placed on other areas during the review, or the review team lacked the expertise to evaluate the 16-inch qualification program.

Also, weaknesses exist with the Navy's formal training program for 16-inch gun operations and maintenance. Our visits to the 16-inch school disclosed that limited hands-on training was being provided due to the lack of training aids. Training films being used at the school were basically 1940s vintage, and I might say that no improvements were noted as recently as two weeks ago by our staff in the structure or available training aids since the time of the explosion. While the Navy developed a draft training plan to improve the 16-inch training courses in September 1989, the plan still awaits final approval and implementation.

Finally, Mr. Chairman, in response to your request we reviewed the Navy's concept of battleship employment. While the battleships, of course, are very capable weapons platforms and have been included in deployment schedules and operational plans, emerging conditions limit their utility. The battleships were reactivated to alleviate existing force structure shortfalls and to help meet the 600-ship goal using existing platforms.

The battleships provide an imposing array of fire power. The Tomahawk missile gives them a significant capability for attacking both land and other surface ships. The Harpoon missiles also contribute to the battleship's capability, and the 16-inch guns are the best source of naval surface fire support for an amphibious assault.

Because of the imposing size and configuration, the Navy believes, also, a battleship's presence can be a strong deterrent in a third world scenario. While the battleship's Tomahawk and Harpoon missiles capability is imposing, I need to point out it is not unique within the Navy. Many other Navy vessels, submarines as well as surface ships, carry these same weapons, and the battleships' contribution to future amphibious warfare may be limited because of the distances of current scenarios versus the capability of the guns.

Furthermore, with only two battleships, personnel tempo restrictions will limit future deployments. Current policies, for example, preclude a ship from deploying for an additional twelve months after it returns from a six month deployment. Thus, with only two ships in the active force, it is unlikely one would be available on short notice should a crisis erupt. The battleships are also labor-intensive, requiring a crew of about fifteen hundred compared, for example, to a crew of about three hundred and sixty on an Aegis cruiser. . . .

Finally, reducing the number of battleships to two, especially with one home-ported on each coast, will compound the manning and training problems that I discussed earlier and further limit availability.

In closing, Mr. Chairman, I do not have to remind anyone here of the budget situation that we are facing generally and the pressures to reduce the defense budget. That leads me to say that because the battleships are costly to maintain and difficult to man, and because of the unanswered safety supportability and mission-related questions, the two remaining battleships seem to be top candidates for deactivation as we look for ways to scale back U.S. forces. . . .

Appendix F

Testimony before the House Banking Subcommittee

On 8 November 1990, Congresswoman Mary Rose Oakar (D-Ohio) convened a hearing on the USS *Iowa* investigation as chairperson of the House Banking, Finance, and Urban Affairs, Economic Stabilization Subcommittee. The jurisdictional authority for this hearing was the committee's responsibility for oversight of the Defense Production Act of 1950.

Congresswoman Oakar's interest went beyond this particular jurisdictional authority. Seven of the men killed in the *Iowa* explosion were from Ohio, and four of those were in the center gun room, where the explosion occurred.

Testifying on this day were Frank C. Conahan of the GAO, Vice Adm. Peter M. Hekman Jr., and myself. Congresswoman Oakar arrived shortly after 10:00 A.M., accompanied by two staffers (the three were the only persons at the committee table), and opened the hearing by saying, "The subcommittee will come to order. Today we are conducting a hearing which will follow up a request from this subcommittee to the General Accounting Office to investigate the April 19, 1989 explosion aboard the USS *Iowa*, with emphasis on safety, training and maintenance."

Following Representative Oakar's opening comments, Frank C. Conahan submitted his statement for the record and verbally outlined the GAO report for Oakar. He reported on the GAO study of any systemic ammunition problems, problems with 16-inch guns or the battleships themselves, and reported that there were none. He noted that the Navy inspector general had concluded that experiments were taking place with projectiles and propellants on the *Iowa* that were improper and unauthorized.

The issue of the Navy's one-officer investigation was discussed. Conahan observed that with a board of inquiry rather than a one-officer investigation, "you have people reporting their evidence and findings to the board, the board is in a position to discuss, challenge, give greater scrutiny and review."

Chair Oakar: Would you say it is a little more objective?

Mr. Conahan: I think it results in a much more objective result, yes, I believe that. I think there is a second feature we need to consider. That is the way they set their parameters. They postulated possible causes for the explosion and then the methodology was essentially to eliminate causes. Contrast that with the Sandia technical investigation, where they keep looking for new causes: Sandia's methodology was not the elimination of causes, but rather the seeking out of causes. . . .

Representative Oakar concluded the GAO portion of the testimony and asked me (Schwoebel) to come to the table.

Chair Oakar: Let me ask the gentleman from Sandia, please, Dr. Schwoebel, would you come forward, please? . . . Do you have a prepared statement?

Mr. Schwoebel: No, I do not, Madam Chair.

Chair Oakar: And I want to compliment GAO for having you do some of the studies and so forth, and I think that your work has been truly outstanding, and we are lucky to have Sandia as part of our ability to understand very technical types of operations and maneuvers, and equipment, and your initial report was of great interest to the Chair. Let me ask you a similar question, because your methodology . . . was somewhat different from the Navy's methodology. Could you describe the difference?

Mr. Schwoebel: The differences . . . between the two approaches is that the Navy undertook a very broad investigation looking at a whole variety of different contributing factors that may have been involved in the explosion. . . . We . . . picked out areas that we thought might benefit from some additional study. . . . So our study was rather prescribed in nature as to the contrast of the Navy's study. . . .

Chair Oakar: Let me take the easier question first. With respect to the black powders, and so forth, the last item you mentioned, how would you describe their condition?

Mr. Schwoebel: The black powder study that had been conducted by the Navy was reviewed in some detail by people at Sandia, and the bottom line is we agree with essentially all of the findings with regard to the black powder, the nature of that material, the ignition characteristics, and so on.

Chair Oakar: Was it safe?

Mr. Schwoebel: Yes.

Chair Oakar: So that was safe to use. Would you explain what you believe may have happened with respect to the explosion? . . . But will you explain what you think took place?

Mr. Schwoebel: Yes. We suggested an alternative scenario in our report to the GAO in May. . . . Our suggested alternative is based on something that we discovered in the course of our investigation . . . that was the fact the propellant, which was aboard the USS *Iowa*, that lot of D846 material, can be initiated by a fracture process. . . . We also know that an overram occurred on that morning. . . . That is to say, that the powder bags were pushed up against the projectile, jammed up against the projectile in a way that could have fractured the propellant. . . .

Chair Oakar: Do you think that the Navy looked at that as an option for what took place? Did they examine that scenario?

Mr. Schwoebel: The scenario that I have just described to you, Madam Chair, really relates to a discovery we made in our investigation. . . . In the initial Navy investigation, impact sensitivity was not considered as an important factor. It was ruled out. . . .

Chair Oakar: . . . Could a mechanical failure of some nature have caused in any way any type of explosion?

Mr. Schwoebel: There is no evidence of mechanical failure that we are aware of, and the Navy really has done a set of rather extensive studies on this. . . .

Chair Oakar: I mean are you going on—when you make that statement is it based on your own evidence, or is it based on—who is the primary source?

Mr. Schwoebel: The primary source is really the Navy—

Chair Oakar: Well, you see, normally I would say, of course, you know, but I am so dismayed at the handling of this particular situation, that I am somewhat quizzical about evidence that at times is based on what you are given. . . .

What followed were discussions of foreign materials, testimony that was in keeping with previously discussed findings. Oakar closed this part of the hearing with a question:

Chair Oakar: I want to just get to one last bottom line question then.

You can't—you have no reason to believe, nor disbelieve, that allegations by the Navy that Clayton Hartwig committed a crime?

Mr. Schwoebel: We can neither prove nor disprove the existence of a chemical initiator.

Chair Oakar: And you—when you can't prove or disprove, in a situation like that, then you would not blame an individual, would you, in this case?

Mr. Schwoebel: The investigation that we took part in was rather prescribed, looking at the technical information that I mentioned at the outset. . . .

Chair Oakar: Mr. Conahan, would you answer the same question?

Mr. Conahan: I believe that the conclusion or the answer to your question does rest on the final technical findings. There was a lot covered over the last year plus in this area, but as I analyze it overall, it does come down to the technical finding, and I don't know when we are ever going to have an answer one way or the other. . . .

Chair Oakar: . . . Thank you, gentlemen, very, very much.

With that, Representative Oakar excused us, and the GAO representatives and Sandians left the hearing. Oakar next invited Admiral Hekman to the table and began the third part of the hearing:

Chair Oakar: Our next witness is Vice Adm. Peter M. Hekman, Jr. We are very, very delighted that you were able to attend, that the Navy was able to send someone of your caliber, Admiral, and we are pleased that you would be here. . . .

Admiral Hekman: Madam Chair, I would like to read a short statement for the record as a point of introduction.

Madam Chair and distinguished members of the subcommittee, I am Vice Admiral Peter M. Hekman, United States Navy, Commander of the Naval Sea Systems Command.

I am here today in response to your request to discuss with you the status of the USS *Iowa* investigation and the Navy's review of the recent GAO draft report entitled Battleships: Issues Arising From the Explosion Aboard the USS *Iowa*.

In September 1989, Madam Chair, you requested the GAO to report to you on the safety of the USS *Iowa*'s equipment and munitions. Subsequently, the Chairman of the Senate Armed Services Committee, Senator Nunn, tasked the GAO to report on the safety of the USS *Iowa* and in November 1989 requested that Sandia National Laboratories in Albuquerque, NM, assist the GAO by undertaking a technical analysis of the Navy's tests.

The Navy was asked to work closely with Sandia Laboratories and the GAO and has done so. All Navy data has been made available to cognizant agencies and the Navy has arranged numerous visits to Navy activities and ships by personnel from both organizations.

I want to assure you that the Navy and Sandia Laboratories are continuing to cooperate closely in order to address the results of Sandia's experiments as well as all other aspects of the testing.

Additionally, the Secretary of the Navy directed that a technical review of all Navy test data and any other data which had been provided to the Navy be conducted. I was assigned that duty by the Chief of Naval Operations on May 31, 1990.

The *Iowa* technical review is ongoing. The Navy, however, has completed comprehensive analysis and testing of the 16-inch powder inventory and conducted shipboard inspections to ensure firing safety with the propellant bags that are aboard the two battleships, the USS *Wisconsin* and USS *Missouri*, will use. This testing was a separate and distinct phase, oriented toward assessing the safety of 16-inch firing by the two ships.

With respect to the ships themselves, every aspect of safety, material, and training was scrutinized. As a result, in September, the Chief of Naval Operations lifted the moratorium for those types of propellant which have been completely tested. The *Wisconsin* has conducted safe and satisfactory gunnery training off San Clemente Island in the Pacific.

Although the technical conditions to lift the firing moratorium on the battleships have been established, the Naval Sea Systems command technical review to determine if the Sandia conclusions could explain the explosion aboard the USS *Iowa* is continuing. The technical review is being conducted in conjunction with the Sandia National Laboratories, the U.S. Army Research Laboratory and appropriate Navy activities.

In view of the ongoing nature of the investigation, it would be premature for me to address any conclusions from this phase of the testing since they remain to be drawn. Conclusions will not be drawn until all obtainable facts have been gathered and assembled.

The draft report of the GAO's investigations of the *Iowa* explosion was received for comment within the past week, and is now under review. It reflects GAO and Sandia's work up to May 25, 1990, but does not reflect the continuing work being conducted by the Navy with the full participation of both the GAO and Sandia. Until staffing within the department of the Navy and the Department of Defense is complete, it would be inappropriate for me to comment on its conclusions.

We look forward to the completion of testing within the next few months unless new testing requirements become known or are revised by unforeseen results.

Madam Chair, that concludes my prepared statement. I would be pleased to answer your questions.

Chair Oakar: Admiral, thank you for coming. I want to, first of all, say that this hearing is intended to arrive at the truth and to ensure that the people who serve us in the Armed Services, and in the Navy in particular, serve us in a very safe atmosphere. . . .

You indicate, and I quote, "It would be premature for me to address any conclusions from this phase of testing since they remain to be drawn. Conclusions will not be drawn until all obtainable facts have been gathered and assembled." . . .

I am wondering why the Navy wasn't so firm in addressing the issue of prematurity with respect to the facts then. Why are you so emphatic now, versus then?

Admiral Hekman: Madam Chair, I was not a party to the original investigation. That was a determination I have to leave with the investigating officer.

Nor have I read or been party to anything other than purely the technical part of this investigation. I have not reviewed, for example, the Naval Investigative Service reports or the FBI reports, or any other information that may have led the investigating officer to his conclusion. So I cannot say it was improper.

Chair Oakar: Haven't you reviewed the other reports, Admiral Milligan's report?

Admiral Hekman: Because I was, first, outside that line of investigation, and, second, Madam Chair, I have been tasked with a technical evaluation, and my conclusions will be drawn on the assemblage of technical facts, and not on circumstantial or on interview or on rumor or on any other type of information that may have been provided in the original investigation.

Chair Oakar: Do you think that is the better way to go, based on technical facts, as opposed to rumor, innuendo, and so forth?

Admiral Hekman: I don't mean to imply the other investigation was based on rumor or innuendo, not at all. The investigation was reportedly very thorough, and—

Chair Oakar: But you have not read it.

Admiral Hekman: I have not read that portion. I read the Sandia report, of course, and, of course, commended action on the Sandia hypothesis prior to their hearing with you, as stated. I have not read the other part. I feel it would be inappropriate for me to read other parts. I prefer to keep my mind purely on the technical side.

Chair Oakar: I am going to ask you a series of questions, Admiral, and I know you have indicated you would rather not, apparently, respond until you complete your study, but this is not a question that I am addressing to you personally. You are representing the Navy here, and so while you may or may not agree with Admiral Milligan's conclusions once you do your technical report, as opposed to his report which apparently was, in part at least, nontechnical. Nonetheless, you are representing—in my understanding you are representing the Navy at this hearing. So it is not a personal element—

Admiral Hekman: I understand that.

Chair Oakar: In terms of the questions I want to get at.

The GAO draft report calls attention to a number of deficiencies with respect to the manning of the USS *Iowa* at the time of the explosion, the shortfall of gunners, gunner's mates, supervisors, the key turret positions filled with lower graded personnel than prescribed in the ship's manning document; the battleship personnel rated lower in several performance and behavioral characteristics, more frequent disciplinarian problems.

Are these, from your technical knowledge, are these deficiencies symptomatic of the conditions aboard other battleships or—including the USS *Iowa* or, pardon me, *Wisconsin*, which is now maneuvering in the Persian Gulf?

Admiral Hekman: Madam Chair, those statistics are not abnormal when one looks at the makeup of the crew. The battleships are not what we would call a high tech ship. About 70 percent of their manning is made up of E-4 and below. These are personnel who have not received the extensive training that your would find, for example, on an Aegis-type cruiser. In my own experience as commander of a cruiser with a five-hundred man crew, less than fifty were at the E-4 level or below. Others were petty officers at least.

These ships were designed in the 1930s for an average education level in the Navy at that time of fifth grade. . . .

Chair Oakar: We don't have a class system in the Navy, do we? Are you telling me these young people are not every bit as worthwhile?

Admiral Hekman: It is not a class system.

Chair Oakar: I am not addressing this at you personally but my goodness, my constituents were reasonably educated. They died for their country unnecessarily?

Admiral Hekman: I only mean to say that their function—

Chair Oakar: Their fathers served on these battleships.

Admiral Hekman: There are functions that have to be performed on another ship of a higher technology level and it takes a different type of person to do that type of function.

Chair Oakar: Do they deserve thorough training none the less?

Admiral Hekman: I don't mean training. That does not mean the crew of the *Iowa* was untrainable or could not have advanced into new positions.

Chair Oakar: We are not talking about upward mobility here. I save that for other hearings I am involved in. I am talking about the training that is mandated to fulfill a standard so that these young people could operate a battleship with the standards. Were the standards for training met on the USS *Iowa* and are they being met to the ultimate capacity of their needs to operate two battleships that are currently operational, one of which is in an extraordinary part of the world right now[?].

Admiral Hekman: I cannot answer for the condition of the USS *Iowa* at the time of the incident. I can say that the Navy has a very well established personnel training qualification program where every person for every watch position and many of the maintenance positions on board every Navy ship, no matter what the type, must go through a very rigorous qualification program. . . .

Chair Oakar: Well how do you explain the Navy's investigation, their own report that some people feel was very premature in terms of its conclusion. Nonetheless, there were some points in there I thought were very interesting. One on page nine, you have not had a chance to read it but I will tell you what it says, "of the fifty-five watch stations manned in Turret I on April 19, 1989, which required formal PQS qualified watch standards, four personnel were PQS qualified, four out of fifty-five."

In Turret II, thirteen out of fifty-one personnel were PQS qualified and in Turret III nine out of sixty-two were PQS qualified. Then they name one of the individuals who was the only officer in Turret I after being onboard only sixteen days, he was not familiar with turret operations, safety or misfire procedures.

Is that what you are talking about in terms of all this quality of training? Is that par for the course?

Admiral Hekman: I cannot answer for what is said at that part of the investigation. . . .

Chair Oakar: Where do you keep the data for the training of the individuals who serve on the battleships, Admiral?

Admiral Hekman: The training records are usually kept by each department and by each division aboard the ships. This varies depending on the size of the ship and depending on how the commanding officer wishes to administer it.

Chair Oakar: Is there no regulation?

Admiral Hekman: There are but it allows the commanding officer, as far as repository, he can do it on the computer, on paper. It is his choice.

Chair Oakar: Do you think that is a good idea in terms of keeping records on these individuals who serve on these ships? Is that true of every major operation?

Admiral Hekman: Yes.

Chair Oakar: Don't you think that is a little slipshod, to allow the whim of the commander to either write it on paper or put it in the computer?

Admiral Hekman: The policy is that he will have records. The records are formatted. There was a requirement at the time of the *Iowa* incident that before a man was transferred from the ship the records that were held within his own department area would then be recorded in his service record as part of his transferring procedure. These records were turned in to the ship's personnel man and the ship's personnel man as part of their requirements transferred them into his records. Then they would look at the qualifications and they would fit you into their organization and they are required to retest him before he can go to the duties on a new ship.

Where he is adequately trained they can make a judgment but each man goes through a new training and qualification program when he transfers to a new ship. The only change that has been made to that system is that as a man completes a qualification now, his department must submit that and have it recorded as part of his report as an ongoing requirement.

Chair Oakar: Is that because of what took place on the USS *Iowa* where nobody has the records and cannot find them?

Admiral Hekman: It was a result of what happened on the *Iowa*.

Chair Oakar: So there is an opportunity for the Navy to improve, right?

Admiral Hekman: Yes, we are always improving.

Chair Oakar: I have had the impression that the Navy, in the past at least, would rather sweep this whole incident under the rug, blame some young man for the incident and then feel you got away with it. It is in America's best interest that you get to the bottom of what truly happened so that we can protect those who currently serve and will serve in the future.

Admiral Hekman: Madam Chairman, I think if you were to check the Navy's record of investigations over time and the actions taken when safety violations or any other incident has occurred, you will find a very commendable record of follow-up, a very commendable record of change, new procedures, new design, new instructions that will follow from that.

Chair Oakar: Admiral, let me tell you something. With all due respect, I don't think there would be any changes if we did not get after you in this case. I would hope that is true.

Admiral Hekman: I believe you will find the record will show otherwise.

Chair Oakar: When I asked for a GAO report and they said there was no training plan for battleship gunnery, no "hands-on" training aids, and that some of the training material and film on 16-inch guns dated back to the 1940s.

Given the history of major accidents with these 16-inch batteries and given the disclosure that these heavy weapons tend to be operated by relatively inexperienced personnel, shouldn't the Navy have taken more precautions in training?

Here we have spent $2 billion for refitting these battleships and we have the GAO recommending that they be decommissioned.

Admiral Hekman: I cannot speak for the GAO recommendation. That is a matter of policy that belongs to CNO. However, I can say we felt fortunate that we still had training films for these guns. The guns have not changed. The procedures have not changed. The films were very good training devices. We were fortunate to have them in inventories.

We had the technical documentation for all the guns within the inventory.

Chair Oakar: We are glad you are going back to the 1940s to train these individuals, but bottom line, do you think these battleships should be decommissioned?

Admiral Hekman: That is not a question that I can answer because it is purely a matter of policy.

Chair Oakar: We are leaving the policy up to a few individuals. Meanwhile, we are seeing these people who serve our country get killed for no good reason. I mean, there is no reason why we have should have more individuals today die in accidents. They have not even experienced combat.

Admiral Hekman: Any part of the Navy operations is by nature a hazardous environment.

Chair Oakar: Admiral, I don't buy that. Of course, you are in a hazardous occupation. I respect that. I respect anyone who serves our country. That is really obvious. But I expect that at the least that America should expect that when they send their sons and daughters to serve, their husbands and wives and grandchildren, that they will have the best possible training, best possible equipment. If we are at fault, the Congress is at fault, or the President is at fault, tell us what to do. The only way we can be forthright in this is if we acknowledge that indeed there have been a few mistakes in the past. . . .

Chair Oakar: . . . Admiral, thank you very much. I really hope and pray that if your mission to arrive at the truth and the technical evidence that you apparently are pursuing finds that indeed beyond any reasonable doubt Clayton

Hartwig was not guilty, I hope that the Navy will acknowledge that publicly. That is the least they should do. The families are very concerned that, they are concerned about what information the Navy needs from the families or anybody before they are going to in a reasonable, simple way apologize.

Admiral Hekman: I understand that. I am sure that that has weighed heavily on the minds of the Chief of Naval Operations and the Secretary over this period of time. I am confident that—my knowledge of those officials is that if there is a reason for change in conclusions, that they will follow up on that and take whatever action is appropriate.

Congresswoman Oakar adjourned the meeting at 12:55 P.M.

Appendix G

Admiral Frank B. Kelso II
Press Conference

Following is a special Defense Department briefing by Adm. Frank B. Kelso II regarding the USS *Iowa* explosion which was given at 12:01 P.M. EDT on Thursday, 17 October 1991:

Good afternoon. I'll make a statement on the USS *Iowa* investigation. This statement is my endorsement on the investigation report.

The investigation of the explosion in Turret II on board the *Iowa* has been the most extensive ever conducted by the Navy. This unprecedented effort had consumed more than two years, during which thousands of scientific tests and experiments, and hundreds of thousands of man-hours have been expended in an attempt to discover the cause of the tragedy, and to ensure the safety of 16-inch guns.

The professionalism and dedication of the scientists, technicians and supporting teams assisting the Navy and Sandia National Laboratories have been extraordinary. Their respective reports reflect [that] a tremendous application of effort and intellect has gone into this investigation.

A review of the process under which the initial investigation was conducted has led to important changes in the Navy procedures applicable to major incidents. Although a more formal investigative form was available at the time of the *Iowa* explosion, it was not used. As a consequence of the *Iowa* experience, the Secretary has issued guidance that requires more formal procedures to be used in major incidents.

These changes include requirements for a hearing or formal board of inquiry, and a higher, clear and convincing standard of proof when the intentional acts of a deceased member are called into question.

The initial *Iowa* investigation stated the opinion that the explosion in Turret II resulted from a wrongful intentional act. Based on all evidence available at the time, two factors led to the Navy's conclusion that intentional human intervention caused the explosion. Extensive laboratory and operational testing did not identify a plausible cause of the accident. Second, microscopic traces of material believed to be foreign to the gun turret environment were found trapped in the projectile's rotating band.

At the time we released our initial investigation on September the 7th, 1989, we stated that future technical testing might result in changes or modifications to these findings and opinions. Ten months later, independent tests by Sandia National Laboratories, using subscale modeling under laboratory conditions, suggested that a possible accidental explosion might result from a high-speed compressive overram of the gun propellant powder. That discovery led to a reevaluation of the *Iowa* explosion.

On 24 May 1990, Navy personnel from the Naval Surface Warfare Center, Dahlgren, Virginia, working with technical experts from Sandia, produced an explosive reaction using a full-scale drop test fixture. The *Iowa* investigation was reopened to pursue this new evidence, and further testing and evaluation resulted in technical reports developed by Sandia and the Naval Sea Systems Command.

The Navy suspended firing of all 16-inch guns after the 24 May explosion reaction, and returned the 16-inch guns to service only after addressing the two crucial components of the Sandia theory: the possible presence of a small number of powder grains in the tare layer of the powder bags, and the potential compressive force that might be focused on those few grains during a high-speed powder ram.

All 16-inch powder bags worldwide were inspected and those found to have a small number of grains in the trim layer were removed from inventory. Additionally, recertification of the gun crews, and a color coded system to delineate clearly the slow-speed ram position, provide additional safeguards to prevent an accidental high-speed powder ram.

These steps eliminated the possibility of a reaction in the 16-inch guns as postulated. During Desert Shield/Desert Storm Operations, USS *Wisconsin* and *Missouri* successfully fired 1,182 16-inch rounds under combat conditions, without incident. There is one conclusion we can draw with confidence. Our battleship 16[-inch] guns and their ammunition are safe to fire. This is a critically important result of our efforts. It is an assurance we owe to all our sailors, their families and the American people.

Despite all the efforts that have gone into the *Iowa* investigation, however, my final conclusion is that there's no certain answer to the question of what caused the tragedy. The Sandia theory affected the foundation upon which the intentional act opinion rested, by producing at least experimentally a possible accidental cause of the explosion. When tested under operational conditions, however, the probability of a Sandia type reaction was found to be lower than what initial subscale laboratory tests had suggested.

The significance of the Sandia theory to the decision making process is that despite an enormously dedicated scientific effort, the theory's relevance to the *Iowa* explosion cannot be proved or disapproved with absolute certainty.

Considering all the evidence now available, the opinion that the explosion on board the USS *Iowa* on 19 April 1989 resulted from a wrongful intentional act, is not conclusively established by the evidence. Neither an intentional act nor an accidental cause can be proved or dismissed given the limits of science and the dynamics of the blast and its aftermath. Without clear and convincing proof, an opinion, no matter how equivocally stated, that an individual may have intentionally brought about his own death and the deaths of forty-six of his shipmates is inappropriate.

Accordingly, the opinion that the explosion resulted from a wrongful intentional act is disapproved. The exact cause of the explosion is unknown.

The initial investigation was an honest attempt to weigh impartially all the evidence as it existed at the time. And indeed, despite the Sandia theory and almost two years of subsequent testing, a substantial body of scientific and expert evidence and analysis continues to support the initial investigation finding that no plausible accidental cause can be established.

However, the initial investigation could not and did not state conclusively that Gunner's Mate Clayton Hartwig caused the blast.

Because there is no conclusive proof to support either theory, the final official Navy position on the cause of the *Iowa* explosion is that the exact cause cannot be determined.

The initial investigation contained a qualified opinion that implicated Gunner's Mate Clayton M. Hartwig, USN, and that opinion was interpreted by many as a conclusive finding of wrongdoing.

For this, on behalf of the US Navy, I extend my sincere regrets to the family of GM2 Hartwig. There is no clear and convincing proof of the cause of the *Iowa* explosion. And the Navy will not imply that a deceased individual is to blame for his own death or the deaths of others without such clear and convincing proof.

I also apologize to all the families of those who died on board USS *Iowa*, that such a long period has passed, and despite all efforts no certain answer regarding the cause of this terrible tragedy can be found.

That ends my statement. I'll now take your questions.

Appendix H

Abbreviated Vitae of Key Technical Personnel at the Time of the Sandia Investigation

Dr. Melvin R. Baer is a Distinguished Member of the Technical Staff in Energetic Materials and Fluid Mechanics. He received his B.S., M.S., and Ph.D. in mechanical engineering from Colorado State University. He joined Sandia in 1976, and his areas of expertise include interior ballistics and explosive effects modeling.

Dr. James A. Borders is Supervisor of Materials Compatibility and Reliability. He received his B.A. in physics from Reed College, his M.S. in physics from the University of Illinois, and his Ph.D. in solid state physics from the University of Illinois. He joined Sandia in 1968, and his areas of expertise include energetic ion analysis, ion implantation, radiation effects in insulators, and surface characterization of materials.

Nora Bess Campbell-Domme is Senior Technical Assistant in Materials Compatibility and Reliability. She received her B.S. in biology and chemistry from the University of New Mexico. She has extensive experience in applied gas chromatography and mass spectroscopy to studies of materials compatibility and identification, failure analysis, and environmental trace analysis.

William B. Chambers is a Member of the Technical Staff in Process Characterization. He received his B.S. in biology and chemistry from the University of New Mexico and joined Sandia in 1985. His areas of expertise includes compositional and trace characterization of materials and inductively coupled plasma-atomic emission spectroscopy.

Paul W. Cooper is a Distinguished Member of the Technical Staff in Engineering Projects and Explosives Applications. He received his B.S. in chemical engineering from New York Polytechnic University. He joined Sandia in 1965 as a Member of the Technical Staff. He has conducted basic research in explosives phenomena and the design and development of explosives and firing components for weapons systems. He is the former editor of the *International Journal of Propellants, Explosives and Pyrotechnics*, and is a member of the Advisory Committee for the International Association of Bomb Technicians and Investigators.

Mark J. Davis is Manager of Metallic Materials. He received his B.S. and M.S. in metallurgical engineering from the University of California. He joined Sandia in 1963. He is an expert in materials and failure analyses and has made notable contributions to subjects as varied as rocket motor explosions and volcanic eruptions.

Dr. Kathleen V. Diegert is a Distinguished Member of the Technical Staff in Statistics, Computing and Human Factors. She earned a B.A. in mathematical sciences from Rice University and an M.S. and Ph.D. in operations research from Cornell University. She joined Sandia in 1980. She specializes in statistical consulting for weapon reliability analyses and probabilistic risk and safety analysis.

Kenneth W. Gwinn is a Senior Member of the Technical Staff in Applied Mechanics. He received both a B.S. and M.S. degree in civil engineering from Oklahoma State University and joined Sandia in 1980. He has extensive experience in impact analyses and shock and vibration of nuclear-waste shipping-cask transportation, and has chaired two ANSI committees in writing standards for this industry. Current assignments deal with the analysis and design of advanced reentry vehicles.

Dr. Steven M. Harris is a Senior Member of the Technical Staff in Detonating Components. He received his B.S., M.S., and Ph.D. in mechanical engineering from Oklahoma State University, where he specialized in heat transfer and fluid flow. He joined Sandia in 1988 and has been the project leader on a hazards-assessment project that deals with energetic material responses to abnormal environments.

Paul F. Hlava is a Senior Member of the Technical Staff in charge of the Electron Microprobe Laboratory. He received his B.S. in geology from the University of Wisconsin and an M.S. in geology at the University of New Mexico. His expertise is in the electron microprobe analysis of a wide variety of materials and failure analyses and contamination of various systems.

Dennis E. Mitchell is Supervisor of Detonating Components. He earned B.S. and M.S. degrees in mechanical engineering from the University of New Mexico and specialized in dynamic response of materials to high-strain-rate loading. He joined Sandia in 1969 and has been involved in all aspects of explosives utilization, performance characterization, and application. He has extensive experience in explosive component design and studies related to energetic materials safety.

Dr. Gerald C. Nelson is a Senior Member of the Technical Staff in Materials Compatibility and Reliability. He received a B.A. in physics and math from St. Olaf College and a Ph.D. in physics from Iowa State University. He has used surface analytical techniques to study material problems and specializes in the application of these techniques to the study of segregation, diffusion, and corrosion of thin films and alloys.

Dr. Karl W. Schuler is a Distinguished Member of the Technical Staff in Applied Mechanics. He received his B.S. in mechanical engineering from Pratt Institute and a Ph.D. in mechanics from the Illinois Institute of Technology. He joined Sandia in 1967. He has worked on a variety of analytical and experimental programs related to viscoelastic wave propagation in polymers, dynamic loading of oil shale, and stress wave propagation in complex weapons structures. He has designed experimental apparatus for high-pressure research, centrifuge testing of geotechnical models, and hypervelocity launchers.

Dr. Richard L. Schwoebel is Director of Systems Evaluation. He earned a B.S. in physics and mathematics from Hamline University and a Ph.D. in engineering physics from Cornell University. He joined Sandia in 1962. He was Supervisor of Surface Kinetics Research, Manager of Materials Research and Development, and Director of Materials and Process Sciences. He was also Director of Components until his current position. He has published extensively in the area of surface physics research and has made notable contributions in the area of high-altitude balloons and manned balloon systems.

Dr. David R. Tallant is Senior Member of the Technical Staff in Chemical Instrumentation Research. He received his B.S. in chemistry and an M.S. and Ph.D. in analytical chemistry from the University of Wisconsin. He joined Sandia in 1976. He has extensive experience in cleaning and contamination control and in high-temperature materials. He is an expert in Raman and fluorescence spectroscopy.

Notes

Chapter 1. Incident

1. "Investigation into the 19 April Explosion in Turret II USS *Iowa* (BB-61)," U.S. Navy Technical Report, Rear Adm. Richard D. Milligan.

2. Ibid.

3. Armor piercing, blank loaded, and plugged (no high explosive charge).

4. It was later determined that none of the deaths were by drowning.

5. Commonly referred to as a JAGMAN investigation in accordance with procedures set forth in the Manual of the Judge Advocate General, chap. 5, pt. C.

Chapter 2. Press Reports of the Navy's Investigation

1. David Smith's testimony was released by a source in the Navy.

2. House, *Joint Hearings before the Investigations Subcommittee and the Defense Policy Panel of the Committee on Armed Services*, 101st Cong., 1st sess., 12, 13, and 21 December 1989.

Chapter 4. The Navy's Report

1. PQS is a training program by which military personnel are qualified to serve in particular positions or functions.

2. In spite of Commander Kocmick's thoughtful concerns, a Navy inspector general review found that the November 1987 firings were properly approved and that the five-bag charge was safe in that specific case. The conclusions of that IG review do not, however, extend to the firings on 19 April 1989.

Chapter 6. House Committee on Armed Services Hearings

1. The Navy has now changed its investigative procedures, and a board will be assembled to review incidents in which there is loss of life.

Chapter 7. Visiting the USS *Iowa*

1. Captain Moosally's testimony, while not directly germane to the technical investigation, was important in terms of establishing a background of critical issues. This

included the questionable manning and general support policies for battleships, absence of training for either officers or enlisted personnel, and lack of a clear employment plan for battleships that established the tactical and strategic use. Appendix D includes important excerpts.

2. A Mast (an on-board hearing by the captain) was held over the wrestling incident, and Clayton Hartwig was reduced in rank. A careful investigation satisfied the *Iowa* command that both men were guilty only of misconduct on watch. Hartwig's subsequent performance was excellent, and he was judged an outstanding petty officer and an expert in the 16-inch gun, approved by a quality review board for reenlistment as a career sailor. (Private communication from Capt. [ret.] Larry Seaquist, former commander of the USS *Iowa*.)

Chapter 8. The Navy and Sandia Technical Teams Meet

1. The Navy representatives were Captain Miceli and Stephen Mitchell of NOS, Indian Head, Maryland; David File and Robert E. Sloan of the Naval Weapons Support Center, Crane, Indiana; and Thomas E. Doran of the Naval Surface Warfare Center at Dahlgren.

2. See Appendix B for a brief resume of previous open-breech explosions.

Chapter 9. The FBI Laboratory

1. A test similar to this was conducted during the Sandia investigation.

Chapter 10. The House Report

1. Preparation of this report involved members of these two committees and the following: Professional Staff—Warren L. Nelson, William T. Fleshman Jr., and Lawrence J. Caviola; Investigative Staff—Jeffrey Phillips and Alan Byroade; Staff Assistants—Kathleen A. Lipovac, Brown J. Sharp II, and Regina S. Yarbrough.

Chapter 12. The Sandia Investigation

1. Abbreviated vitae for those extensively involved in the Sandia technical investigation can be found in Appendix H.

Chapter 13. Impact Ignition

1. There were also several exchange visits among the materials analysis personnel from Sandia and Crane to discuss the details of the various procedures that were being used.

Chapter 14. Senate Armed Services Committee Hearing

1. This is the letter that resulted from my conversation with Rick DeBobes regarding Sandia's observations of impact ignition and the implications for gun crew safety.

2. The Navy claimed that calcium and chlorine found on the rotating band of the projectile were residues of a chemical ignitor placed between the propellant bags by the gun captain.

3. The Navy also believed that other residues found on the rotating band were of three glycols from a chemical ignitor.

4. Two of the materials were glycols. The third was incorrectly identified by the Navy as a glycol but was actually a phenol.

5. A fragment of PET material was found on the rotating band and thought by the Navy to be a portion of a plastic bag used to contain a chemical ignitor.

6. The interface between the first and second bag is the most probable site for ignition because the kinetic energy of the rammer and four propellant bags is available to fracture pellets at this location.

Chapter 15. Overdue Contacts

1. Capt. Fred P. Moosally Jr. testified before the Senate Armed Services Committee on Monday, 11 December 1989.

Chapter 16. Gun-Scale Testing at Dahlgren

1. Many of these were civilian personnel at Dahlgren.

2. I have not been able to establish the exact number of trim-layer pellets, but twenty was approximately the dividing line.

Chapter 20. Toward a Conclusion

1. House, *Testimony before Joint Committees of the House*, 101st Cong., 1st sess., 13 December 1989 (hereafter cited as Testimony, followed by names of those testifying and date of testimony).

2. Testimony, GMG3 Kendall L. Truitt, 20 April 1989.

3. Testimony, Larry S. Sanders, 26 April 1989.

4. Testimony, GMG3 Murray J. Cunningham, 26 April 1989.

5. Testimony, GMG1 Dale E. Mortensen, 21 April 1989.

6. At this point Admiral Milligan was still under the impression that Lawrence was serving as center gun captain.

Chapter 21. Reviewing Our Conclusions with Admiral Kelso

1. "USS *Iowa* Explosion, Sandia National Laboratories' Final Technical Report, GAO/NSIAD-91-4S, August 1991" (a publication of "Final Report—Sandia National Laboratories Review of the USS *Iowa* Incident").

Index

ABOUT THE AUTHOR

Richard L. Schwoebel was born and raised in North Dakota. He graduated from Hamline University in 1953 with a degree in physics and mathematics, and subsequently received a Ph.D. from Cornell University in Engineering Physics. Prior to pursuing his graduate degree Schwoebel was an engineer with General Mills, Inc. He participated in several notable high-altitude balloon programs, one of which included codeveloping a high-altitude air sampling system that collected debris from the first Russian thermonuclear tests. He was also the flight and technical director for the first crossing of the Atlantic by manned balloon in 1978, and for a transcontinental flight in 1980.

In 1962 Schwoebel joined Sandia National Laboratories in Albuquerque, where he later became director of various scientific and engineering organizations. At the request of the Senate Armed Services Committee he organized and led an independent investigation by Sandia of an explosion aboard the battleship USS *Iowa*. He testified before this committee in May 1990, presenting results that seriously questioned the Navy's investigation.

Schwoebel retired from Sandia in 1995. He resides in Albuquerque with his wife, Jennie.

The Naval Institute Press is the book-publishing arm of the U.S. Naval Institute, a private, nonprofit, membership society for sea service professionals and others who share an interest in naval and maritime affairs. Established in 1873 at the U.S. Naval Academy in Annapolis, Maryland, where its offices remain today, the Naval Institute has members worldwide.

Members of the Naval Institute support the education programs of the society and receive the influential monthly magazine *Proceedings* and discounts on fine nautical prints and on ship and aircraft photos. They also have access to the transcripts of the Institute's Oral History Program and get discounted admission to any of the Institute-sponsored seminars offered around the country.

The Naval Institute also publishes *Naval History* magazine. This colorful bimonthly is filled with entertaining and thought-provoking articles, first-person reminiscences, and dramatic art and photography. Members receive a discount on *Naval History* subscriptions.

The Naval Institute's book-publishing program, begun in 1898 with basic guides to naval practices, has broadened its scope in recent years to include books of more general interest. Now the Naval Institute Press publishes about one hundred titles each year, ranging from how-to books on boating and navigation to battle histories, biographies, ship and aircraft guides, and novels. Institute members receive discounts of 20 to 50 percent on the Press's nearly six hundred books in print.

Full-time students are eligible for special half-price membership rates. Life memberships are also available.

For a free catalog describing Naval Institute Press books currently available, and for further information about subscribing to *Naval History* magazine or about joining the U.S. Naval Institute, please write to:

Membership Department
U.S. Naval Institute
291 Wood Road
Annapolis, MD 21402-5035

Telephone: (800) 233-8764
Fax: (410) 269-7940
Web address: www.usni.org